offbeat nimzo-Indian

by Chris Ward

EVERYMAN CHESS

Gloucester Publishers plc   www.everymanchess.com

First published in 2005 by Gloucester Publishers plc (formerly Everyman Publishers plc), Northburgh House, 10 Northburgh Street, London EC1V 0AT

British Library Cataloguing-in-Publication Data
A catalogue record for this book is available from the British Library.

ISBN 1 85744 369 1

Distributed in North America by The Globe Pequot Press, P.O Box 480, 246 Goose Lane, Guilford, CT 06437-0480.

All other sales enquiries should be directed to Everyman Chess, Northburgh House, 10 Northburgh Street, London EC1V 0AT
tel: 020 7253 7887 fax: 020 7490 3708
email: info@everymanchess.com
website: www.everymanchess.com

To my brother Edward; thanks for all your help.

EVERYMAN CHESS SERIES (formerly Cadogan Chess)
Chief advisor: Garry Kasparov
Commissioning editor: Byron Jacobs
General editor: John Emms

Typeset and edited by First Rank Publishing, Brighton.
Cover design by Horatio Monteverde.
Production by Navigator Guides.
Printed and bound in the US by Versa Press.

CONTENTS

Bibliography   4

Introduction   5

1 d4 ♘f6 2 c4 e6 3 ♘c3 ♗b4

1   The Main Line Open Sämisch (4 f3 d5 5 a3 ♗xc3+ 6 bxc3 c5)   9

2   4 f3 d5 5 a3: Alternatives to the Main Line   40

3   4 f3: Others   54

4   The Stand-alone Sämisch (4 a3 ♗xc3+ 5 bxc3)   69

5   4 ♗g5 (The Leningrad Variation)   85

6   4 g3   108

7   4 ♕b3   125

8   Very Rare Fourth Moves for White   135

Index of Complete Games   143

BIBLIOGRAPHY

Books

Easy Guide to the Nimzo-Indian, John Emms (Everyman 1998)
Encyclopaedia of Chess Openings Volume E (3rd edition, Sahovski Informator 1998)
New In Chess 1 d4 Keybook (New In Chess 1983)
Nimzo-Indian Kasparov Variation, Chris Ward (Everyman 2003)
Nunn's Chess Openings, John Nunn, Graham Burgess, John Emms & Joe Gallagher
(Everyman 1999)
Play the 4 f3 Nimzo-Indian, Yuri Yakovich (Gambit 2004)

Periodicals

Chess Informants 1-91
Chess Today
ChessBase Magazine
Chesspublishing.com
New In Chess Yearbooks 1-73

Databases

Mega Corr 3
Mega Database 2005
The Week in Chess 1-535

INTRODUCTION

Welcome to *Offbeat Nimzo-Indian* in which basically I'm going to be taking a look at the more unusual white approaches to meeting the Nimzo-Indian Defence: 1 d4 ♘f6 2 c4 e6 3 ♘c3 ♗b4.

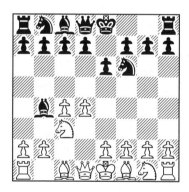

The diagram above is the starting position of the highly respected defence that I myself have employed as Black ever since the word go. White's 1 d4 and then 2 c4 was actually sneakily preparing for world domination via e2-e4 too but Black has put the breaks on that plan for now by pinning the c3-knight. The obvious drawback of 3...♗b4 is that Black must be prepared to concede this bishop for the knight. In such a scenario it could well be that Black will seek a closed game where a knight may be superior to a

bishop or it could well be that he will gain a lead in development whilst White continues to move pawns in a quest for central control. The doubled c-pawn structure immediately crops up in the Sämisch variation characterised by the move 4 a3.

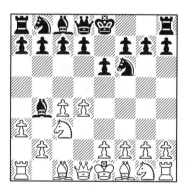

The Sämisch

I have always been a 1 d4 player as White, and as a junior this was the line that I first adopted. Perhaps back then there was the hope that Black might fall for 4...♗a5?? 5 b4 ♗b6 6 c5 but, that aside, it just seemed to clarify the situation.

Often in the Nimzo Black takes on c3 without any provocation and in that respect it may seem like a waste of a move to play 4 a3. Indeed it could also be argued that the move is detrimental as a hole is created on b3 and White's dark-squared bishop is deprived of access to the a3-square. The advantage, however, is that White will never have to worry about Black preserving his dark-squared bishop, and without having committed any of his kingside (e.g. a knight to f3) he can now get on with the formation he desires. That formation often includes a pawn on f3 and, if allowed, then a pawn on e4 too. The pieces will slot in around the pawns.

Probably it is a little harsh to refer to the many of this book's fourth moves as 'offbeat' but really it's all relative. Amongst the world's elite 4 ♕c2 and 4 e3 are the most popular variations, with 4 ♘f3 also having a big following.

That's not to say though that top players haven't dabbled in this book's offerings because they most certainly have. Indeed, take 4 f3 for example:

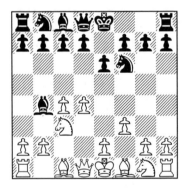

4 f3 (Open Sämisch)

This kind of updated Sämisch was first brought to my attention by the games of the super-GM Alexei Shirov. White immediately battles to force his e-pawn to e4 and deems this more relevant than 4 a3, particularly if that move can be omitted altogether. The reader will soon discover why there is a tendency for 4 f3 and 4 a3 to transpose to the same position and hence why two of the

chapters involve Sämisch and 4 f3 intersections. That is not always the case though, thus justifying the inclusion of a 'stand alone' chapter for each move each as well.

Barring a couple of the rare fourth move alternatives detailed in the book's final chapter, I have tried everything against the Nimzo-Indian, with my teenage years focussing on an early counter-pin:

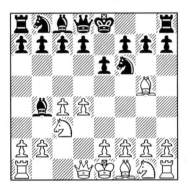

The Leningrad

If one assumes that White intends castling kingside then developing the queenside bishop seems a little illogical at this particular juncture. However, 4 ♗g5 always held an appeal for me and indeed as a grandmaster I returned to it for a period with (if I say so myself!) excellent results. The justification for prioritising this bishop move is that White may not want it locked inside the pawn that may only make it to e3, and a decision on the kingside development hasn't been made yet. The latter may sound like a lame reason but the fact is that it may depend on how Black continues that dictates whether White wants a pawn or a knight on f3 and indeed whether the king's knight wants to go to f3, e2 or even h3.

The majority of this book is dedicated to 4 a3, 4 f3 and 4 ♗g5 where, as well as transpositions, often similar plans are encountered both for White and Black. Other moves are discussed though including a favourite of the

Austrian GM Rudolf Spielmann.

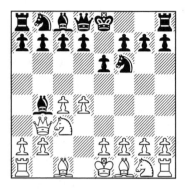

4 ♕b3 (Spielmann variation)

This is a crafty attempt to gain a tempo on the far more popular 'Classical' variation because unlike 4 ♕c2 it immediately puts the question to Black's bishop. Upon the continuation 4...♗xc3+(?!) 5 ♕xc3 one would have to say that White's early queen sortie would have been a definite success. White would have gained a bishop for a knight without compromising his pawn structure and without even having to expend time on a2-a3. The catch is of course that Black shouldn't concede his bishop so cheaply, and indeed after the more sensible 4...c5, for example, the white queen is arguably more vulnerably placed and certainly in the way of a b-pawn advance. Usually less common lines such as 4 ♕b3 are employed by strong players only as surprise weapons when they are hoping to catch their opponents unprepared. It could cost Black dearly not to take them seriously.

What I do not discuss in this book is 4 ♘f3 and, in particular, the following two positions:

See following diagrams

Although the first of the two may share some of its characteristics with the Leningrad there is unlikely to be an exact overlap. That is because although they both involve the move ♗g5, a queenside fianchetto is devoid of point should White easily arrange f2-f3 and e2-e4. White has extra pawn options without his knight on f3 but of course Black certainly need not employ 4...b6?! after 4 ♗g5.

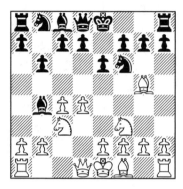

4 ♘f3 b6 5 ♗g5

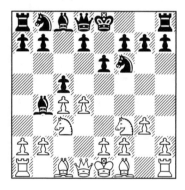

4 ♘f3 c5 5 g3

It's also worth noting here and now that if contemplating ...d7-d5 after having already included ...b7-b6, Black should be sure to remember the white queen check on a4. I can tell you that many a (usually!) strong player has blundered in this manner.

I concentrated on these two positions (and indeed the one after 4 ♘f3 0-0 5 ♗g5) in my recent book entitled *Nimzo-Indian Kasparov Variation*. During my years as an International Master I reached the second position on numerous occasions. However, after becoming dissatisfied with 4 ♘f3 b6 (preferring to play Black!), I graduated to 4 g3 instead.

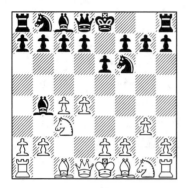

4 g3

In the main my outings with the above position led me directly into the realms of the Kasparov Nimzo via 4...c5 5 ♘f3, although it seemed to me that my opponents often mechanically played 4...c5 without much thought. Indeed I later concluded that Black was probably better off delaying this move and possibly adopting a set-up pairing ...d7-d6 and ...e6-e5 or a quick ...d7-d5. I study the alternatives to 4...c5 in Chapter 6.

In case anyone was wondering, there is no bias shown in this book. Some White players could easily be tempted by many of lines covered whilst Black should also be well prepared. I have encountered both sides of these positions and when it comes to assessments I am merely telling the truth!

One truth is that this is an ambitious project. There have been books on the Sämisch, books on the Leningrad and more recently books on 4 f3 and yet I've attempted to encompass these and more into just one text! Frankly, writing opening books can be a nightmare as these days there are huge amounts of practical games available, often even in what one might otherwise deem as comparative sidelines. The emphasis in this book has been on selecting relatively recent encounters that demonstrate instructive or interesting ideas. It is always possible to learn from strong players' games although the odd lower level game is included if justified by the entertainment value!

Enjoy!

Chris Ward,
Beckenham,
March 2005

CHAPTER ONE

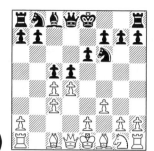

The Main Line Open Sämisch
(4 f3 d5 5 a3 ♗xc3+ 6 bxc3 c5)

1 d4 ♘f6 2 c4 e6 3 ♘c3 ♗b4 4 f3 d5 5 a3 ♗xc3+ 6 bxc3 c5

In this first chapter I'm dealing with the popular position reached after 4 f3 d5 5 a3 ♗xc3+ 6 bxc3 c5, which of course also arises via the move order 4 a3 ♗xc3+ 5 bxc3 c5 6 f3 d5. The main move for White here is the immediate capture in the centre with 7 cxd5, and this is the subject of Games 2-11. The advantage of this move is that Black must make an immediate decision on how to re-capture – in Game 1 White refrains from this capture but Black doesn't face any real difficulties.

After 7 cxd5 Black has a choice of two re-captures (7...♕xd5? 8 e4! isn't worth considering). The advantage of 7...exd5 (Games 2-4) is obvious – White will have to work a little hard to get his pawn to e4. In fact White normally begins with the modest 8 e3, after which Black can try the tricky 8...♕c7 (Game 2) or the more usual 8...0-0 (Games 3-4).

7...♘xd5 is featured in the majority of games here (Games 5-11) because, put quite simply, it is much more popular. White may get a free run at e2-e4, but for now he needs to bear in mind the threat to his c-pawn, which is not so easy to deal with as it first appears. In Games 5-7 White defends his c-pawn with either 8 ♕d2 (the least common option) or 8 ♕d3. The advantages that 8 ♕d3 has over 8 ♕d2 are that it adds extra support to e4 and c4, eyes up the b5-square and doesn't obstruct the dark-squared bishop. The disadvantages are that it potentially obstructs its own light-squared bishop and it is vulnerable to attack from Black's remaining bishop.

Trends dictate that 8 dxc5 now super-seded both of the white queen moves in popularity, and it is probably not unfair to say that 8 dxc5 is the main line of the 4 f3 Nimzo. The big question then is 'what is Black's best response?' In Game 8 Black plays 8...f5, dissuading White from playing e2-e4. More popular, however, is 8...♕a5 (Games 10-11), immediately hitting the weaknesses on c3 and c5. We end the chapter with a look at the rare but logical-looking 8...♘d7, which has been used by English GM and Nimzo expert Michael Adams.

Game 1
G.Sagalchik-V.Akopian
New York 1998

---

1 d4 ♘f6 2 c4 e6 3 ♘c3 ♗b4 4 a3 ♗xc3+ 5 bxc3 c5 6 f3 d5 7 e3?!

Actually, it seems a little harsh to be suggesting that this move is dubious, but really it is a little wet for such a sharp system. When White plays f2-f3 so quickly, ideally he wants to get e2-e4 played in one move rather than pussyfooting around with e2-e3.

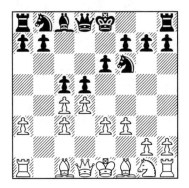

Black players who are frightened by ...♘xd5 (after cxd5) because of the speed in which e2-e4 arrives, may not be so worried about recapturing that way next turn as White will have effectively wasted a tempo.

7...0-0

Instead 7...♘c6 8 ♖b1 0-0 includes a different approach to the text, but after 9 cxd5 ♘xd5 10 ♕d2 ♕e7 11 ♗d3 cxd4 12 cxd4 e5 Black's position was definitely starting to look very satisfactory. White has the bishop pair but his own king is starting to look shaky on the open board. Indeed White's 'extra' centre pawn wasn't looking like such a bonus after the continuation 13 ♘e2 exd4 14 exd4 ♗e6 15 0-0 ♖ac8 16 ♖e1 ♖fd8, and indeed 17 ♔h1 b6 18 f4 ♕f6 19 ♘g3 ♕xd4 in fact saw it simply drop off in the game J.Bick-V.Milov, Biel 2003.

Similarly to the main game, Black could select the immediate 7...♕c7!?. The Croatian grandmaster Bogdan Lalic prefers that to 7...dxc4 despite the following impressive encounter: 8 ♗xc4 ♕c7 9 ♕c2 (White had to deal with the threats on the c-file but should also consider 9 ♗a2!? and 10 ♕d3!?) 9...e5 10 d5 (probably White should eliminate Black's next move by playing 10 e4!? himself) 10...e4!? 11 ♗b5+? (11 fxe4 0-0 12 ♘f3

♘bd7 13 ♗b5!? c4 14 0-0 would be fairly unclear but the text merely swaps off a rare developed piece!) 11...♗d7 12 ♗xd7+ ♘bxd7 13 c4 0-0 14 f4 b5! (correctly pressurising White, who is severely underdeveloped) 15 ♗b2 bxc4 16 ♗xf6? (White is worse but this doesn't help the situation) 16...♘xf6 17 ♕xc4 ♕a5+ 18 ♔e2 ♖ab8 19 ♔f2 ♘g4+ 20 ♔g3 ♘xe3 21 ♕xe4 ♖fe8 22 ♕d3 c4 0-1 F.Santos Olivera-B.Lalic, Dos Hermanas 2004.

8 ♗d3

After 8 cxd5 ♘xd5 9 ♘e2 White may then feel silly about taking two moves to get his pawn to e4. Indeed, whilst 9...cxd4 10 cxd4 ♘c6 11 e4 ♘b6 looks fine for Black because a knight or two can eye up the c4-square, 10...f5!? is also interesting.

8...♕c7

There is certainly no compulsion for Black to commit anything yet, although 8...dxc4!? 9 ♗xc4 ♕c7 would see him achieving Bogdan Lalic's recent position (see the note to Black's previous move) but with ...0-0 in for free. Black has scored very highly from that position too, with the second player going on to convert the full point after 10 ♘e2 cxd4 11 ♕xd4 (already it seems to me that White is worse as he won't be able to drum up enough play to compensate him for his weak queenside pawns) 11...♘c6 12 ♕c5 ♘d7 13 ♕b5 ♘ce5 14 ♗a2 ♘c5 15 0-0 b6 16 c4 ♗a6 17 ♕b4 ♖ac8 18 ♗b2 ♘ed3 19 ♕d2 ♘xb2 20 ♕xb2 ♘d3 21 ♕c3 ♗xc4 22 ♗xc4 ♕xc4 23 ♕xc4 ♖xc4 in G.Sagalchik-Y.Dokhoian, Nabereznye Chelny 1988.

9 ♕b3

This doesn't look very attractive but White had to do something about the threats to his c-pawns. After 9 ♕c2 dxc4 10 ♗xc4, 10...b6 is still perfectly plausible but an obvious danger to White is shown in the following: 10...♗d7 11 ♘e2 cxd4 12 cxd4 ♖c8 0-1 J.Fischer-D.Adla, Badalona 1993. Yes, the c-file is a big concern and it's worth observing 9 cxd5 cxd4! too.

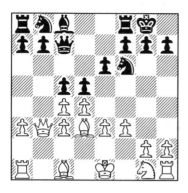

9...b6

Supporting the c5-pawn but more importantly preparing the challenging ...♗a6.

Also very reasonable is 9...♘c6 which threatens to embarrass the white queen via ...♘a5. Then very ugly for White was 10 dxc5 ♘e5 11 ♗e2 ♕xc5 12 cxd5 exd5 13 ♕b4 ♕c7! 14 ♘h3 ♗xh3 15 gxh3 ♕d7 16 ♕h4 ♖ac8 17 ♔f2 ♕f5 18 ♕f4 ♘d3+ 19 ♗xd3 ♕xd3 20 ♖a2 ♖xc3 21 ♖d2 ♖c2 22 ♖hd1 ♖fc8 23 ♔e1 ♕c3 0-1, as seen in P.Mas Recorda-M.Serrano Pertinez, Barcelona 2001.

10 cxd5 exd5

Another drawback of 9 ♕b3 is that now Black threatens a simple fork.

11 ♕b1 ♗a6!

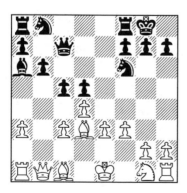

As White can't realistically avoid the trade, this offer of a swap eliminates White's bishop pair, leaving his remaining one locked inside the pawn structure. Later you will see situations whereby a similar structure can be favourable for White but here he has wasted far too much time.

12 ♗xa6 ♘xa6 13 ♘e2 cxd4

Black is prepared to saddle himself with an isolated d-pawn because of the c-file domination that the pawn exchange entails.

14 cxd4 ♕c4 15 ♖a2 ♖ac8 16 0-0 ♘c7

16...♖c6!?, intending to treble the major pieces on the c-file, looks even more convincing but Black clearly wanted to relocate his knight to sunnier climes.

17 a4

After 17 ♖c2 ♕b5 White's f1-rook doesn't communicate with its compatriot quickly enough.

17...♖fe8 18 ♘g3 g6

Keeping the white knight out of an excellent post on f5, but now White has bought himself some time.

19 ♗d2

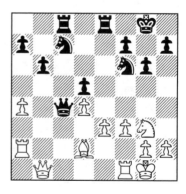

I promised I wouldn't lie to you and I won't. Suddenly White's position is looking a bit brighter. Unlike Black he has the chance to exchange off his isolated pawn and he can even make Black's queenside a target. His pawn chain from the h- to the d-files controls some useful squares and now he is ready to challenge for the c-file.

19...♘e6

For Black's part, e6 is clearly a much better square for the knight than a6.

20 a5 bxa5

And definitely not 20...b5?? 21 ♖c1, trapping the queen.

21 ♖c1 ♛a6 22 ♖xa5

With all things considered, probably 22 ♖xc8!? ♖xc8 23 ♖xa5 leaves White with the upper hand.

22...♖xc1+ 23 ♛xc1 ♛b6 24 ♛a1 ♖e7 25 ♘e2 ♖b7 26 ♘c3

White is getting to grips with the black isolanis.

26...♛c7!? 27 ♛a2

27 ♘xd5 ♘xd5 28 ♖xd5 ♛c2 29 ♛c3 ♛d1+ 30 ♔f2 (or 30 ♗e1 ♖b2!!, with this rook being untouchable and serious problems inevitable on g2) 30...♖c7 is the sort of counterplay that Black is after.

27...♛b8 28 ♗e1?!

Black was threatening 28...♖b2 but there is definitely the feeling that things are starting to turn. Instead 28 ♘xd5!? ♘xd5 29 ♛xd5 ♖b1+ 30 ♔f2 ♛xh2 31 ♖xa7 looks very plausible as actually Black has the weaker of the two kings.

28...♖b2 29 ♛a4 ♘g5!

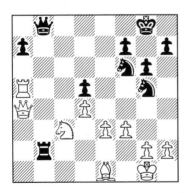

With White seemingly playing around the edges, Black starts to mount an offensive.

30 f4

This looks like a really ugly move but the concept of ...♘xf3+ would have left Black's queen and rook combining in awesome fashion.

30...♘g4

If White was starting to worry here then

he would have been perfectly justified! Even the straightforward 30...♘ge4 31 ♘xe4 ♘xe4 would leave Black with a superbly posted knight. Note 32 ♖xa7 ♖b1 33 ♔f1 ♔g7, when White's position is really uncomfortable.

31 ♖b5?

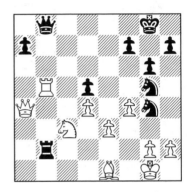

31 ♖xa7? is dealt with beautifully by 31...♖xg2+!! 32 ♔xg2 ♛b2+ 33 ♔g3 ♛xh2+ 34 ♔xg4 ♛g2+ 35 ♗g3 ♛h3+ 36 ♔xg5 h6+ 37 ♔f6 ♛e6 mate, but 31 ♘d1!? looks like some sort of a defence. Black has all the fun though.

31...♖xg2+!!

Excellent stuff!

32 ♔xg2 ♘xe3+

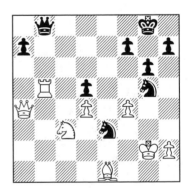

33 ♔g3?

This loses by force but 33 ♔f2 ♛xf4+ 34 ♔e2 ♘g2! would also leave Black with a wicked attack.

33...♘f1+! 34 ♔g2

Alternatives are no better, e.g. 34 ♔g4 ♕c8+ 35 ♔xg5 ♕f5+ 36 ♔h6 ♕h5 mate.

34...♕xf4!

Even more deadly than the queen and knight pairing is the queen and two knights 'pairing'! Mate is threatened via ...♘e3+.

35 ♗f2 ♘e3+!

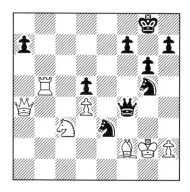

36 ♗xe3 ♕f3+!! 0-1

A lovely way to wrap things up. Mate will follow with 37...♘h3.

Game 2
S.Volkov-A.Istratescu
Korinthos 2002

---

1 d4 ♘f6 2 c4 e6 3 ♘c3 ♗b4 4 f3

Reiterating my transpositional spiel, our previous encounter saw 4 a3 but after Black's sixth move we reach the same position anyway.

4...d5 5 a3 ♗xc3+ 6 bxc3 c5 7 cxd5 exd5

The more popular 7...♘xd5 will be discussed in Games 5-11.

8 e3 ♕c7

The flexible 8...0-0 is covered in the next two games but there is a case for the text as it puts a spanner in White's works. Specifically, White can't develop naturally with 9 ♗d3? (intending 10 ♘e2) because it falls foul of 9...cxd4 when the queen check on c3 is serious.

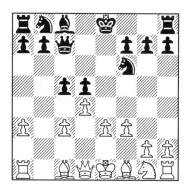

9 ♘e2

The main alternative is 9 ♖a2

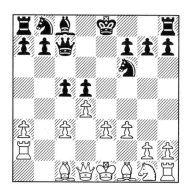

and that sneaky move is a common theme in these scenarios. The rook guards the second rank where it is also available to switch from one place to another and, perhaps above all, it is now no longer vulnerable to a fork on c3. Now Black must decide whether or not to enter an early trade of pawns:

a) 9...♗f5 10 ♘e2 ♘c6 11 g4 ♗e6 12 ♘f4 when, according to Ftacnik, both 12...h6 13 ♗d3 0-0-0 14 0-0 g5 15 ♘xe6 fxe6 and 12...0-0-0 13 g5 ♘d7 leave White with a slight edge. I wouldn't disagree with that as certainly he retains his bishop pair. He also has a space advantage, but it's not clear where his king belongs and Black's position is quite solid.

b) 9...cxd4!? 10 cxd4 ♗f5 claims the b1-h7 diagonal before White has a chance to play

♗d3. This move is very logical but, at the same time, it's double-edged as White can attack the bishop with his kingside pawns. Time to branch out:

b1) After 11 g4 ♗g6 12 h4!? the simple 12...h5 13 g5 ♘g8 14 ♘e2 ♘e7 is fairly unclear due to some weak white holes. However, Black can also dabble in something like 12...♘bd7!? 13 h5 ♗b1 (White should decline the 'offering' 13...♗e4 and settle for an edge via 14 ♗g2 ♗d3 15 ♕xd3! ♕xc1+ 16 ♔f2) 14 ♖b2 ♕g3+ 15 ♔d2 (or 15 ♖f2 ♖c8 16 ♘e2 ♕c7 17 g5 ♗c2 18 ♕d2 ♘g8 with a bizarre position) 15...♘e4+ (or even 15...♗e4!?) 16 fxe4 ♗xe4 17 ♘e2 ♕f2 18 ♖h3 ♘b6. I would say that Black gets some excitement for his piece but perhaps White should try to simplify via 19 ♖xb6 axb6 20 ♕e1.

b2) 11 ♘e2 ♘bd7! 12 g4 ♗g6

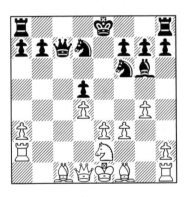

is quite complex but Black seems to have his fair share of the play, for example:

b21) 13 h4 ♖c8 14 h5 ♗c2.

b22) 13 ♘f4 ♖c8 14 ♗d2 ♗c2 15 ♕a1 (Black also had the initiative after 15 ♕c1 g5 16 ♘e2 h5! in J.Pomes Marcet-M.Suba, Castellar del Valles 1994) 15...g5 16 ♗d3 ♗xd3 17 ♘xd3 h5 18 gxh5 ♖xh5 was comfortably better for Black, who went on to win in B.Halldorsson-I.Sokolov, Reykjavik 2000.

b23) 13 a4 0-0 14 h4 ♖ac8 15 ♖a3 ♕d6 16 h5 ♗c2 17 ♕d2 ♘e4!? (the less radical 17...♘b6 is also a consideration) 18 fxe4

♗xe4 19 ♖g1 (or 19 ♖h3 ♗c2 20 ♕d1 ♖fc8 when Black had very good compensation for the piece in Wells-Suba, London 1991, a game that Black went on to win) 19...♖c2 20 ♕d1 ♖fc8 21 ♖a1 ♕h2 when Black is winning.

I can recall grandmaster John Emms and myself analysing many of the above lines in the days before Fritz arrived on the scene to spoil a lot of the tactics!

Regarding other White ninth moves, though it solves a development problem it makes no sense to seek a bishop trade via 9 ♗b5+. 9 ♗d2 is not very energetic whilst the jury is still out on the 9 g4 0-0 10 ♘e2 ♖e8 11 ♗g2 ♘c6 12 0-0, as seen in V.Moskalenko-P.Mascaro March, Mallorca 2000. White's bishops will always have potential but I still suspect that most White players wouldn't be ecstatic with their short-term control here.

9...♘c6

As you will notice a big strategical debate in these lines is the tactical versus positional elements that arise from the pawn structure derived by 9...cxd4 10 cxd4. Although Black gets the isolated pawn on d5, ironically after 10...♗f5 11 g4 ♗c2 12 ♕d2 h6 13 a4 ♗h7 14 ♗a3 (this bishop is a real pain!) 14...♘c6 15 ♘c3 a6 16 ♖c1 ♕a5 17 ♗e2 0-0-0 18 ♕b2 ♖he8 19 ♔f2 ♗e6 20 ♗c5 ♗d7 21 ♗b6 ♕b4 22 ♕xb4 ♘xb4 23 ♘xd5+ Black had suffered tactically too in V.Moskalenko-

N.Mitkov, Sitges 2000.

A big name for Black in these ...exd5 variations is the Rumanian GM Mikhail Suba and that is why we should take 9...h5, securing the f5-square for the bishop, very seriously. It's easy to see how things could get very murky, although after the 10 c4 cxd4 11 ♘xd4 0-0 12 cxd5 ♘xd5 13 ♕b3 ♘d7 14 e4 ♘f4 15 ♘b5 ♕b8 16 ♕c3 ♘e6 17 ♗c4 ♘b6 18 ♗xe6 of V.Moskalenko-M.Suba, Alicante 2000 I'm not sure why White offered a draw as the threat of ♘c7 with or without ♗f4 looks rather powerful.

10 dxc5

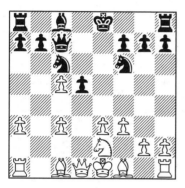

White takes the opportunity to grab the pawn which leads to a typical Nimzo-Indian structure. White has an extra pawn but all three of his queenside ones are isolated. If Black recoups the one on c5 then he will have pressure against the pawn on c3 but in the interim White has control of many useful squares.

10...0-0 11 ♘f4

Upon 11 ♘d4 Black should of course not be interested in a trade and should instead prefer 11...♘e5.

11...♕a5 12 ♕b3 ♕xc5

White wins this game but as it stands now it is difficult to say that Black is worse. Yes, the white bishops could be very useful in the endgame but in the meantime the black knights can make a nuisance of themselves. Although the pawn on f3 prevents an intru-

sion on e4, the obvious downside is that the e3-pawn is weak.

13 ♗e2 ♗d7

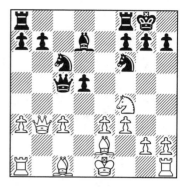

The alternative 13...♖e8 also looks very sensible seeing as White can't castle because of 14...♖xe3!.

14 ♔f2

Thanks to the control and cover that the f3-pawn offers, the white king is quite safe here.

14...♘a5 15 ♕b4 ♖ac8 16 ♖d1 ♖fe8 17 ♖a2 ♘c4

I think that generally speaking the key to this middlegame is either not swapping off the queens or at the very least not swapping them off under unfavourable circumstances. Here 17...♕c7 isn't unappealing as after 18 ♘xd5 ♘xd5 19 ♖xd5 Black would have 19...♗e6.

18 ♖d4

18 ♘xd5 isn't that stunning a tactic, e.g. 18...♘xd5 19 ♕xc5 ♖xc5 20 ♗xc4 ♘xc3 21 ♖xd7 ♖xc4 22 ♖a1 ♘a4 23 ♗d2 ♘c5 with approximate equality.

18...♘b6 19 ♗d2 ♗a4 20 ♖b2

20...♕xb4?!

One unfavourable consequence of this is ironing out White's queenside pawn structure.

21 axb4 a6 22 b5 ♘c4

After 22...axb5 23 ♗xb5 ♗xb5 24 ♖xb5 White has lost one of the bishop duo but has significant pressure against both of Black's isolated pawns.

23 ♗xc4 dxc4

Now we have an opposite-coloured bishops scenario but White has reasonable winning chances because of his superbly placed rook on d4.

24 bxa6 bxa6 25 ♖b6 ♗b5 26 e4

Now White's kingside pawns and his bishop work well together by controlling squares of both colours.

26...♖b8 27 ♖bd6 ♖b7 28 ♗c1 ♘d7 29 ♗a3 f6 30 ♘d5 ♘e5 31 ♘e3 ♖c7 32 h4 ♖c6 33 ♖6d5 ♖ce6 34 ♘f5

Black succeeds in maintaining a strong knight but his other pieces are devoid of activity.

34...♘f7 35 ♖c5 g6 36 ♘e3 f5

Upon 36...♘e5 37 ♖c7 Black would suffer on the sixth rank and so instead he looks to get a piece of the action.

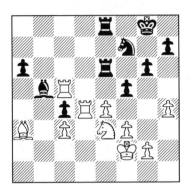

37 ♘d5 ♘e5 38 ♖c7 ♘c6 39 exf5 gxf5 40 ♖f4

This has all been very instructive. Note how Black's bishop has been a bystander.

40...♘e5 41 ♖xf5

A key pawn is bagged.

41...♘d7 42 g4 ♖e2+ 43 ♔g3 ♖a2 44 ♗c5 ♖d2 45 ♗d4 1-0

Game 3

V.Tipu-L.Henry

Canadian Ch., Toronto 2004

1 d4 ♘f6 2 c4 e6 3 ♘c3 ♗b4 4 f3 d5 5 a3 ♗xc3+ 6 bxc3 0-0 7 cxd5 exd5 8 e3 c5

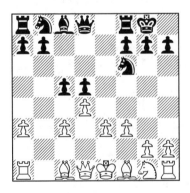

Black actually castled here on move six but, for all intents and purposes, through transposition I am treating it as the more popular move than the previous game's

8...♕c7 (with the move order 1 d4 ♘f6 2 c4 e6 3 ♘c3 ♗b4 4 f3 d5 5 a3 ♗xc3+ 6 bxc3 c5 7 cxd5 exd5 8 e3 0-0).

9 ♗d3

This is available now because there is no immediate threat on c3 by the 'still at home' black queen.

9...♖e8

The main move here is 9...b6, which is up next. In this game I just want to illustrate the lesser-seen alternatives. Aside from the text, also featured in practice has been 9...♘c6 10 ♘e2 ♖e8 11 0-0. Due mainly to the potential of building up a big centre, results have been in White's favour, with one particularly entertaining continuing 11...♕d6 12 ♘g3!? ♗d7 13 ♖a2 ♖ac8 14 ♔h1 a5 15 ♖af2 a4 16 ♗c2 b5 17 e4! cxd4 18 cxd4 dxe4 19 ♘xe4! ♘xe4 20 fxe4 ♘xd4 (or of course 20...♕xd4? 21 ♖d2) 21 ♗b2! ♖xc2! 22 ♖xc2 ♖xe4 23 ♖d2 ♖h4 24 h3! ♗xh3 25 ♔g1! ♕g3 26 ♗xd4 ♗e6 27 ♗e5! ♕e3+ 28 ♖df2 ♕b6 29 ♕d6 ♕xd6 30 ♗xd6 with White going on to convert the endgame in V.Golod-S.Solomon, Hoogeveen 1998.

10 ♘e2 b6 11 0-0 ♗b7?

I have selected this game primarily to show the reader just how badly things can go for Black if White succeeds in his aims. The text is too passive and really this bishop should seek a trade on a6.

12 ♘g3

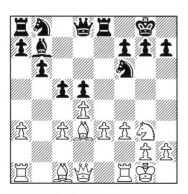

The f5-square is just begging to be in-

vaded and Black is always going to be reluctant to play ...g6 because of the dark holes that would be created.

12...♘c6 13 ♖a2!?

Sliding along the second rank is a sensible way to introduce this rook into action.

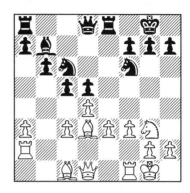

13...♖c8 14 ♔h1

White is preparing for e3-e4 and takes time out to remove his king from the a7-g1 diagonal.

14...♔h8

Black in turn moves his king so that ♗xh7 wouldn't be check should he ever get the chance to take on d4.

15 ♖e2 cxd4 16 cxd4 ♘a5 17 e4

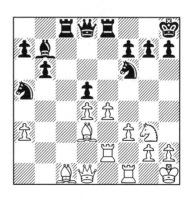

17...♘c4

This is a good square for the knight but after White's next move it seems that this is all that Black has. On the face of it I'm tempted to say that Black must really try

17...dxe4 but after 18 fxe4 he can't get away with 18...♛xd4 because of 19 ♗b2 ♛d7 20 ♖xf6! gxf6 21 ♗xf6+ ♔g8 22 ♖d2!. Threats include ♗c4 when Black will suffer down the draughty g-file.

18 e5 ♘g8 19 f4

Very natural, with one obvious plan being to charge this pawn straight down to f6. White's position is about as good it gets without being material up, and it is an extremely nice one to play.

19...b5 20 ♗b1

Basically White is spoilt for choice, with the ensuing queen and bishop alignment being a good plan amongst several others.

20...♖c7 21 ♛d3 g6 22 f5

The only debate at the moment is 'on which square is White going to deliver checkmate?'

22...♗c8 23 ♖ef2 a5

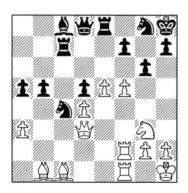

At least Black has been consistent, but I doubt that White allocated much time to trying to rebuff Black's queenside advances!

24 e6!

Putting f7 and hence also g6 under severe pressure.

24...fxe6 25 fxg6 1-0

Despite remaining equal in material terms, Black decides it is time to throw in the towel. One can't really blame him for this decision: his king is bereft of useful defenders while White has a huge armada of pieces ready to descend.

Game 4

Y.Yakovich-D.Campora

Santo Antonio 2001

1 d4 ♘f6 2 c4 e6 3 ♘c3 ♗b4 4 f3 d5 5 a3 ♗xc3+ 6 bxc3 c5 7 cxd5 exd5 8 e3 0-0 9 ♗d3 b6

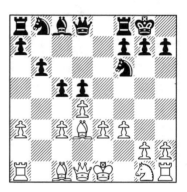

Arguably the main variation within 7...exd5; Black immediately sets about trying to trade off a set of bishops.

10 ♘e2 ♗a6 11 0-0

Practical play suggests that this is more accurate than 11 ♗xa6 ♘xa6 12 ♛d3 as the black knight is on a very reasonable track after 12...♘c7 and, besides, 12...♛c8 is not bad either.

Although it's logical to want to preserve the bishop, it takes a brave man to attempt the likes of 11 ♗b1 ♖e8 12 g4 ♘c6 13 ♘g3 g6 14 ♔f2. There are a few of those in Indonesia though, and 14...cxd4 15 cxd4 ♖c8 16 h4 was double-edged in U.Adianto-C.Garma Genting 1995.

11...♖e8

White has a very simple plan and after 11...♗xd3 12 ♛xd3 ♘c6 13 e4! it starts to get realised. Again pointing out the danger to Black was the following: 13...cxd4 14 cxd4 dxe4 15 fxe4 ♛e7 (if White succeeds in maintaining his two pawns abreast then he has excellent chances of keeping the advantage; if, however, he is forced to move his e-pawn to e5, thus allowing a blockade on the light squares, then Black will be happy) 16 ♘g3 ♖ad8 17 ♗b2 ♖fe8 18 ♖ae1! (the correct rook as the other one is well placed on the f-file) 18...♘e5 19 ♕b3 ♘g6 20 ♘f5 ♕d7 21 ♕f3! (White is already in an overwhelming position as the threat of ♘xg7 is very hard to meet) 21...♖e6 22 d5 ♖xe4 23 ♘h6+! (23 ♖xe4 ♘xe4 24 ♕xe4 ♕xd5 25 ♕xd5 ♖xd5 26 ♘xg7 also does the job for White, but this is much prettier) 23...♔f8 (23...gxh6 24 ♕xf6 is crushing) 24 ♖xe4 ♘xe4 25 ♘xf7 ♘d2 26 ♗xg7+!! ♔e8 (both 26...♔xg7 27 ♕f6+ ♔f8 28 ♘e5+ and 26...♔g8 27 ♕f6 are also devastating) 27 ♘d6+ 1-0 G.Lazovic-R.Zelcic, Pula 1999.

12 ♘g3

12 ♖a2!? and 12 g4!? come into the picture too, but a swift transfer of the knight is arguably the most appealing.

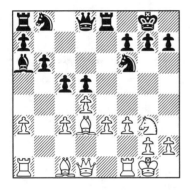

12...♗xd3

After 12...♕d7 probably White's most accurate is 13 ♗f5!? (note that 13 e4? dxe4 14 fxe4 cxd4 15 ♗xa6 ♘xa6 16 cxd4 ♘xe4 basically just drops a pawn) 13...♕b5 when after 14 ♖e1 ♕c4, rather than simply 15 ♗b2, he can try 15 e4!? intending 15...♕xc3 16 ♗g5 ♕xd4+ 17 ♕xd4 cxd4 18 ♗xf6 gxf6 19 exd5. In the event of all this, all of a sudden White would find himself in a completely winning position!

13 ♗f5 looks sensible against 12...♕c8 too as there Black doesn't even have the option

of ...♕b5.

13 ♕xd3 ♘c6 14 ♖a2

14 ♗b2 ♖c8 15 ♖ad1 cxd4 16 cxd4 ♘a5 17 e4 ♕c7 18 e5 ♘d7 19 ♘f5 ♘c4 20 ♗c1 b5 21 f4 ♘f8 22 ♖f3 ♖e6 23 ♘g3 ♖c6 24 ♖ff1 ♕b6 25 ♔h1 b4 26 axb4 ♕xb4 27 f5 ♘b2 28 ♗xb2 ♕xb2 29 ♕f3 ♕b5 30 ♘h5 ♖8c7 31 ♕g3 g6 32 ♘f6+ ♔h8 33 e6 fxe6 34 fxe6 ♘xe6 35 ♕e5 ♖f7 36 ♘xd5+ ♔g8 37 ♖xf7 1-0 A.Kalka-W.Rosen, Germany 2003 is certainly food for thought but it's not that convincing. I like the look of the rook swinger as now White is able to double rooks on either the f-file or the e-file.

14...♖c8

The 14...♕d7 15 ♖e2 ♖e6 16 ♗b2 ♖d8 17 ♖d1 cxd4 18 cxd4 ♘e8 19 e4 ♘e7 20 e5 ♖c8 21 f4 of A.Khalifman-V.Bologan, Prague (rapid) 2002 was assessed as clearly better for White, and as Black is unable to erect a blockade on f5, it is easy to understand why.

15 ♖e2 ♖e6 16 ♗b2 cxd4 17 cxd4 ♘a5 18 e4!

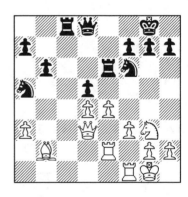

White has made plenty of useful preparatory moves and so there is no need to delay this any longer.

18...♖ec6 19 e5 ♘e8 20 f4

Could Black secure a pawn on f5 now, then he would be okay. However, he can't!

20...♘c4 21 f5 f6

White's pawns are very intimidating and sooner or later White was going to play this move himself.

22 ♘h5

Strong passed pawn though it might be, there is no need for 22 e6 as it would concede the d6-square. Instead it makes more sense to build up pressure against f6 and g7.

22...♘xb2 23 ♖xb2 ♖c3 24 ♕e2

Unfortunately for Black, control of the c-file is not going to keep the white queen out of the attack!

24...fxe5 25 dxe5 ♕g5 26 f6!

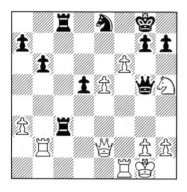

Pressurising g7 further and threatening an obvious advance.

26...♖8c7 27 ♘f4

27 ♕b5 ♕xh5 28 f7+ also looks rather embarrassing.

27...♖c1 28 f7+! ♖xf7

After 28...♔xf7 White would win material via 29 ♘xd5+ (rather than 29 ♘h3+? ♕f5!).

29 ♖xc1 ♕xf4 30 ♕d2 ♕xe5 31 ♖e1 ♕b8 32 ♕xd5

The dust has settled and Black has just one pawn for the exchange. As the minor piece is a knight his drawing chances are very slim. When up against a ruthless GM that translates to about zero!

32...♘f6 33 ♕c4 ♕f8 34 ♖be2 ♔h8 35 a4 h6 36 h3 ♖d7 37 ♕c2 ♕f7 38 ♖e6 ♖c7 39 ♕d3 ♖d7 40 ♕c2 ♖c7 41 ♖c6 ♖xc6 42 ♕xc6 ♔h7 43 ♕c2+ ♔g8 44 ♕c8+ ♔h7 45 ♕f5+ ♔g8 46 ♕e6 ♘d5 47 ♕c8+ ♔h7 48 ♕c2+ ♕g6 49 ♕xg6+ ♔xg6 50 ♖e5 ♘c3 51 ♖e7 ♘xa4 52 ♖xa7 ♘c5 53 ♖c7 ♘a4 54 ♖c4 ♘c5 55 ♖b4 ♘d7 56 ♖d4 ♘f6 57 ♖d6

Nobody said that it wouldn't be a grind though!

57...h5 58 ♖xb6 h4 59 ♔f2 ♔f5 60 ♖b5+ ♔f4 61 ♖b4+ ♔g5 62 ♔f3 ♔h5 63 ♖b6 ♘g8 64 ♔f4 g5+ 65 ♔f5 ♘e7+ 66 ♔e6 ♘g8 67 ♔f7 1-0

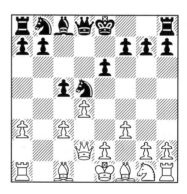

Game 5
Nguyen Chi Minh-E.Van den Doel
French League 2003

1 d4 ♘f6 2 c4 e6 3 ♘c3 ♗b4 4 f3 d5 5 a3 ♗xc3+ 6 bxc3 c5 7 cxd5 ♘xd5

And so appears the more popular recapture.

8 ♕d2

This is the least common of the three white options that I will discuss. Given that White has plenty of minor pieces still at home it hardly seems ideal to want to guard c3 with the queen. However, in anything to do with f2-f3 White must remember that his king is a trifle exposed, and 8 ♗d2? is refuted by 8...cxd4 9 cxd4 ♕h4+!.

8...f5!?

Bearing in mind the aforementioned queen check, this move is aimed at making it awkward for White to get in e2-e4. It is of course far from forced, and I need to say something about the alternatives:

a) 8...cxd4 9 cxd4 ♘c6 (9...f5 is again playable as it puts the breaks on e2-e4 because of that h4 check) 10 e4 ♘b6 11 ♗b5 (Black has nothing to fear from 11 ♗b2 ♘a4! 12 ♗b5 ♘xb2 13 ♗xc6+ bxc6 14 ♕xb2 ♗a6!) 11...0-0 12 ♘e2 ♗d7! 13 0-0 ♘e5!. Black forces a trade of bishops, and the more pieces that get traded the more that extra centre pawn is going to be a target rather than a strength.

b) 8...♕a5 9 e4! and now:

b1) Upon 9...♘xc3 10 ♗b2 cxd4 11 ♘e2 White would get one of his pawns back. He would still remain one pawn down but would be, unusually for this variation, in the situation of having a lead in development. His terrific bishop pair would provide good compensation.

b2) 9...♕xc3 10 ♖b1 ♕xd2+ 11 ♗xd2 ♘c7 12 dxc5. White has the advantage in these type of endings: although isolated, White's queenside pawns can often clamp down on Black; he has a half open e-file, and often his excellent bishop pair prevents Black from ganging up on the c5-pawn.

c) 8...♘c6 9 e4 ♘b6 10 ♗b5 ♗d7 11 dxc5 ♘e5 12 ♗e2 ♘a4 leads to a kind of mix of the previous two lines. White's pieces are awkward here though, and 13 ♕d6 f6 14 ♗d2 ♖c8 15 ♖b1 ♘xc5 16 ♘h3 ♕e7 17 ♕xe7+ ♔xe7 18 ♘f2 b6 is easier for Black to play as 19 0-0 ♘a4 20 ♖fc1 ♘c4 21 ♗xc4 ♖xc4 proved in A.Jakab-R.Ruck, Hungary 2002, with Black going on to win.

9 e3

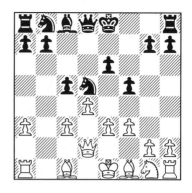

The continuation 9 c4 ♘f6 10 e3 0-0 11 ♘h3 ♘c6 12 ♗b2 highlights some interesting aspects about the position. The e5-square is an outpost while the backward e6-pawn is an obvious target. However, an inevitable trade on d4 would leave White with more pawn islands and his structure open to attack from many different angles. After 12...b6 13 ♖d1 cxd4 14 exd4 ♗a6 15 ♘f4 ♖e8 16 ♕c2 ♖c8 17 ♔f2 ♘a5 18 c5 ♗xf1 19 ♖hxf1 ♘d5 20 ♘xd5 ♕xd5 (F.Kirwald-D.Gutsche, Germany 2000) another significant feature was the bad bishop versus potentially good knight.

9...0-0 10 ♘h3

Black has little to fear from 10 ♗d3 cxd4 11 cxd4 ♘c6 12 ♘e2 e5 and the white knight isn't exactly spoilt for choice.

10...♘c6

Due to the weakness on e6, the concept of 10...b6 is not quite so attractive now, although 10...cxd4 11 cxd4 ♘c6 12 ♖b1 b6 13 ♗e2 ♕h4+ 14 ♔f1 ♗b7 15 ♕e1 ♕e7 16 f4 ♖ac8 turned out very nicely for Black in Nguyen Chi Minh-K.Le Quang, Bagneux 2002.

11 ♖b1

11 c4 ♘b6 12 dxc5 ♘d7 13 ♕d6 ♕f6 14 ♖b1 ♖d8 15 ♕d2 ♘xc5 16 ♕c2 e5 17 f4 b6 18 ♗b2 ♗b7 19 ♘g5 ♕g6 20 ♗e2 exf4 21 ♘f3 fxe3 22 ♘h4 ♕g5 23 ♘f3 ♕xg2 24 ♖f1 ♘e4 25 c5 ♘d2 was a comprehensive black victory in D.Kumaran-P.Wells, Hastings

1991/92, while upon both 11 &d3 or 11 &e2 Black should trade on d4 and get in ...e6-e5.

11...e5

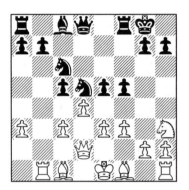

Black could swap on d4 first, but this game is very instructive.

12 dxc5

It's the same old story. White is sort of half a pawn up and has the bishop pair, but his structure isn't great and his pieces don't coordinate well.

12...♔h8

Sidestepping any potential pins on the knight.

13 ♘f2 &e6 14 &b5 ♕e7 15 c4 ♘f6 16 ♕d6 ♖fd8!

Of course Black shouldn't be tempted to take on d6 but the text demonstrates how Black can handle the endgame too.

17 ♕xe7 ♘xe7

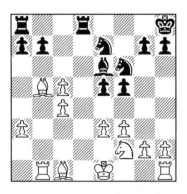

The problem here for White is that his light-squared bishop is a little offside and his dark-squared bishop can't easily guard the c5-pawn.

18 &b2 ♘g6 19 h4

Fair enough. If White were able to budge the g6-knight then the e5-pawn would drop.

19...h5 20 ♘h3

Again this is difficult to criticise as g5 looks like a good square for a white knight to make its home.

20...♖ac8 21 ♘g5 &g8

Up to now analysis engines prefer White, but this is where the likes of Fritz start to change their mind!

22 ♔e2

White certainly can't return the pawn under favourable circumstances with 22 c6 bxc6 23 &a6 ♖b8 as the pin is extremely awkward and ironically it is the other bishop that is in most danger (i.e. to ...♖b6). The text seems to put the king in the firing line, but White hardly desires an invasion of his second rank and the h1-rook is to some extent tied to the defence of the h4-pawn.

22...a6 23 &a4 &xc4+ 24 ♔e1 ♖xc5 25 ♖c1 ♖d3 0-1

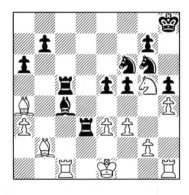

How quickly things can change! White has gone from being a pawn up to a pawn down in a short space of time and more material looks set to follow. On top of that, White is no better off development-wise and all these features combine to provoke a resignation.

Game 6
B.Lalic-O.Jovanic
Zadar 2004

1 d4 ♘f6 2 c4 e6 3 ♘c3 ♗b4 4 f3 d5 5 a3 ♗xc3+ 6 bxc3 c5 7 cxd5 ♘xd5 8 ♕d3

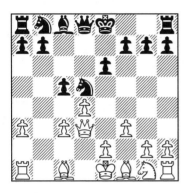

8...b6, preparing ...♗a6, looks like the most obvious way to exploit what is after all another queen move. However, that is up in the next game, and here I want to discuss the main alternatives.

8...cxd4

Although in the main game Black makes a home for his knight on b6, as the c-pawns are still on after 8...0-0 9 e4, the three main retreats are:

a) 9...♘c7?! 10 ♗e3 ♘c6 11 ♘h3 cxd4 12 cxd4 e5 13 d5 ♘d4 14 ♗xd4 exd4 15 ♘f2 ♕f6 16 ♖d1 and in A.Bandza-V.Zhidkov, Rimavska Sobota 1990 White was able to round up Black's d-pawn. The problem with the knight on c7 is that it prevents Black's ...♕a5 option. It also doesn't control the c6-square and can either get in the way of or be a liability on the c-file.

b) 9...♘e7 10 f4!? (recently 10 dxc5 ♕a5 11 ♕c4 ♘d7 12 ♗e3 ♘c6 13 ♘h3 ♕c7 14 ♗e2 ♘a5 15 ♕b4 ♘c6 16 ♕b5 a6 17 ♕a4 ♘a5 18 ♖b1 ♘xc5 19 ♕b4 ♘d7 20 0-0 ♘c6 21 ♕b2 ♘a5 22 ♕b4 ♘c6 23 ♕a4 b5 24 ♕c2 ♘b6 was hardly a raging success in Dao

Thien Hai-Wu Shaobin, Ho Chi Minh City 2003 – White has to get his knight out somehow; 10 ♘h3 ♘bc6 11 ♗e3 ♕a5! leaves White struggling to hold d4, whilst 10 ♘e2 leads to obvious congestion)

and now:

b1) We know that 4 f3 was popularised by Alexei Shirov and it is always worth studying his games. After 10...♕a5 11 ♗d2 ♕a4 12 ♕b1 ♗d7 13 ♘f3 ♗c6 14 ♗d3 ♘d7 15 0-0 h6 16 f5! he had done well in the development stakes and had already got an attack under way in A.Shirov-Ki.Georgiev, Manila Olympiad 1992.

b2) 10...b6 11 ♕e3 ♕c7 12 ♘f3 ♗b7 (12...♗a6 13 ♗xa6 ♘xa6 14 0-0 ♖ae8 15 ♗b2 ♕b7 16 ♖ae1 f5 17 ♕d3 ♘c7 18 c4 would reach, by transposition, A.Shirov-H.Olafsson Reykjavik 1992, in which White developed a very comfortable initiative) 13 ♖b1 (in looking for an improvement, perhaps this is where White should start) 13...♖c8! 14 ♗d3 ♗a6 (it looks as though Black has lost a tempo by stopping off at b7 but now he is ready to utilise the c-file) 15 ♗xa6 ♘xa6 16 0-0 cxd4 17 cxd4 ♕c3 18 ♕e2 ♕c4 19 ♕e3 ♕c3 20 ♕e2 ♕c4 21 ♕e3 ½-½ T.Hillarp Persson-J.Timman, Malmö 2003 – Black would be fine in the endgame and so instead the outcome is a repetition.

c) 9...♘f6 10 ♗g5!? (10 ♘h3 cxd4 11 cxd4 ♘c6 12 ♗b2 ♕e7 13 ♘f2 ♖d8 14 ♗e2 ♘h5 15 ♕e3 ♕c7 16 0-0 ♕f4 17 ♕d3 ♕h4 18 g3

♘xg3 19 hxg3 ♕xg3+ 20 ♔h1 ♕h4+ 21 ♔g2 ♕g5+ 22 ♔h2 ♕h4+ 23 ♔g2 ♕g5+ 24 ♔h2 ½-½ was Y.Yakovich-S.Kishnev, Munich 1992) 10...cxd4 11 cxd4 b6 12 e5 ♕d5 13 ♕d2 ♘fd7 14 ♗d3 ♘c5 15 dxc5 ♕xe5+ 16 ♔f2 ♕xa1 17 ♗e4 ♘d7 18 ♗xa8 ♘xc5 19 ♗e7 with a material advantage but still work to be done in S.Volkov-S.Ivanov, St Petersburg 1998.

8...♘c6 is of course possible but isn't of much independent significance as after 9 e4 ♘de7 10 ♗e3 there is nothing better than 10...0-0.

9 cxd4 0-0 10 e4 ♘b6

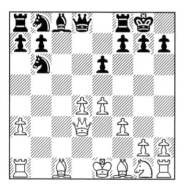

After 10...♘e7 again Shirov's 11 f4!?, vacating the f3-square for the knight, would be very applicable.

11 ♘h3

Over ten years ago 11 ♗e3 ♘c6 12 ♗e2 f5 13 ♖d1 was all the rage but after 13...♗d7 Black was getting his fair share of the results. White maintains that attractive pawn structure but he can't ignore his kingside forever. Perhaps critical then is 14 ♘h3 fxe4 15 fxe4 e5 16 d5 ♗xh3 (White retains control after 16...♘d4?! 17 ♗xd4 exd4 18 ♘f2) 17 dxc6 ♕h4+ 18 g3 ♕e7 which to me looks a little double-edged. If White can obtain an endgame via ♕d6 then he would probably stand quite well but he must guard against ...♗g2, and 19 ♖g1 ♖ad8!? brings home the positioning of the white king.

11...♘c6 12 ♗e3

Under different circumstances 12 ♗b2? might be reasonable as the bishop could cause some damage pointing towards the black king. Here though it walks into 12...♕a4!, spelling very bad news for the d-pawn.

12...f5!

The correct move. Black is right to want to strike out at White's pawn centre and, in contrast to the notes to White's 11th move, the way he is handling this is to look to exclude ...♗d7 altogether.

13 ♗e2

After 13 ♖d1?! Black doesn't have to transpose to the previously mentioned variation and can instead tackle 13...fxe4 14 ♕xe4 ♘d5 15 ♘g5?! ♖f5! as after 16 ♘xe6 ♕e7 White would be justified in feeling rather nervous.

Also 13 ♘f4 fxe4 14 fxe4 e5 15 dxe5 ♕g5!? sees Black taking the game to White.

13...fxe4

Black certainly can't be worse after 13...e5!? 14 dxe5 ♕xd3 15 ♗xd3 ♘xe5 16 ♗c2 fxe4 17 ♘g5 exf3 18 ♗xh7+ ♔h8 19 0-0 ♗f5 either.

14 fxe4

One interesting (far from forced) variation runs 14 ♕xe4 ♘d5 15 ♘g5 ♖f5 16 ♘xe6 ♕e7 17 ♕xf5 ♘xe3 18 ♕e4 ♘xg2+ 19 ♔f2 ♗xe6 20 ♔xg2 ♖d8 and clearly Black has compensation for the exchange.

14...e5!

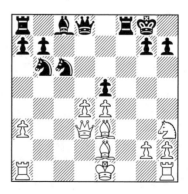

15 d5 ♗xh3 16 gxh3

16 dxc6? is not a viable option because of 16...♗xg2 when 17 ♖g1? gets slaughtered by 17...♕h4+ 18 ♔d2 ♖ad8.

16...♕h4+ 17 ♔d2 ♘d4!

Without a doubt the best way to go. The text effectively eliminates one of the bishops and looks to expose the white king further.

18 ♗xd4 exd4 19 ♕xd4 ♖ae8

A fairly natural selection although 19...♖ac8!?, keeping the white king in the centre looks sensible too.

20 ♖hg1 ♕h6+

21 ♔c3?

After the game Bogdan criticised this move, with the Croatian GM instead claiming that after 21 ♔c2 ♖f7 22 ♖g3 ♕f4 23 ♗d3 White would stand slightly better. However, in light of the tactical response 23...♘c4! I'm not sure that I can agree. Certainly I would feel uncomfortable playing White.

Generally speaking Black clearly has reasonable compensation for the pawn as White has some isolanis and his king is weak. However, although White's centre pawns can be blockaded on the dark squares, obviously they offer serious potential.

21...♖f7

21...♕xh3+? is a mistake because of 22 ♖g3 ♕d7 23 ♖xg7+! ♕xg7 24 ♖g1, but 21...♘a4+!? is certainly a candidate because of 22 ♕xa4? (or 22 ♔b3? ♖xe4!) 22...♕e3+

23 ♗d3 ♖c8+.

22 ♖g3 ♘xd5+!

22...♕xe4?! is not as tempting as it might seem because after 23 ♕xe4 ♕f6+ 24 ♔b3 ♕xa1 25 d6 surprisingly Black doesn't have any checks.

23 ♕xd5

Upon 23 exd5 ♖xe2 the pawn count is level but the white king is all over the shop.

23...♕f6+ 24 ♔c2!

After 24 ♕d4? ♖c8+ 25 ♗c4 b5 26 ♕xf6 ♖xc4+ 27 ♔b3 ♖xf6 White faces a grim rook and pawn endgame.

24...♖d8?

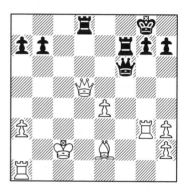

After 24...♕xa1 25 ♗c4 ♕f6 the likely outcome would be a draw but because of time trouble now both players start to make mistakes.

25 ♕a2?

25 ♕c4! ♕xa1 26 ♖f3 ♖df8 27 ♖xf7 ♖xf7 28 ♕c8+ ♖f8 29 ♗c4+ is winning for White but Black now returns the error.

25...♕f2?

Yes, Black could have drawn via 25...♖c8+ 26 ♔d1 ♕d4+ 27 ♖d3 ♕g1+ 28 ♔d2 ♕g5+ and, although he is probably losing now, a draw was probably the fair result. The remaining symbols are provided by Bogdan Lalic, who was probably happy to get the whole ordeal over with!

26 ♕c4 b5 27 ♕xb5 ♖c7+ 28 ♔b3 a6!? 29 ♗c4+?? ♔h8 30 ♖d1 ♖dc8! 31 ♕d5?! ♕b6+ 32 ♔a2 ♖xc4 33 ♖b3 ♕c7

34 ☐d2 h6 35 e5! ☐c5 36 ☖d6 ☐c2+ 37 ☐xc2 ☖xc2+ 38 ☐b2 ☖c4+ 39 ☗a1 ☖c1+ 40 ☗a2 ☖c4+ 41 ☗a1 ☖c1+ 42 ☗a2 ☖c4+ 43 ☗a1 ½-½

Game 7

A.Shirov-'Canchess'
Internet (Simultaneous Display) 2000

---

1 d4 ☖f6 2 c4 e6 3 ☖c3 ☗b4 4 f3 d5 5 a3 ☗xc3+ 6 bxc3 c5 7 cxd5 ☖xd5 8 ☖d3 b6!?

The recommended antidote to the more advanced of the white queen move options. Black of course needs his queen's knight to be still at home in order to facilitate ....☗a6. Shirov had big problems against this move which, against top-level opponents at least, eventually persuaded the Latvian to give up on 8 ☖d3. Clearly in this encounter he decided to give it another whirl.

9 e4 ☗a6 10 ☖d2

Arguably the most ambitious continuation here is trying to preserve the bishop pair via 10 c4. Unfortunately, after 10...☖e7 11 d5 exd5 White is of course unable to recapture with the c-pawn. Hence 12 exd5 0-0 when a knight blockade on d6 is inevitable. White has a superb diagonal for his bishop along the b2-g7 diagonal and, given time, could really get his bishop pair working well together. However, as things stand he is well behind in development and (often a later criticism of the 4 f3 line), the white f-pawn would rather be back home!

Incidentally 10...☖c7 is not that dissimilar and 10...☖f6!: 11 e5!? ☖fd7 12 ☖e4 cxd4! 13 ☖xa8 ☖c5 14 ☐b1 ☖c7! is (though not forced) also something that White needs to consider as his queen has severe problems just staying alive.

While I'm here, 10 ☖c2 ☗xf1 11 ☗xf1 offers White nothing as 11...☖e7 12 dxc5 bxc5 13 ☖e2 0-0 14 g3 ☖d7 15 ☗g2 ☖e5 16 ☐d1 ☖a5 17 ☐b1 ☖a6 18 a4 ☐ab8 19 ☗e3 ☖c4 20 ☖f4 ☖7c6 21 ☖e2 g5! 22 ☐xb8 ☐xb8 23

☖xc4 ☖xc4 24 ☗xc5 gxf4 25 gxf4 a6 26 ☐d7 ☐c8 27 ☗f2 ☖b2 28 ☐d2 ☖xa4 29 ☐a2 ☖xc3 30 ☐xa6 f5 31 ☐a3 ☖b5 32 ☐a6 ☗f7 33 ☗h3 ☖d6 34 ☗c5 ☖e8 35 ☐b6 ☖f6 36 exf5 exf5 37 ☗d6 ☗g6 38 ☗e5 ☖d7 39 ☐a6 0-1 B.Halldorsson-N.De Firmian, Reykjavik 2003 recently demonstrated.

10...☗xf1 11 ☗xf1 ☖e7

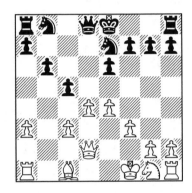

12 ☖e2

After 12 dxc5 Black should avoid the endgame for now with 12...☖d7!. This type of positional pawn sacrifice is a common theme in these lines as after 13 cxb6 axb6 Black would have play in the shape of two half-open files against White's isolated queenside pawns. In practice Black has preferred 13...☖xb6 when after 14 ☖d4 few would disagree that 14...☖c5 15 ☖b4 ☖a6+ 16 c4 ☐c8 17 ☖e2 0-0 offers Black reasonable play. However, also providing food for thought is the recent 14...☖a6+ 15 ☗f2 e5 16 ☖e3 ☖b6 17 ☖h3 ☖c4 18 ☖e2 ☐b8 19 ☐d1 0-0 20 ☐a2 ☖a4 21 ☖c2 ☐b3 22 ☐d7 ☖c6 23 ☐b7 ☖b6 24 ☐c7 ☖a5 25 ☐xa7 ☖bc4 26 ☖d3 ☖c6 27 ☐c2 ☖c5+ 28 ☗e3 ☖xa3 29 ☗g3 ☐bb8 30 ☗f2 ☖a4 31 ☐c1 ☐bd8 32 ☖e2 ☖c6 33 ☗g1 ☐d2 34 ☖xd2 ☖xd2 35 ☐xa5 ☖b3 36 ☐ca1 ☖g6+ 37 ☗h4 ☖xa1 38 ☐xa1 ☖xg2 39 ☗c5 ☐c8 40 ☗b4 ☖xf3 0-1 M.Kirszenberg-T.Hinks Edwards, Paris 2004. I certainly wouldn't say that Black was winning all along, but clearly life isn't easy for White!

12...♘bc6

When I originally annotated this game for Chesspublishing.com I remarked '12...0-0 13 a4 ♘bc6 14 ♔f2 ♘a5 15 ♕a2 has previously been assessed as equal by Shirov. One wonders though whether he had 13 h4!? up his sleeve in the event of 12... 0-0 too.' After that comment came the following encounter: 13 h4!? ♕d7 14 h5 f5 15 h6 g6 16 exf5 ♘xf5 17 dxc5 bxc5 18 ♔f2 ♕e7 19 ♕g5 ♕f7 20 ♕g4 ♘d7 21 ♗g5 ♘d6 22 ♖ad1 ♘e5 23 ♕f4 ♘dc4 24 ♕xf7+ ♖xf7 25 ♖h4 ♘xa3 26 ♖e4 ♘ac4 27 ♔e1 ♘b2 28 ♖xe5 ♘xd1 29 ♔xd1, T.Hillarp Persson-T.Sammalvuo, Swedish Team Championship 2003. Surprisingly White went on to lose in this encounter, but of course he definitely shouldn't have. Indeed the h-pawn lunge seems very worthy of attention. The disadvantage for Black of 12...0-0 is that his king is destined to be attacked. The advantage (particularly when comparing it to our main game) is that at least he gets his king's rook into the game.

13 h4!?

The same theme as discussed after the possibility of 12 dxc5 is applicable here too. Namely, after 13 dxc5 Black should eschew the endgame 13...bxc5 14 ♕xd8+ ♖xd8 15 ♗e3 ♘a5 16 ♖b1 ♘c4 17 ♔f2, which is a definite edge to White, in favour of preserving the queens (for now at least). As it happens, two ways of doing that have proven more than adequate for Black:

a) 13...♕c7!? 14 ♕f4 (or 14 ♕d6 when 14...♕xd6 15 cxd6 ♘c8 16 ♘d4 ♘xd4 17 cxd4 ♘xd6 is a level endgame although Black could also continue his queen-swapping avoidance policy with 14...♕b7!?) 14...e5! 15 ♕g4 0-0 16 ♔f2 ♘a5 17 cxb6 ♕xb6+! 18 ♗e3 ♕c6!. White remains a pawn up, but that's the end of the good news! Threats for Black, including ...♘a5-c4 and ...f7-f5, are starting to loom large.

b) 13...♕c8!? 14 ♕e3 0-0! 15 cxb6 ♖d8! 16 ♔f2 axb6 17 ♖b1 ♘e5 18 ♕xb6 is, for the time being at least, two pawns for White, but both 18...♘d3+!? and 18...♘c4! are at least of some concern to White's king and queen.

13...h6

It's logical for Black to want to get some dark-squared control and, in view of White's h-pawn aspirations, prevent weaknesses in his camp. This of course may have been the case if White had got in h5-h6, but all the same it might have been more in the spirit of things to take up the challenge with 13...0-0. Referring back to my comments to Black's 12th move, Black does have an ...f5 break available to try and expose the white monarch situated on the f-file. Possibly a lot rests on the correct assessment of that previously mentioned all-Swedish encounter that comes as a direct transposition.

14 ♖h3

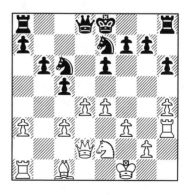

This is the other option that 13 h4!? brings with it: the chance of a 'rook swinger'.

14...♕c7

Black's play looks a little bizarre when it comes to the defence of the g-pawn. However, 14...0-0 15 ♖g3 is surprisingly dangerous as illustrated by 15...♔h8 16 ♖xg7!! ♔xg7 17 ♕xh6+ ♔g8 18 ♘f4 – there is no good defence to 19 ♘h5.

15 ♖g3 ♖g8 16 dxc5 bxc5

Regarding the failure to make this recapture, the positional pawn sacrifice would be nothing like as good now because Black's own king position is far from secure and his king's rook is out of the game.

17 ♕f4 ♕xf4

At the very least providing White with a simple bishop-for-knight advantage in the endgame; in retrospect perhaps keeping the queens on would offer Black more play. An obvious candidate is 17...♘e5!? but it's not clear what's going to happen to Black's king.

18 ♘xf4 ♖b8

18...0-0-0 would be more satisfactory from the perspective of Black's king's rook, but the possible variation 19 ♗e3 c4 20 ♖b1 e5 21 ♘d5 ♘xd5 22 exd5 ♖xd5 23 ♖g4 still favours White.

19 ♘h5!

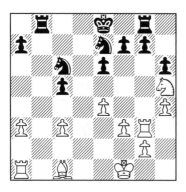

Obvious, but this attack of the g7-pawn is also very strong.

19...♘g6

Almost out of the blue Black is in big trouble, for example 19...♔f8 falling foul of 20 ♖xg7! ♖xg7 21 ♗xh6.

20 ♗xh6! gxh6 21 ♘f6+

The key to this neat tactic is that there is no place for the black king that will escape the material-winning h4-h5.

21...♔e7 22 ♘xg8+ ♖xg8 23 h5

The point of course is that the pin guarantees the win of the knight.

23...♔f6 24 hxg6 fxg6 25 ♖b1

And why not? The rest is easy.

25...♖b8 26 ♖xb8 ♘xb8 27 ♔e2 ♘d7 28 f4 e5 29 ♖d3 1-0

Game 8

T.Hillarp Persson-P.Lehikoinen
Reykjavik 2004

---

1 d4 ♘f6 2 c4 e6 3 ♘c3 ♗b4 4 f3 d5 5 a3 ♗xc3+ 6 bxc3 c5 7 cxd5 ♘xd5 8 dxc5

Finally we come to White's main move.

8...f5

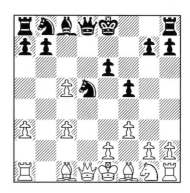

The next two games will investigate 8...♕a5 and the chapter will end with the lesser-seen 8...♘d7. Anyway, regarding the text, as usual this move is aimed at dissuading the advance e2-e4.

9 ♘h3

The English GM Peter Wells is a bit of a theoretician and it is notable that he likes this move. Nevertheless, it is definitely worth taking a brief look at the alternatives:

a) 9 ♕c2 0-0 10 e4 fxe4 11 fxe4 ♘f4 12 ♘f3 ♕c7 13 ♗e3 ♘d7 14 ♗c4 ♘xc5 15 0-0

♗d7 has been reached on a few occasions, and the general opinion is that it is fairly balanced – White has the bishop pair but Black has the better queenside pawn structure.

As well as 9...0-0, 9...f4!? is very playable as 10 ♗xf4?! ♘xf4 11 ♕a4+ ♘c6 12 ♕xf4 e5 leaves White with an ugly pawn structure and an embarrassing kingside development, while 10 e4 fxe3 would transpose to 'c' below. Also, the intriguing 10 g3 0-0 11 c4 ♘e3 12 ♗xe3 fxe3 13 ♕c3 ♘c6 14 ♕xe3 e5 15 ♖c1 ♗f5 16 ♗h3 ♘d4 17 ♗xf5 ♘xf5 18 ♕c3 ♕e7 19 ♘h3 e4 20 ♘f4 exf3 21 ♕xf3 ♘e3 22 ♖c3 ♖ae8 23 ♔f2 ♘f5 24 ♕d5+ ♔h8 25 ♖b1 g5 26 ♖xb7 ♕f6 27 ♖f3 gxf4 28 ♖xf4 ♕h6 29 h4 ♖xe2+ 30 ♔xe2 ♘xg3+ 31 ♔d3 ♕xf4 32 ♕d4+ ♕xd4+ 33 ♔xd4 ♘f5+ 34 ♔e5 ♘e3 35 ♖xa7 ♘xc4+ 36 ♔d5 ♘e3+ 37 ♔c6 ♘f5 38 ♖a4 ♖c8+ 39 ♔b6 ♘e7 40 ♖d4 ♔g7 41 a4 ♔f7 42 a5 ½-½ of M.Cebalo-I.Naumkin, Reggio Emilia 2004 suggests that Black has reasonable play for the (roughly!) one-and-a-half pawns deficit.

b) 9 c4 ♕f6!?

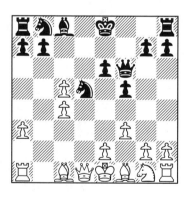

10 ♗d2 (or 10 ♗g5 ♕xg5 11 cxd5 when each of 11...exd5, 11...0-0 and 11...f4 looks playable – even if White escapes a pawn ahead, that big hole on e3 is always going to provide Black with something to work with) 10...♘e7 (or 10...♘c3 11 ♕c1 ♘a4 when White has the usual kingside development problems and Black will have no trouble regaining one of those c-pawns) 11 ♘h3

♘bc6 12 ♘f4 0-0 13 e3 ♘g6 14 ♘xg6 ♕xg6 15 ♗c3 e5 with an equal position, V.Ragozin-A.Sokolsky, Kiev 1954.

c) 9 e4 fxe4 10 ♕c2 will merely transpose to 'a' above unless Black plays something other than 10...0-0. I would have said that it is a reasonable move order for White to employ if he wants to avoid the 9 ♕c2 f4!? possibility, but in fact they could still come to the same thing.

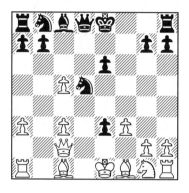

Yes, 9 e4 fxe4 10 ♕c2 e3 (the best 'something' other than 10...0-0) and 9 ♕c2 f4!? 10 e4!? fxe3 both reach the position illustrated above. After 11 ♗d3 ♘d7 two obvious variations stand out (note I'm not including 12 ♗xh7?? ♕h4+!):

c1) 12 c4 ♕a5+! (taking advantage of the fact that White can't use the d2-square) 13 ♔f1 ♘f4 14 ♗xe3 (14 ♗xh7 ♕xc5 leaves White's army mainly undeveloped and certainly poorly coordinated) 14...♘xd3 15 ♕xd3 0-0 16 ♕d6 ♕c3!? when Black is more than happy to offload his e-pawn as in its absence Black's pieces will spring to life. There also looks nothing wrong with 13...♘5f6 intending ...♘xc5 next. Now we might see 14 c6 if White decides that he may as well expend a tempo to split the black queenside pawns, but that's not a big problem for Black's potentially very active position. Besides, 14...♘e5!? must be okay as well as it looks too greedy to snatch the b-pawn.

c2) 12 ♘e2 ♘xc5 13 0-0 ♘xd3 14 ♕xd3

0-0 15 ♗xe3 when both 15...♗d7 and 15 ...b6 look fine for Black, who (because of the knight's attack on White's bishop) threatens to bring his own bishop to the e2-a6 diagonal. It would also settle for a home on b7 or c6. Either way, just as in 'c1' Black has nothing to fear.

9...0-0 10 c4!?

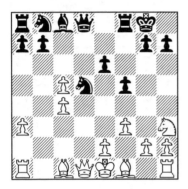

Far more critical than the bland 10 ♘f4.

10...♘f6

In view of the unfavourable endgames available to Black, probably his better practical option is to dabble in something like 10...♕h4+!? 11 ♘f2 and now:

a) Though the game ended in a draw, 11...♘f6 12 e3 ♘c6 13 ♗e2 ♖d8 14 ♕c2 ♘d7 15 0-0 ♘xc5 16 ♗b2 b6 17 ♘d3! ♕h6 18 f4 ♘e4 19 ♖f3! ♕h4 20 ♖h3 ♕e7 21 ♗f3 (G.Ligterink-G.Miralles Cannes 1990) was, with all things considered, generally deemed to have left White with an edge, the potential pressure against g7 and control of the outpost on e5 being the main reasons.

b) 11...♕f6!? 12 ♗d2 ♘e7 when the c-pawns could still be a pain but Black will be able to get some dark-squared control via ...e6-e5 and can then hopefully complete his development. Personally, I think I prefer this to 12...♘c3 13 ♕c1 ♘a4 14 ♗g5 ♕f7 15 ♘d3 ♘d7 which White went on to win in A.Beliavsky-L.Portisch, Amsterdam 1990.

11 ♕xd8 ♖xd8 12 ♘f2 ♘a6?!

Black seeks to regain his pawn quickly but,

seeing as he doesn't, this knight ends up offside here. Instead 12...♘c6 13 e3 e5 14 ♗b2 ♗e6 isn't too bad for Black, but putting the clamps on the second player's queenside with the immediate 13 ♖b1!? may be more problematic for Black as it is trickier for him to get his bishop out. Indeed after 13...e5 14 ♘d3, upon 14...♖b8 White can delay e2-e3 in favour of pressurising the e5-pawn further by 15 ♗b2.

13 ♘d3 ♗d7

After 13...♘d7 White will play 14 ♗e3 anyway when Black can't even employ the standard positional pawn sacrifice 14...b6?! because of 15 c6!.

14 ♗e3

Also not ridiculous is 14 ♗f4 as after 14...♖ac8 15 ♗d6 Black can't play 15...♘e8? because of 16 ♗e7.

14...♗c6 15 ♖g1

Not the only plan, but I've noticed that in many of his games as White Tiger has a tendency to seek out the break g2-g4.

15...♖dc8

This looks like a funny move but with c5 currently well guarded and the e5-square also under White's control, it's difficult to make a good recommendation.

16 ♖b1

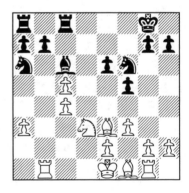

Having played the Nimzo-Indian all my life with both colours I've had a bit of experience in positions where White has been saddled with doubled (and sometimes even trebled) isolated c-pawns. It is not too hard to imagine how they can be weak and easily picked off by enemy rooks, but often they can also be a strength. Here is such an occasion with the ones on c4 and c5 controlling some very useful squares. Typically White's dark-squared bishop works well with them (its enemy counterpart will of course be absent) and, as demonstrated here, the half-open b-file is also a big plus.

16...g6 17 h4 ♔f7 18 ♗d4 ♘d7 19 g4!

Always the Swedish grandmaster's idea – his ultimate goal is action for his king's rook.

19...♖e8 20 gxf5 exf5 21 ♔f2 ♖ac8 22 h5

Continuing the chiselling process.

22...♖c7 23 hxg6+ hxg6 24 ♖h1

The bishop on d4 is an absolute monster.

24...♘f8 25 ♘e5+ ♔e7 26 ♖g1 g5 27 ♘xc6+

Correctly avoiding 27 ♖xg5?? ♘e6.

27...bxc6 28 ♗e5 ♖d7 29 ♖xg5

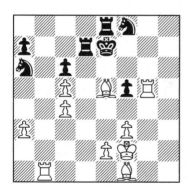

Black's position is collapsing like a deck of cards. It's all over bar the shouting.

29...♘xc5 30 ♖xf5 ♖b7 31 ♖xb7+ ♘xb7 32 ♗h3 ♘d7 33 ♖h5 ♔d8 34 ♗d4 ♘b6 35 ♖h7 1-0

Game 9
S.Volkov-V.Jeremic
Korinthos 2004

---

1 d4 ♘f6 2 c4 e6 3 ♘c3 ♗b4 4 f3 d5 5

a3 ♗xc3+ 6 bxc3 c5 7 cxd5 ♘xd5 8 dxc5 ♕a5

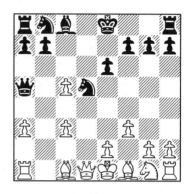

I haven't mentioned it before but I'm sure the reader observed that 8...♘xc3? 9 ♕xd8+ ♔xd8 10 ♗b2 ♘a4 11 ♗xg7 ♖g8 12 ♗d4 ♘c6 13 ♗f2 is very undesirable. The text move attacks c3 with a second piece and removes her majesty from the same file as the white queen.

9 e4 ♘f6

First up, it is necessary to know that 9...♘xc3? 10 ♕d2 is especially bad for Black in the event of 10...♕xc5? 11 ♗b2. Not only is the g7-pawn under threat but 11...♘a4 walks into 12 ♖c1. Meanwhile, 10...♘c6 11 ♗b2 ♘a4 12 ♕xa5 ♘xa5 13 ♗xg7 doesn't exactly lose but it's not great! White has the bishop pair, and his dark-squared one in particular will rule the roost. Similarly, 9...♕xc3+? should be avoided as 10 ♗d2 ♕e5 11 ♘e2 ♘f6 12 ♗c3 will quite clearly favour White – again look out for 12...♕xc5 13 ♖c1.

Hence Black must retreat his knight, and a key move for White to look out for is 9...♘c7 10 ♕d4! (the same queen centralisation could also apply after 9...♘e7 although, as you'll discover in the next game, 10 ♗e3 tends to be favoured). Results have definitely favoured White here, e.g. 10...f6 11 ♕b4 (the most straightforward) 11...♘c6 12 ♕xa5 ♘xa5 13 ♖b1 ♗d7 14 ♗e3 e5 15 ♘e2 ♘e6 16 ♘c1 ♔e7 17 ♘b3 ♘xb3 18 ♖xb3 ♖ab8

19 ♗b5 ♖hc8 20 ♗xd7 ♔xd7 21 ♖b5 a6 22 ♖a5 ♖c6 23 ♔e2 ♖bc8 24 ♖b1 ♖8c7 25 ♖d1+ ♔e7 26 ♖d5 when in I.Khenkin-A.Ayas Fernandez, Andorra 2004 White had consolidated his extra pawn and was able to grind out a win.

Also worthy of consideration is 11 f4, which recently saw the fascinating 11...♘c6 12 ♕c4 e5 13 f5 g6 14 ♗d3 ♗d7 15 ♘e2 ♘e7 16 fxg6 hxg6 17 ♖b1 0-0-0 18 ♕b4 ♕xb4 19 cxb4 ♗h3 20 gxh3 ♖xd3 21 0-0 ♖dxh3 22 ♖xf6 ♖xh2 23 ♘g3 ♖c2 24 ♗e3 ♖c3 25 ♗f2 ♘b5 26 ♖e6 ♘c6 27 ♖xg6 ♖xa3 28 ♘f5 ♖ah3 29 ♔g2 ♖h2+ 30 ♔f3 ♘cd4+ 31 ♗xd4 ♘xd4+ 32 ♘xd4 exd4 33 ♖d1 ♖d8 34 ♖d6 ♖f8+ 35 ♔g3 ♖h7 36 ♖g6 ♖d7 ½-½ M.Bluvshtein-V.Kotronias, Hastings 2004/05.

10 ♗e3

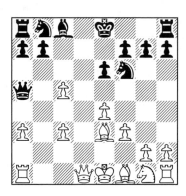

Also instructive was 10 ♖b1 0-0 11 ♖b5 ♕xc3+ 12 ♔f2 ♕e5 13 ♗b2 ♕c7 14 ♕d6 ♘e8 15 ♕xc7 ♘xc7 16 ♖b3 ♘c6 17 f4 f5 18 e5 ♖d8 19 ♘f3 ♘d5 20 g3 ♘a5 21 ♖d3 b6 22 cxb6 axb6 23 ♘d4 ♘b7 24 ♗g2 ♘c5 25 ♖dd1 ♗b7 26 ♘b5 ♖ab8 27 ♘d6 when White retained an edge throughout in V.Milov-E.Magerramov, Berlin 1993. The c5-pawn is of far more importance to White than its compatriot on c3 which, when present, obstructs activity along the b2-g7 diagonal.

10...0-0

10...♕xc3+ 11 ♔f2 0-0 12 ♘e2 ♕a5 13 ♕d2 ♕xd2 14 ♗xd2 ♘c6 15 ♗e3 ♖d8 16 ♘c3 merely gives White a risk-free endgame advantage, but 10...♘fd7!? played on this specific move has actually scored rather well for Black in practical play. Whilst 11 ♕d4 0-0 12 ♕b4 ♕c7 13 a4 ♘c6 14 ♕a3 ♘a5 15 ♘h3 b6 16 cxb6 axb6 17 ♕b4 ♘c6 18 ♕b2 ♘a5 19 ♕b4 ♘c6 ½-½ D.Zagorskis-J.Nilssen, Copenhagen 1998 is of independent significance, 11 ♕b3 0-0 would transpose to the notes to White's next move. Retreating the f6-knight is not such a strange idea as the e4-pawn is currently shutting it out of the action. It's also an interesting concept to hold back on ...0-0 for a move, even if with the king on e8 it is vulnerable to a check on b5.
11 ♔f2!?

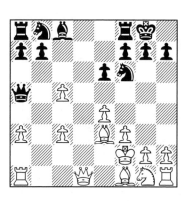

White has to do something with his king eventually and this keeps the white queen options open. Nevertheless I do need to talk about 11 ♕b3 ♘fd7!? (Black immediately gets to the point of attacking the c5-pawn; on the debate of which knight, note how 11...♘a6 12 ♗xa6 ♕xa6 13 ♘e2 e5 14 c4 ♗e6 15 ♕b5 ♗xc4 16 ♕xa6 ♗xa6 17 ♔f2 ♖ac8 18 ♖hd1 ♖fd8 19 ♘c3 ♔f8 20 a4 ♖xd1 21 ♖xd1 b6 22 ♖d6 ♔e8 23 a5 ♘d7 24 axb6 axb6 25 ♘d5 ♗b7 26 cxb6 wasn't much fun for Black in V.Moskalenko-A.Shneider, Lvov 1985) 12 a4 ♕c7 13 ♕a3 b6! (surely a familiar theme by now: rather than spending a decade trying to round up the c5-pawn, as we have seen previously

Black is often advised to turn it into a real pawn sacrifice in order to get play for his major pieces) 14 a5! bxc5. Now 15 a6 c4 16 ♕a5 ♕xa5 17 ♖xa5 ♘c6 18 ♖a2 ♖b8 19 ♗xc4 ♘de5 20 ♗e2 ♖d8 21 ♔f2 ♖b1 22 g4 f5 23 ♔g2 ended up as an eventual victory for White in F.Berkes-Z.Almasi, Budapest 2004. I'm certainly not saying that White is winning in this variation, but one conclusion is clear: if White can maintain some initiative then in practice it is better for him to eschew Black's offering of ...b7-b6.

Another point is that Black should play with reasonable urgency, as giving White time will allow him to consolidate. In particular, Black should try to avoid White parking a knight on d5 as was recently the case in G.Lettieri-F.Guido, Verona 2005. Here play continued 11 ♕b3 ♘c6 (as I just mentioned, it is better to attack the c-pawn immediately) 12 ♗b5 ♕c7 13 ♗xc6 ♕xc6 14 ♘e2 e5 15 ♖b1 ♖b8 16 c4 ♗e6 17 ♘c3 ♖fc8 18 ♘d5 ♔f8 19 0-0 ♘d7 20 ♕c3 f6 21 f4! exf4 22 ♖xf4 ♗f7 23 ♖bf1 ♖e8 24 ♗d4 ♖e6 25 e5 ♘xc5 26 exf6 g6 27 ♕g3 ♘d7 28 ♕g5 ♕xc4 29 ♗xa7 ♖e4 30 ♖xe4 ♕xe4 31 ♘c3 ♕e6 32 ♗xb8 ♘xb8 33 ♕h6+ ♔e8 34 ♕d2 1-0. For a not-so-high rated player, that was a very well handled game.

11...♘fd7!

11...♘c6 12 ♕b3 ♕c7 13 ♘e2 e5 14 ♖b1 ♘a5 15 ♕b4 ♗e6 16 ♘g3 favoured White in S.Volkov-B.Macieja, European Team Championship, Batumi 1999. He won't lose his c5-pawn yet, and he is only a move away from activating his king's rook.

12 ♖b1 ♖d8

12...b6 is, as we know, thematic but the 13 cxb6 axb6 14 ♗b5 ♕xa3 15 ♘e2 ♕e7 16 ♖a1 ♖xa1 17 ♕xa1 ♘c5 18 ♖b1 of M.Ulibin-J.Barkhagen, Stockholm 2002 again shows the advantage of returning the extra pawn to buy time for development. I sound like a broken record, but the bishop pair offers White a slight plus.

13 ♕b3 ♕c7 14 ♖d1

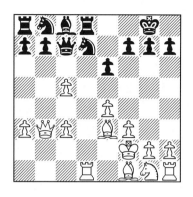

14...♖f8!

Last turn White had indirectly protected the c5-pawn via the pin on the rook. This move of course simply unpins it.

15 ♕c4

More common is 15 ♕b4, although White has hardly set the house on fire regarding results. That said, after 15...♘c6 16 ♕a4 ♘a5 17 ♕b4 ♘c6 18 ♕a4 ♘a5 19 ♕b5 a6 20 ♕b4 ♘c6 21 ♕a4 ♘a5 the latest finesse of 22 ♘h3 ♘xc5 23 ♕b4 b6 24 ♖b1 ♘d7 25 ♗xb6 ♘xb6 26 ♕xb6 ♕xc3 27 ♗e2 ♘c6 28 ♖hc1 ♕d4+ 29 ♔e1! ♕xb6 30 ♖xb6 gave White something to work with in M.Ulibin-R.Tischbierek, Biel 2004.

In T.Hillarp Persson-V.Ikonnikov, Barcelona 2003 Black broke with the 16...♘a5 trend: 16...♘ce5!? 17 ♕d4 ♘c6 18 ♕d6 ♕a5 19 ♕g3 ♘xc5 20 ♘e2 f5 21 exf5 ♖xf5 22 ♔g1 e5 23 h4 ♗e6 frankly worked out quite well for Black, although of course White didn't need to venture his queen into the d6-square.

15...♘c6 16 ♘e2 b6!?

Black doesn't need to play this but what follows demonstrates the sort of counterplay that can be received through this pawn sacrifice.

17 cxb6

After 17 ♘g3 bxc5, 18 ♗xc5? is unplayable because of 18...♘a5, but without that the black knights gear up for action.

17...axb6 18 ♘d4 ♘c5

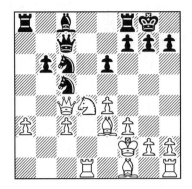

19 ♘b5

In retrospect perhaps something like 19 ♘xc6 ♕xc6 20 ♕b5 ♕xb5 21 ♗xb5 ♖xa3 22 ♖d6 would be more prudent, although actually Black isn't obliged to trade queens.

19...♕e5 20 ♗e2 ♖a4 21 ♕a2 ♗a6

I'm not saying that White should lose this game but it is quite a tricky position for a human to handle. With a rating of well over 2600, Mr Volkov is no mug!

22 c4?!

I don't like this move as although it supports the knight, the pawn blocks out the queen and relinquishes control of the b4-square.

22...f5!

Now Black has play on both sides of the board.

23 exf5 ♗xb5 24 cxb5 ♘b4 25 ♕b1?!

Given his time again White would probably opt to bail out with 25 ♕d2 ♕xf5 26 ♗xc5 ♕xc5+ 27 ♕e3 ♕xe3+ 28 ♔xe3 ♖xa3+ 29 ♔f2 ♖a2 30 ♖he1 and a likely draw.

25...♘d5

I'm not going to bang on about the two bishops here as the threat from the black queen and knights is obvious!

26 ♗d2 ♖xf5

And let's not forget the black rooks!

27 ♕a1 ♖d4!

A queen swap definitely isn't on Black's agenda!

28 g4

White is getting desperate.

28...♘e4+! 29 ♔e1 ♘ec3 30 ♗xc3 ♘xc3 31 ♖d2

Or of course 31 ♕xc3 ♖xd1+, netting the queen. This is turning into a complete nightmare for White.

31...♖xd2 32 ♔xd2 ♕xe2+ 33 ♔xc3 ♖c5+ 0-1

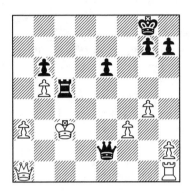

Mate is forced.

Game 10
A.Beliavsky-N.De Firmian
Sigeman & Co, Malmö 2004

---

1 d4 ♘f6 2 c4 e6 3 ♘c3 ♗b4 4 f3 d5 5 a3 ♗xc3+ 6 bxc3 c5 7 cxd5 ♘xd5 8 dxc5 ♕a5 9 e4 ♘e7

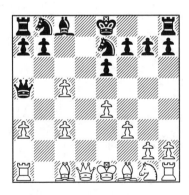

10 ♗e3

Comparing 9...♘e7 to the comments I

made in the previous game about 9...♘c7, here 10 ♕d4 hasn't proven to be that successful for White because after 10...0-0 11 ♕b4 Black has available the most satisfactory retreat 11...♕c7.

10...0-0

Again 10...♕xc3+?! isn't so hot as after 11 ♔f2 0-0 12 ♘e2 ♕a5 13 ♕d2 any endgames will favour White. However, 10...♘d7, sharing ideas with the next game, is slightly different. White should choose between 11 ♕d4 or 11 ♕b3. Regarding the latter, in contrast to the previous game 11...♘c6 12 ♗b5 ♕c7 13 ♘h3 0-0 14 ♘f2 ♘a5 15 ♕b4 ♘c6 16 ♕a4 ♘ce5 17 ♕d4 ♘c6 18 ♗xc6 ♕xc6 19 0-0 b6 20 cxb6 axb6 21 ♘d3 leaves White with nothing to fear. It's the same pawn structure but he dominates the centre and 21...♖a5 22 ♘b4 ♕a8 23 ♘c2 ♖a4 24 ♕d6 ♕a5 25 ♘b4 ♕e5 26 ♕xe5 ♘xe5 27 ♗xb6 was easily converted in M.Cebalo-O.Jovanic, Zagreb 2004.

11 ♕b3

I'm not sure I buy into the 11 ♖b1 ♘d7 12 ♗b5 ♖d8 13 ♕b3 ♘e5 14 ♔f2 ♗d7 15 ♘e2 ♗xb5 16 ♕xb5 ♘d3+ 17 ♔g3 ♕c7+ 18 ♔h3 ♖d7 19 g3 of S.Volkov-P.Jaracz, Bad Wiessee 2004 even though White went on to win. Volkov is undoubtedly a leading expert in this line but in the same year of 2004 after 11 ♖b1 he lost to the greedy 11...♕xc3+ 12 ♔f2 ♕xa3 and drew against 11...♖d8 12 ♕b3 ♘a6.

11...♕c7

With the other knight on e7, again 11...♘a6 must be a candidate and actually 12 ♘h3 ♗d7 13 ♗e2 ♖ab8 14 ♗f4 e5!? 15 ♗xe5 ♘xc5 16 ♕b4 ♘d3+ 17 ♗xd3 ♕xe5 18 f4?! ♕c7 19 ♕xe7? ♕xc3+ 20 ♔e2 ♗g4+ 0-1 V.Jianu-A.Kalinin, Sozina 2004 is a game White will want to forget in a hurry.

12 ♖b1

12 ♘h3 e5 13 ♘f2 ♘ec6 is an alternative approach when White could still employ 14 ♖b1 to try to tie Black down to the defence of his b-pawn or else travel the road of 14

♗e2 ♗e6 15 ♕c2 ♘d7 16 0-0 ♘a5 17 ♘d3. Although White guards c5, the bishop on e2 is a little out of it and for Black the c4-square must count for something.

12...♘ec6 13 f4!?

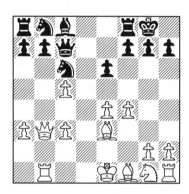

Finally something a little different! Not that it's entirely a new idea as previously we have seen Shirov himself employ this move in order to ready f3 for the knight.

13...♘a5 14 ♕d1!? ♖d8 15 ♕h5

Entertaining stuff. The white queen has transferred to the kingside where of course the minor pieces still rest at home!

15...♘d7 16 ♘f3

White can see Black's threat but plumps for development anyway. That said, although it seems harsh to actually criticise this move, possibly 16 ♗d3!?, intending to meet 16...♘f6 with 17 ♕e2, might have been better, whilst 16 ♖d1!? also has its plus points.

16...♘f6 17 ♕h4 ♘xe4 18 ♗d4

This is a superbly placed bishop which understandably Black is now quite eager to eliminate.

18...♘c6 19 ♗d3 ♘xd4 20 cxd4

White has lost his bishop but has improved his pawn structure.

20...♕a5+

After 20...♘f6 21 0-0 White could easily mount a serious offensive. Hence Black ensures that his won't be the only king to be targeted.

21 ♔e2?

It takes too long to castle by hand after this, and White should instead prefer the (only temporary) self-pin 21 ♖b4!.

21...♘c3+

Regarding that dodgy white king position, instead of this 21...♖xd4!? looks quite promising for Black.

22 ♔f2

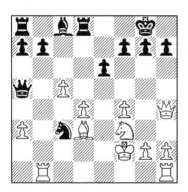

22...h6

Upon 22...♘xb1?! 23 ♕xh7+ ♔f8 24 ♖xb1 White would have tremendous play for the exchange.

23 ♖b3

White has a bind on e5 and pieces slowly aiming at Black's king, but he must be careful. Although Black is yet to complete his development, things could easily go horribly wrong for the first player as he has more pawn islands and some obvious targets within his own camp.

23...♗d7 24 ♖c1 ♘d5

A considerable number of very natural moves are played throughout this middlegame and overall an assessment of 'dynamic equality' couldn't be far off the mark. Okay, what that basically means then is that White has the better of the first half of this game and Black the better of the second!

25 ♔g1 ♗c6 26 f5

White wants to make further inroads towards the black monarch but now Black will have the e-file to work with.

26...exf5 27 ♗xf5 ♖e8 28 ♕f2 ♕a4 29

♘d2 ♖e7 30 ♗c2 ♖ae8 31 ♖g3

Just when it seemed as though White had abandoned his attacking aspirations he returns for more!

31...♕a6 32 ♖f1 ♕e2 33 ♗d3 ♕xf2+ 34 ♖xf2 ♖e1+ 35 ♖f1 ♘f4 36 ♗c4 ♘e2+ 37 ♗xe2 ♖1xe2 38 ♘f3 ♖8e4

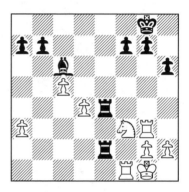

Clearly the tide has turned although Nick doesn't seem to do quite enough for Black to gain the full point.

39 ♖f2 ♖2e3 40 ♖d2 ♖xa3 41 d5 ♖a1+ 42 ♔f2 ♗b5 43 ♖h3

The only satisfactory way to avoid the mate on f1.

43...♗d7

Instead 43...♖f1+ 44 ♔g3 ♖c1 45 d6 ♗d7 looks very powerful, but arguably the main point of interest in this game is White's novel opening approach.

44 ♖h5 f6 45 d6 ♖c1 46 ♖b2 b6 47 cxb6 axb6 48 ♖d5

After the alternative 48 ♖xb6 ♖c2+ 49 ♔f1 ♖a4 White would suffer on the back rank.

48...b5 49 ♘d2 ♖e5 50 ♖xe5 fxe5 51 ♘f3 ♖c5 52 ♖e2 ♖d5 53 ♘xe5 ♖xd6 54 ♘xd7 ♖xd7 55 ♖e8+ ♔f7 56 ♖b8 ♖d5 57 ♔e2 ♔e7 58 h4 ♖c5 59 g4 ♖c2+ 60 ♔e3 ♖c3+ 61 ♔f4 ♖c5 ½-½

One grandmaster shows another the usual amount of respect. Well, that and Black can't make much progress without risking things on the kingside!

Game 11
A.Beliavsky-A.Kunte
Pune 2004

1 d4 ♘f6 2 c4 e6 3 ♘c3 ♗b4 4 f3 d5 5 a3 ♗xc3+ 6 bxc3 c5 7 cxd5 ♘xd5 8 dxc5 ♘d7!?

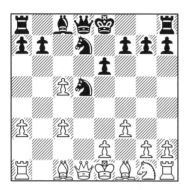

In my opinion the fact that English GM Michael Adams has favoured this move should make us all sit up and take note. With the text Black shows that he is eager to regain the c5-pawn but prefers not to commit the queen.

9 e4

A continuation not yet seen is 9 c6!? bxc6 10 e4. It looks to me as though 10...♘xc3 11 ♕d4 ♕h4+ (or 11...♕f6 12 e5!) 12 g3 ♕f6 13 e5! ♘xe5 14 ♕xc3 ♘d3+ 15 ♕xd3 ♕xa1 16 ♕c2 ♗d7 17 ♗d3 is excellent for White and so Black may just have to retreat his knight. Presumably with a symmetrical pawn structure (i.e. both sides having isolated a- and c-pawns) White's bishop pair should give him a niggling edge, although eventually Black should be able to arrange ...♗a6.

9...♘e7 10 ♗e3 0-0

Of course Black could still employ 10...♕a5 but if he doesn't venture out with it now it won't be chased back later!

11 ♗b5

11 ♕b3?! has less point now as the c3-pawn isn't even attacked. Instead of 11...♕a5

12 ♕b4 ♕c7, Black should of course opt for the immediate 11...♕c7! when he stands well upon either 12 ♕c4 ♘e5 13 ♕b4 ♖d8 (the d3-square is ripe for an invasion and as usual White lags behind in development) or 12 a4 ♘xc5 13 ♕a3 b6 14 a5 ♗b7 (Mickey went on to win in J.Pomes Marcet-M.Adams, Mainz 2001).

Black's idea then is to develop the queen on c7, although 11 ♘h3 ♕c7!? 12 ♕d6 ♕a5 is sneaky! With that in mind, perhaps White's most flexible is 11 ♖b1!? as after 11...♕c7?! 12 ♕d6!, 12...♕a5? is unplayable because ...♕xc3+ will no longer be a fork. Hence 11...♕a5 12 ♕b3 ♕c7, returning more to the realms of our previous game.

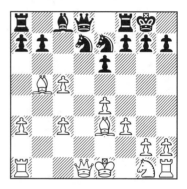

11...♕a5

Basically it seems that Black has the choice of where he wants the white queen to be when he parks his own queen on c7. The immediate deployment encourages some crazy lines, e.g. 11...♕c7 12 ♕d6 (or 12 ♗xd7 ♖d8!) 12...♕a5 13 ♗xd7 (maybe 13 ♖b1!? is stronger) 13...♕xc3+ 14 ♔f2 ♕xa1 15 ♕xe7 ♗xd7 16 ♕xd7 ♖ad8 17 ♕b5 ♖d1 – White has two pieces for a rook but will struggle to complete his kingside development.

12 ♕b3 ♕c7

The alternative 12...e5 13 ♘e2 ♕c7 14 ♗xd7 ♗xd7 would transpose to the main game.

13 ♗xd7 ♗xd7 14 ♘e2

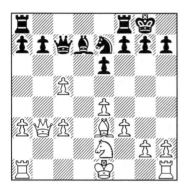

14...e5!?

14...♘c6 has proven to be okay in practice too, e.g. 15 c4 (15 0-0 e5 16 ♖fd1 ♘a5 17 ♕b4 ♘c6 18 ♕b3 ♘a5 19 ♕b4 ♘c6, J.Cox-J.Emms, London 2005, can hardly be deemed as a winning attempt for White, but it does also highlight Black's difficulties in reaching positions in which he can create winning chances) 15...e5 16 ♘c3 ♖ab8 (16...♘d4?! 17 ♗xd4 exd4 18 ♘d5 ♕xc5 19 ♕xb7 d3 20 ♕b4 was a successful smash-and-grab raid in M.Bluvshtein-T.Roussel Roozmon, Montreal 2002) 17 ♘d5 ♕a5+ 18 ♔f2 f5 19 exf5 ♗xf5 20 ♖hd1 ♕d8 21 ♔g1 ♕h4. Well, objectively I suppose White is slightly better, but actually Black went on to win in M.Ulibin-A.Cherniaev, Biel 2004. Mind you, Alexander plays a lot in England and he is a very slippery customer!

15 ♖b1 ♖ab8 16 0-0 ♘c6

16...♗e6 17 ♕b5 (17 c4 ♘c6 18 ♖fd1 would transpose to our main game) 17...♘c6 18 ♖fd1 ♖fd8 19 c4 ♖xd1+ 20 ♖xd1 ♕a5 21 ♕b3 ♕a6 22 ♖d5 ♘a5 23 ♕b5 ♘xc4 24 ♕xa6 bxa6 25 ♖d3 was roughly equal in R.Palliser-D.Gormally, British Rapidplay Championship, Halifax 2004.

17 ♖fd1 ♗e6 18 c4

The pawn is of course weak here and destined to drop off. However, it only got in the way and the 18 ♕a4 ♘a5 19 ♗f2 ♖fd8 20 ♖xd8+ ♖xd8 21 ♘g3 of E.Ovod-V.Sanchez Martin, Oropesa del Mar 2000 doesn't really constitute an improvement.

18...♘a5 19 ♕b4 ♘xc4 20 ♗f2 ♕c6

20...a5 and 20...b6 are obvious alternatives; they both look reasonable but are unlikely to change the outcome of this game.

21 ♘g3 g6 22 ♘f1 ♖fd8 23 ♖xd8+ ♖xd8 24 ♕xb7

White grabs a pawn but Black's counterplay soon becomes self-evident.

24...♕xb7 25 ♖xb7 ♖d1 26 ♗h4 ♘d2 27 ♔f2 ♖xf1+ 28 ♔e2 ♖b1

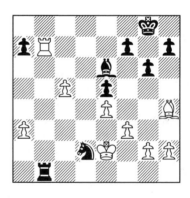

Black is a piece for a pawn up but it is that pawn that saves White's blushes.

29 c6 ♘b3 30 ♗f6 ♘d4+ ½-½

Summary

The first conclusion to draw from this extensive chapter is that 7 cxd5 is White's best move. I started with this ...d7-d5 and ...c7-c5 variation first because it is considered to be the main line, and the big question revolves around how Black should recapture after 7 cxd5. My opinion is that taking back with the knight is rock-solid, but against sensible white play it is extremely difficult for Black to win such positions. Invariably, White tries to consolidate an extra c-pawn after 8 dxc5 (the eighth move queen options haven't achieved great results in practice) and retains the two bishops, but ironically in many games most of his efforts are spent trying to manoeuvre his remaining knight to a good square. If dxc5 has occurred, Black always has the semi-pawn sacrifice ...b7-b6 in his armoury.

Regarding specifics, Adams's 9...♘d7 (see Game 11) encourages rare (for this line) and interesting complications. However, although not committing the black queen has a certain appeal, it could be that my simple (though yet to be seen) 10 c6!? promises White a small but lasting edge. The chances are that with best play there is still a draw, but it is far from clear that that is the case after 7...exd5. Those lines are far more double-edged and, although my gut feeling is that the truth lies with White, often he is living on a knife-edge. He could easily build up a big centre when his beautiful bishop pair watches while the heavy pieces destroy the black king. On the other hand, he could get lumbered with a bad bishop while Black invades down the c-file! 7...exd5 is arguably dubious but offers Black the best winning chances. Frankly though, if he is dead set on defeating 4 f3 then he might be better off investigating the ideas of the next two chapters.

1 d4 ♘f6 2 c4 e6 3 ♘c3 ♗b4 4 f3 d5 5 a3 ♗xc3+ 6 bxc3 c5 7 cxd5

> 7 e3 – *Game 1*

7...♘xd5

> 7...exd5 8 e3 (D)
>> 8...♕c7 – *Game 2*
>> 8...0-0 9 ♗d3: 9...b6 – *Game 4*; 9...♖e8 – *Game 3*

8 dxc5

> 8 ♕d2 – *Game 5*
> 8 ♕d3 (D): 8...b6 – *Game 7*; 8...cxd4 – *Game 6*

8...♕a5

> 8...♘d7 – *Game 11*; 8...f5 – *Game 8*

9 e4 (D) ♘e7 – *Game 10*; 9...♘f6 – *Game 9*

8 e3   8 ♕d3   9 e4

CHAPTER TWO

4 f3 d5 5 a3: Alternatives to the Main Line

1 d4 ♘f6 2 c4 e6 3 ♘c3 ♗b4 4 f3 d5 5 a3

Whilst the majority of this chapter will be spent looking at Black's options of preserving his dark-squared bishop, in the first couple of games I want to take a look at him conceding it as in the main line of Chapter 1 but then employing alternatives to the standard move 6...c5.

In Game 12 I investigate the consequences of Black's castling (relatively) early, while Game 13 then concentrates on the apparently anti-positional pawn advance 6...c6.

Of course Black is under no obligation to exchange on c3 and there is a certain logic to keeping the bishop given that White has weakened his kingside with f2-f3, even if this means White can build up a centre. In Game 14 I take a look at the provocative 5...♗d6, while the final two games in this chapter concentrate on the more popular move 5...♗e7.

Game 12
V.Moskalenko-J.Lopez Martinez
Paretana 1999

1 d4 ♘f6 2 c4 e6 3 ♘c3 ♗b4 4 f3 d5 5 a3 ♗xc3+ 6 bxc3

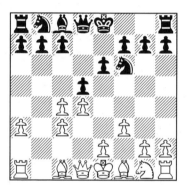

6...0-0

I would first like to mention that after 6...b6?!, 7 cxd5 exd5 8 e3 0-0 9 ♗d3 c5 10 ♘e2 would transpose to the 6...c5 7 cxd5 exd5 section of the previous chapter. Here 9...♗a6 10 ♗xa6 ♘xa6 11 ♕d3 ♕c8 12 ♘e2 c5 13 0-0 ♖e8 14 ♘g3 ♕b7 15 ♖a2 b5 16 ♖e2 b4 17 cxb4 cxb4 18 ♖b2 ♖ab8 19 ♗d2, where White craftily bagged a pawn in I.Novikov-R.Furdzik, New York 2002, is not of serious independent significance. However, it's probably fair to say that White can take advantage of Black's inferior move order by playing 7 ♗g5!?. It is of course very nice to get the bishop outside the pawn chain (i.e. move it before playing e2-e3), and 7...♘bd7 8 cxd5 exd5 9 e3 h6 10 ♗h4 0-0 11 ♗d3

♗b7 12 ♘e2 feels like a pleasant Queen's Gambit Declined for White in which expending a tempo on a2-a3 was worth it to net Black's dark-squared bishop. With all due respect to the players involved, it's not the highest level encounter, but 12...♖e8 13 ♗f2 ♖c8 14 0-0 ♕e7 15 ♘g3 ♘f8 16 ♘f5 ♕d7 17 g4 ♘e6 18 ♗g3 g6 19 ♗e5 ♘h7 20 ♘xh6+ ♔f8 21 f4 c5 22 f5 gxf5 23 ♗xf5 ♖e7 24 ♗xh7 1-0 B.Szabo-M,Tamas, Budapest 2004 clearly demonstrates how things can quickly go sour for Black.

7 cxd5

7 ♗g5 isn't as attractive now because Black can try to punish White for his poor development. Specifically. Black should not play 7...b6? which, in line with my comments to 6...b6?!, would justify White's play. Instead he should aim to hit White's queenside more quickly, and 7...c6 8 ♘h3 ♘bd7 9 ♘f2 ♕a5 (a pawn on b6 prevents this possibility) 10 ♕d2 dxc4 11 e4 b5 12 ♗e2 c5! 13 dxc5 ♗b7, as seen in I.Manor-E.Rozentalis, Israel 1999, looks like a very sensible approach. As you will see in the next game, the Lithuanian GM is quite keen on this ...c6 move, but after 7 ♗g5 it is no surprise that 7...c5 has its followers too.

Of course 7 e3 is possible but, just as I commented in the very first game of the book, it's not very ambitious.

7...exd5

With ...0-0 taking the place of the previous chapter's ...c5, now 7...♘xd5? is just a mistake because of 8 e4!. An amusing hunting sequence runs 8...♘xc3 9 ♕b3 ♕xd4 10 ♗b2 ♕e3+ 11 ♗e2 ♘d5 12 ♕xe3 ♘xe3 13 ♔f2 ♘c2 14 ♖c1 – yes, the knight is trapped!

8 e3 ♗f5

If Black played for a quick ...c7-c5 (i.e. now!) then we would return to the realms of the previous chapter. That aside, Black must play actively in order to avoid simply reaching an inferior QGD. Specifically, Black should try to do something with this bishop and this is the alternative to bringing it out to

a6.

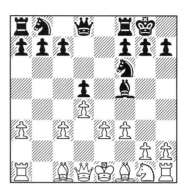

9 ♘e2 c5

The point of 8...♗f5 was to take first dibs on the b1-h7 diagonal (upon 8...c5, as we know, White could have made it his own with 9 ♗d3). White is up for the challenge though and intends to try and punish Black for his boldness.

As a taster for the main game, check out 9...♖e8:

a) I bet the world's greatest player was miffed by 10 ♘f4 c5 11 g4 ♗xg4?! 12 fxg4 ♘e4 13 h4 ♘c6 14 ♗g2 ♘xc3 15 ♕d3 cxd4 16 0-0 ♕xh4 17 exd4 ♘e4 18 ♗e3 ♖ad8 19 ♖ab1 ♘f6 20 ♖f3 ♕xg4 21 ♖xb7 ♘a5 22 ♖xa7 ♘c4 23 ♘xd5?? ♘xd5 24 ♗f2 (presumably here he realised that after 24 ♕xc4 ♘xe3 25 ♕xf7+ ♔h8 Black was guarding g7 and hence he had thrown away a winning position!) 24...♘d6 25 ♖g3 ♕f5 26 ♕xf5 ♘xf5 27 ♖b3 ♘f4 28 ♖bb7 ♘d6 29 ♖d7 ♘xg2 30 ♔xg2 ♖xd7 31 ♖xd7 ♘e4 32 ♗e1 ♘f6 0-1 G.Kasparov-N.Bradbury London (simultaneous display) 1983, but knowing Neil I'm sure he would have been very sympathetic!

b) 10 ♘g3 ♗g6 11 ♗d3 ♗xd3 12 ♕xd3 ♘bd7 13 0-0 c6?! is too passive and White's position has all the potential. He can build up a big pawn centre and swing his knight into action. Come to think of it, it's as if I wrote the script!: 14 ♖b1 ♕c7 15 e4 ♘b6 16 e5 ♘fd7 17 f4 f6 18 ♘h5 fxe5 19 ♕g3 ♖e7 20

fxe5 ♘f8 21 ♗g5 ♖f7 22 ♘f4 ♖e8 23 ♖f2
♘e6 24 ♘xe6 ♖xe6 25 ♖bf1 ♖xf2 26 ♕xf2
h6 27 ♕f8+ 1-0 H.Nordahl-M.Egeland, Alta
2003.

Similarly, there is 9...♘bd7 10 g4 (essentially White tends to choose between this or
♘g3, or of course both!) 10...♘xg4?! (again a
little suspicious; unless there is anything concrete, pieces are always going to be better
than pawns) 11 fxg4 ♕h4+ 12 ♔d2 ♗e4 13
♖g1 ♘b6 14 ♖g3 ♘c4+ 15 ♔e1 ♖ae8 16
♘f4 g5 17 ♘h3 f5 18 gxf5 ♗xf5 19 ♗xc4
dxc4 20 ♘xg5 ♕xh2 21 ♕f3 ♔h8 22 ♕g2
♕h4 23 ♖a2 ♗g4 24 ♖f2 ♖xf2 25 ♔xf2
♖f8+ 26 ♔g1 h5 27 e4 1-0 V.Malaniuk-
V.Dydyshko, Minsk 1988 – Black only managed a few checks.

10 g4

Easily the most testing move and the sort
of reason why players choose 4 f3 in the first
place!

10...♗d7

Firstly, 10...♘xg4? 11 fxg4 ♕h4+ 12 ♔d2
♗e4 13 ♖g1 is never going to be adequate.
The really provocative move is 10...♗g6.
Now 11 h4 h6 12 ♘f4 ♘bd7 is a tough one
to call. In fact 13 ♘xg6?! fxg6 14 ♗d3 ♕c7!
is slightly worrying for White as he has plenty
of weaknesses in his camp. Perhaps something like 13 ♖g1 could be tried instead, but
theoretically speaking the more cautious 11
♘f4 ♘bd7 12 ♗g2 ♖c8 13 0-0 is held in
higher regard, e.g. 13...♘b6 14 ♖a2 ♖c7 15
h3 ♖e8 16 h4 h6 17 ♘xg6 fxg6 18 ♕d3 ♖c6
19 a4 ♘h7 20 dxc5 ♖xc5 21 ♕xg6 ♘f8 22
♕d3 ♕xh4 23 ♗a3 ♖c7 24 a5 ♘c4 25
♕xd5+ ♔h8 26 ♕b5 ♖e5 27 ♕b4 ♘e6 28
a6 b6 29 ♗c1 ♘xe3 30 ♕d6 ♘c4 31 ♕d3
♖ec5 32 ♖e2 ♖5c6 33 ♖fe1 ♘f8 34 ♖e8 and
White went on to win in V.Malaniuk-
I.Naumkin, Tashkent 1987.

11 ♗g2 ♗c6 12 0-0 ♘bd7 13 ♘g3

White's bishops lay in waiting while the
knight looks for a good home. I wouldn't
fancy Black's position here as White has an
obvious expansion plan on the kingside

whereas it's going to take ages for the extra
black b-pawn to have an impact.

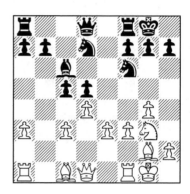

13...♘b6

This knight wanted the c4-square and
Black didn't want to saddle himself with an
isolated d-pawn via 13...cxd4.

14 dxc5!

Unfortunately White is ready to take advantage of the situation. This move is more
about acquiring the d4-square than grabbing
a pawn.

14...♘a4 15 ♕d4

This outpost would be an excellent home
for any white piece.

15...♕a5 16 g5 ♘e8 17 ♘f5 ♕xc5

After 17...♘xc5 18 ♕b4! Black would be
forced to iron out White's pawns.

18 ♕xc5 ♘xc5 19 a4

White has the bishop pair and generally
the more active position; playing Black would
be no fun.

19...♘c7 20 ♗a3 ♘7a6 21 ♘e7+ ♔h8 22 c4!

Eliminating one of White's two weaknesses and Black is about to eliminate the
other!

22...♗xa4 23 cxd5

The material situation remains level but
now White has only one pawn island.

23...♖fe8 24 d6 ♖ad8 25 ♗b2! ♖xd6

No doubt Black could see what was coming but the white knight was going to return
to f5 anyway.

26 ♗xg7+! ♔xg7 27 ♘f5+ ♔g6 28 ♘xd6 ♖xe3 29 f4

The immediate 29 ♘xb7 was on too but I'm just being pedantic. The point is in the bag.

29...b6 30 h4 ♗b3 31 f5+ ♔h5 32 ♖f4 ♖g3 33 ♘e8 1-0

Game 13
Y.Yakovich-G.Tunik
Russian Ch., Krasnodar 2002

---

1 d4 ♘f6 2 c4 e6 3 ♘c3 ♗b4 4 f3 d5 5 a3 ♗xc3+ 6 bxc3 c6

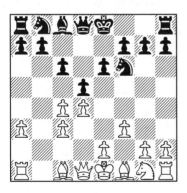

This idea pioneered by Rozentalis looks on the face of it very odd. Black has traded off his dark-squared bishop, but rather than putting pawns on dark squares he appears to be planting them on light squares instead! This policy doesn't seem so appealing to

Black's remaining bishop but in fact there is method in his madness. Black bolsters the d5-pawn but actually intends the standard ...b7-b6 and ...♗a6 plan that in the long term could actually leave White with the only bishop and a bad one at that! In particular the move ...c7-c6 makes available a ...♕a5 option should White get fruity with his dark-squared bishop and, after a future cxd5, ...cxd5, means that a black rook or two can get action down the c-file.

7 ♕c2!?

a) Regarding my comments to Black's previous move, the tame 7 e3 (arguably deserving a '?!') tends to fit in with Black's plans, for example:

a1) The immediate 7...b6 is playable but after 8 cxd5 cxd5 Black mustn't forget what could otherwise be an embarrassing queen check on a4. Hence he will probably have to castle before employing ...♗a6 anyway, although incidentally 9 ♗b5+ ♗d7 10 ♗d3 ♘c6 11 ♘e2 e5! is another idea to look out for.

a2) 7...0-0 8 ♗d3 (8 ♘h3 b6 9 cxd5 cxd5 10 a4 ♗a6 11 ♗xa6 ♘xa6 12 ♕d3 ♕c8 was also very reasonable for Black in H.Nordahl-E.Rozentalis, Gausdal 2003 – White's bishop isn't that bad a piece but the c3-pawn will have to remain in place) 8...b6 9 cxd5 (9 ♘e2 ♗a6 10 cxd5 cxd5 is a transposition, while the jury is out on 9 e4, which is a gambit now because after 9...dxe4 10 fxe4 ♘xe4 there is the check on h4 to consider; probably White continues with 11 ♘f3, which is a pawn for Black but from White's angle it looks better than the Blackmar-Diemer Gambit!) 9...cxd5 10 ♘e2 ♗a6 11 ♗xa6 ♘xa6 12 0-0 ♘c7 13 ♕d3 ♕c8 14 e4 ♕a6 15 ♕c2 ♖ac8 16 e5 ♘d7 17 f4 f6 18 ♗b2 ♕c4 19 a4 fxe5 20 fxe5 ♖xf1+ 21 ♖xf1 ♖f8 22 ♖xf8+ ♔xf8 23 ♘f4 b5 24 axb5 ♘xb5 when the presence of a bad bishop and having to deal with an outside passed pawn led to White's downfall in M.Kantorik-K.Sundararajan, Olomouc 2004.

b) In view of this White should adopt a

more direct approach. Central domination is typically White's plan and, aside from the main move (7 ♕c2), White can also consider 7 e4!? straight away. After 7...dxe4 8 fxe4 White is threatening to advance his e-pawn further. Nobody in their right mind would consider taking that pawn – the greedy 8...♘xe4 9 ♕g4! ♘f6 10 ♕xg7 ♖g8 11 ♕h6 should probably be good for White as Black could easily suffer on the dark squares. Compared to similar positions that could be reached via the French Defence, e.g. 1 e4 e6 2 d4 d5 3 ♘c3 ♗b4 4 a3 ♗xc3+ 5 bxc3 ♘xe4 6 ♕g4 ♘f6 7 ♕xg7 ♖g8 8 ♕h6, White also has the bonus of a half-open f-file.

Thus the thematic response is 8...e5!. Now 9 ♘f3 ♕a5 10 ♕d3 exd4 11 ♗d2 dxc3 12 ♗xc3 ♕d8 13 ♕xd8+ ♔xd8 has occurred in a number of Volkov games. It looks as though he believes in it, with 14 ♘g5 ♗e6 15 ♗e2 ♘a6 16 0-0 ♔e7 17 ♖ad1 ♘c5 18 e5 ♘fd7 19 ♖d6 ♘a4 20 ♗b4 c5 21 ♘xe6 fxe6 22 ♗g4 ♘f8 23 ♗e1 h6 24 ♗h5 g6 25 ♗h4+ ♔e8 26 ♗xg6+ ♘xg6 27 ♖xe6+ ♔d7 28 ♖d6+ ♔c8 29 ♖xg6 ♘b6 30 ♖f7 1-0 S.Volkov-P.Genov, Korinthos 2002 being one successful attempt. There are plenty of possible improvements for Black along the way though, with ...♘xe4 worth looking into on either move nine or ten.

7...0-0

When your minor pieces are still at home there is always going to be some concern, but nevertheless 7...b6 8 cxd5 cxd5 9 e4 feels attractive for White as Black doesn't have time right now for ...♗a6 and the e-pawn is on the march.

Another advantage of 6...c6 is that after 7...dxc4 8 e4 b5 9 a4 the b5-pawn is well supported. In this instance 6 ♕c2 is definitely a pawn sacrifice and reminds me a lot of certain Semi-Slav lines. White's compensation is clear: he has a lovely central pawn duo and a fantastic unchallenged dark-squared bishop. My own experiences in this type of

position have nevertheless taught me that they are very double edged. White's light-squared bishop can get a little shut in whilst the eventual advance e4-e5 will donate the excellent outpost on d5 to a black knight. For Black's part he will always be looking to try and arrange ...c6-c5 in order to try to realise his extra pawn advantage.

8 e4

Upon 8 cxd5 cxd5 9 e4 Black should respond with 9...dxe4 10 fxe4 e5!. Following 11 d5 White has a half-open f-file to work with, but he also has more pawn islands and consequently Black has some attractive potential blockading squares for his knights.

8...dxe4 9 fxe4

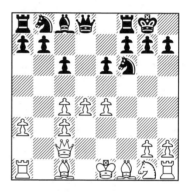

9...e5

Black must get this move in before White does. Although this pawn isn't guarded, needless to say White isn't going to jump at the chance to acquire two sets of doubled isolated pawns!

10 ♘f3 exd4

10...♘bd7 11 ♗d3 c5 12 0-0 gives away less ground, but with the tension in the position Black has problems developing his own bishop. On the other hand White has a superb dark-squared bishop, and even after a future advance of d4-d5 he has good chances to do something on the kingside.

11 e5!?

After 11 cxd4 Black tried to attack White's centre in the game S.Lahtela-'Anfaenger2', playchess.com 2004 with 11...♗g4, but after 12 ♗b2 ♗xf3 13 gxf3 ♘h5 14 0-0-0 White should have been very happy with his position. However. I suspect that 11...♖e8! is critical, intending to meet 12 e5 with 12...c5! 13 ♗e2 cxd4 as 14 exf6?? runs into 14...d3. Note that 12 ♗d3 ♘xe4 13 0-0 f5 14 ♖e1 ♘d7 15 ♗xe4 ♘f6 is an amusing sequence that would also be fine for Black.

11...♖e8 12 ♗d3

12 cxd4 c5! transposes to my previous note.

12...dxc3 13 0-0

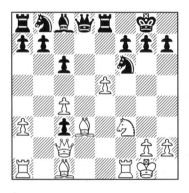

13...♖xe5!?

After 13...♘g4 14 ♗xh7+ ♔h8 15 ♘g5! ♕d4+ 16 ♔h1 ♘xe5 17 ♗f4 ♘bd7 18 ♖ae1 White would have a tremendous initiative, and so instead Black sacrifices the exchange.

14 ♘xe5 ♕d4+ 15 ♔h1

Instead I prefer 15 ♕f2! ♕xe5 16 ♗e3 when the threats of ♗d4 and ♖ae1 make it difficult for Black to complete his development.

15...♕xe5 16 ♗f4

Black currently has three pawns for the exchange, but White's big lead in development and, indeed, excellent pieces leave him as slight favourite.

16...♕a5 17 ♗d6 ♗e6 18 ♖ab1 b6 19 ♖bc1 ♘bd7

Now Black has got this move in, his position is rock-solid. No doubt White had considered sacrificing the exchange himself with

♖xf6 on moves 18 and 19 but, barring those (and White's missed opportunity on move 15), a draw is on the cards.

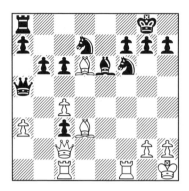

20 ♕xc3 ♕xc3 21 ♖xc3 c5 22 h3 ♖c8 23 a4 ♘b8 24 ♗xb8 ♖xb8 25 a5 ♖d8 26 ♗f5 ♗xf5 27 ♖xf5 ♔f8 28 ♖e5 ♖d1+ 29 ♔h2 ♘d7 30 ♖ee3 ♖d4 31 ♖cd3 ♖xd3 32 ♖xd3 ♔e7 33 ♔g3 ♘e5 34 axb6 axb6 35 ♖c3 g5 36 ♔f2 ½-½

> *Game 14*
> # M.Norberg-R.Sasata
> Correspondence 1999

1 d4 ♘f6 2 c4 e6 3 ♘c3 ♗b4 4 f3 d5 5 a3 ♗d6

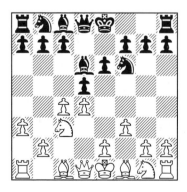

Coming clean, the truth is that this game did in fact involve 5...♗e7 (the subject of the next game), but as it quickly transposes to 5...♗d6 I've doctored the scoresheet a little.

Anyway, regarding this slightly odd-looking retreat, it's actually got some sneaky ideas behind it. It eyes up a few of White's dark squares (a black queen check on h4 would be nice around about now!) and supports the central challenge ...e6-e5. Also, an interesting comparison can be made with the Queen's Gambit Declined after 6 ♗g5 ♗e7. Yes, Black has effectively lost two tempi by moving his bishop three times. However, White's gained free moves are a2-a3 (useful unless White wanted to castle queenside) and f2-f3 (probably detrimental, particularly if he loses his dark-squared bishop).

6 e4

A number of strong players seem to prefer 6 c5 ♗e7 7 b4 (7 e4?! now is too greedy and is well met by 7...dxe4 8 fxe4 e5! as the d-pawn can't advance because of the hanging c-pawn), which of course gains considerable space on the queenside. Now e5 becomes a big square and White certainly would rather not have his pawn on f3. Something like 7...b6 8 e3 (arguably Black was better after 8 ♗g5 bxc5 9 bxc5 h6 10 ♗xf6 ♗xf6 11 f4 ♘d7 12 ♕a4 c6! 13 ♖c1 ♕c7 14 e3 g5!? in T.Hillarp Persson-A.Beliavsky, Malmö 2004) 8...0-0 9 ♗d2 c6 10 f4 a5 11 ♘f3 ♗a6 looks like a reasonable sequence with a draw being agreed after 12 ♗xa6 ♘xa6 13 ♘e5 axb4 14 ♘xc6 ♕c7 15 ♘xe7+ ♕xe7 16 axb4 in S.Volkov-J.Gustafsson, playchess.com 2004.

Tempting though it may be, taking the pressure off the centre with 6 c5 hasn't proven to be a great winning attempt.

6...c5

6...dxe4 7 fxe4 e5 is surprisingly rare, and I can't see any particular reason for that. Surely Black has nothing to fear from the endgame 8 dxe5 ♗xe5 9 ♕xd8+ ♔xd8, whilst the defendable structure after 8 d5 is the subject of the next game.

7 cxd5 exd5 8 dxc5

The antidote to 8 e5 is of course 8...cxd4 9 ♕xd4 ♘c6 10 ♗b5 (or 10 ♕e3? d4) 10...♕e7.

8...♗xc5

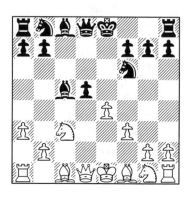

9 e5!

A pawn is up for grabs immediately on d5, but 9 ♘xd5 ♘xd5 10 ♕xd5 ♕b6 leaves Black with super compensation for the pawn. Even in the game White is weak along the b6-g1 diagonal but at least the text forces a black piece to retreat.

9...♘fd7

There is no future in 9...♘h5 because after 10 ♕xd5 ♕h4+ 11 g3 ♘xg3 12 hxg3 ♕xh1 (or 12...♕xg3+ 13 ♔d1 ♗xg1 14 ♗b5+ when at the very least ♘e2 is available to gain a significant material advantage) 13 ♕xc5 the white queen both attacks c8 and protects the g1-knight.

10 ♕xd5 0-0

Or:

a) After 10...♗xg1 11 ♖xg1 ♕b6, the simplest is 12 ♕d6!: 12...♕xg1? 13 ♘d5 ♘c6 (and 13...♕c5 14 ♘c7+ ♔d8 15 ♗g5+ f6 16 ♘e6+) 14 ♘c7+ ♔d8 15 ♗g5+ f6 16 exf6 is curtains for Black, whilst a queen swap on d6 is a pawn-up ending and more for White. Instead of 11...♕b6, going it alone with the queen via 11...♕h4+!? 12 g3 ♕xh2 13 ♖g2 ♕h5 leaves the rest of Black's pieces looking silly, and both 14 ♕d6 and 14 e6! leave White well in control and probably close to winning.

b) Upon 10...♕b6, 11 ♘e4! is a powerful response as after 11...0-0! 12 ♘xc5 Black can't avoid a queen swap with 12...♘xc5 because of 13 ♗e3.

c) Probably the best practical try for Black is 10...♘c6!? and only after 11 f4 play 11...♕b6. It's not clear whether Black really has enough after 12 ♘f3 ♗f2+ 13 ♔e2, but a trick worth watching out for is 11 ♘e4?! ♕a5+! – White's queen is loose.

11 f4

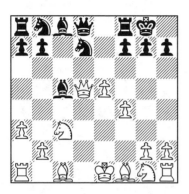

11...♗xg1

After 11...♕b6 12 ♘f3 ♗f2+ 13 ♔e2 ♘c5 14 b4 ♖d8 15 bxc5 ♗xc5 16 ♖b1 ♕a5, a 'playing it safe' human-style advantage can be achieved via 17 ♖b5 ♕xb5+ 18 ♘xb5 ♖xd5 19 ♘c7 ♖d7 20 ♘xa8 b6 21 ♗e3 ♗b7 22 ♗xc5 bxc5 23 ♔e3 ♗xa8 24 ♗b5. However, I suspect that Fritz and co could come up with bigger advantages along the way.

12 ♖xg1 ♕b6

Not for the first time Black can regain his pawn via 12...♕h4+? 13 g3 ♕xh2, but 14 ♕g2 merely offers him the prospect of a grim ending.

13 ♖h1

This seems preferable to 13 ♘e2, although we mustn't forget that now White can't castle!

13...♘c6

After 13...♘c5?! a favourable endgame was forced via 14 b4 ♘e6 15 ♘a4 ♕c7 16 ♗e3 ♘c6 17 ♕d6 in B.Gelfand-B.Spassky, Linares 1990. As well as the extra pawn White always has that bishop pair, whilst his 'exposed' king can easily find itself nicely

centralised in the endgame.

14 ♕b5 ♘d4

Black can't avoid a queen trade without compromising his position.

15 ♕xb6 ♘xb6 16 ♗d3 ♖d8 17 ♗e3

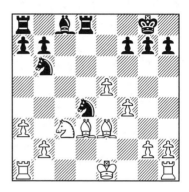

17...♘f3+

White was threatening to completely solidify via 0-0-0 and, though the text doesn't work, neither did the 17...♘b3 18 ♖d1 ♖xd3 19 ♖xd3 ♗f5 20 ♘e4 ♘a1 21 ♖xb6 axb6 22 ♔e2 ♗xe4 23 ♖d4 1-0 of Y.Yakovich-D.Piza Cortizo, Cordoba 1991.

18 gxf3 ♖xd3 19 ♗xb6 axb6 20 ♖d1 ♖xd1+ 21 ♔xd1 ♗e6

Funnily enough now Black has that bishop-for-knight advantage, but nevertheless it's the extra pawn that is the decisive factor.

22 ♘e4 ♔f8 23 ♔e2 ♖c8 24 ♖d1 ♔e7 25 ♘d6 ♖c7 26 f5 ♗b3 27 ♖d3 ♗c4 28 ♘xc4 ♖xc4 29 ♔e3 ♖c2 30 ♖b3 1-0

Game 15
A.Summerscale-L.Yudasin
World Open, Philadelphia 2002

---

1 d4 ♘f6 2 c4 e6 3 ♘c3 ♗b4 4 f3 d5 5 a3 ♗e7

This isn't as provocative as the previously seen 5...♗d6, but White is obviously going to continue to work on his central pawn structure all the same.

6 e4 c5

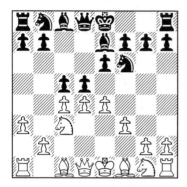

6...dxe4 7 fxe4 e5 appears in the next game, but for now we see Black striking at White's centre once more with ...c7-c5.

7 e5

If those handling the white side of the opening are impressed with his chances in the previous game then they could also give 7 cxd5 exd5 8 dxc5 a whirl as 8....♗xc5 9 e5 is a direct transposition. Black does though have a practical alternative at his disposal in the form of 8...d4, when I'm not sure that White should get embroiled in the likes of 9 ♘b5 ♗xc5 10 ♗f4 0-0 11 ♘c7 ♘h5. Instead 9 ♘a4 0-0 10 ♘e2 ♘c6 11 b4 looks critical. I'm suspicious as to whether Black has enough for the pawn, although 11...b5 12 cxb6 axb6 13 ♘f4 ♗b7 14 ♗b5 ♘a7 15 ♗d3 ♗c6 16 0-0 ♘b5 17 ♕c2 ♖c8 18 ♕e2 ♘c3 19 ♘xc3 dxc3 20 ♗e3 went from what looks like a position of strength to 20...♗d6 21 ♗a6 ♖b8 22 ♘d3 ♕c7 23 ♖fc1 ♗xh2+ 24 ♔f1 ♘h5 25 ♗f2 ♗a4 and what doesn't! Black went on to win in J.Ehlvest-L.Yudasin, New York 2003 after 26 b5 ♖fd8 27 ♘b4 ♖d2 28 ♕xd2 cxd2 29 ♖xc7 ♗xc7 30 ♔e2 d1♕+ 31 ♖xd1 ♘f4+ 32 ♔e1 ♘xg2+ 33 ♔d2 ♖d8+ 34 ♘d5 ♗xd1 35 ♔xd1 ♘f4.

7...♘fd7 8 cxd5 exd5 9 f4!?

Bolstering e5 and facilitating ♘f3, this has a certain appeal to it. Nevertheless, by way of alternatives White should also consider:

a) 9 dxc5 ♗xc5 transposes to the contentious position of the previous game. Black

isn't compelled to do that though, and indeed 9...♘c6 10 ♕xd5 0-0 11 ♗e3 ♘dxe5 12 ♕xd8 ♖xd8 13 ♔f2 occurred in J.Ehlvest-L.Yudasin, New York 2003. With all things considered, White's queenside pawn majority probably gives him the edge.

b) 9 ♘xd5 cxd4 10 ♘xe7 ♕xe7 11 f4 f6 when White should probably choose between 12 ♕xd4 fxe5 13 ♕e3 ♘c6 14 ♘f3 and 12 ♘f3 fxe5 13 ♗c4!?, neither of which theory has been able to make a definite assessment on.

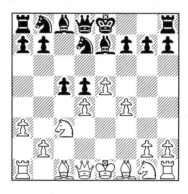

9...cxd4

It is very tempting to lure the queen into the centre but there is also an argument for 9...♘c6 10 ♘f3 cxd4 11 ♘xd4 0-0 as 12 ♘xd5? runs into 12...♘dxe5! 13 ♘xe7+ ♕xe7 14 fxe5 ♕h4+. Also after 12 ♗e3 there is no compulsion for Black to park his knight on b6, and indeed 12...♘c5 is very plausible. Hence to keep the pressure on Black (in particular forcing a decision on the c6-knight) White might care to try 12 ♗b5!?.

10 ♕xd4 ♘b6

Yes, the drawback of Black's previous move is that he must guard the isolated d-pawn before he can gain that tempo on White's queen.

11 ♗d3 0-0 12 ♘f3 f6

It seems logical to strike out at White's centre but this advance weakens Black's kingside and doesn't solve the problem of the isolani.

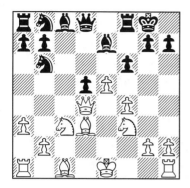

13 exf6 ♗xf6 14 ♕f2 ♘c6

Although the black rook is already on a good file, perhaps it would have made more sense for Black to hassle the white king while he had the chance. Indeed something like 14...♖e8+!? 15 ♘e2 ♘c4 16 ♖a2 ♕a5+ 17 b4 ♕a4 might have been irritating for White.

15 0-0 ♗xc3

Mixing things up but also conceding an important bishop.

16 bxc3 ♕f6 17 ♕c2 h6?!

17...♗f5! is thematic, but I suppose after 18 ♗xf5 ♕xf5 19 ♕xf5 ♖xf5 20 ♖e1 Black can kiss goodbye to any realistic winning chances – a draw is the most likely outcome.

18 ♗e3 ♘c4 19 ♗c5 ♖e8

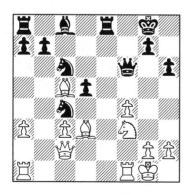

20 ♘e5!

Black has four pieces attacking this square whilst White only defends it once. Nevertheless, it is an excellent move for opening up

more lines.

20...♘6xe5 21 fxe5 ♕c6

Black dare not consider 21...♕xe5, e.g. 22 ♗g6 ♖d8 23 ♖ae1 ♕c7 24 ♗f7+ ♔h8 25 ♗d4 with a fantastic position for White and a devastating threat of ♗xg7+.

22 ♕f2!

Threatening ♕f7+ but also simply transferring the queen to the kingside.

22...♗e6 23 ♗d4 ♖f8 24 ♕g3 ♖xf1+ 25 ♖xf1 ♕e8

Necessary to prevent ♕g6, but now White has got the wind between his sails.

26 ♖f6!

As the g-pawn is pinned this rook threatens the h6-pawn and is of course invulnerable where it stands.

26...♔h8 27 ♕h4 ♕d7

Now 27...gxf6 would have been crushed by the reply 28 ♕xh6+ ♔g8 29 ♕h7+ ♔f8 30 ♗c5+.

28 ♗f5!

White is looking to get his dark-squared bishop in on the act. 28...♗xf5 29 ♖xh6+ gxh6 (or 29...♔g8 30 ♖h8+ ♔f7 31 ♖xa8) 30 e6+ is just what White has in mind!

28...♖e8 29 ♖xe6! ♖xe6 30 ♕g4

The rook is pinned to the queen and so this nets significant material. A wonderful demonstration of the power of the bishop pair by the English GM.

30...♕b5 31 ♗xe6 ♕b1+ 32 ♔f2 ♕c2+ 33 ♕e2 ♕c1 34 ♗xd5 ♕f4+ 35 ♕f3 1-0

Game 16
C.Van Buskirk-R.Del Pilar
Agoura Hills 2004

1 d4 ♘f6 2 c4 e6 3 ♘c3 ♗b4 4 f3 d5 5 a3 ♗e7 6 e4 dxe4 7 fxe4 e5

Planting a pawn here prevents White's pawn advance, and of course 8 dxe5? would be extremely ugly for White now.

8 d5

The structure now reached dictates that there is a very interesting middlegame ahead. White has serious pawn potential on the queenside up to d5 and could conceivably put the half-open f-file to good use too. However, in the short-term White is very weak along the c5-g1 diagonal and Black has a number of ways to try and exploit that.

8...♗c5

Clearly the text gets straight to the crux of the matter but Black has a number of other approaches too:

a) 8...c6 9 ♘f3 0-0 10 ♗d3 ♗g4 all seems too automatic for my liking and both 11 h3 and 11 0-0 here have scored well for White.

b) Similarly, 8...0-0 9 ♘f3 ♗g4 doesn't do much for me either. Mind you, although 10 h3 ♗xf3 11 ♕xf3 a5 12 ♗d3 ♗c5 13 ♖b1 c6 14 ♗e3 ♘bd7 15 0-0 ♕b6 16 ♗xc5 ♕xc5+ 17 ♔h2 a4 18 ♖bd1 ♘b6 19 ♕g3 ♘fd7 20 ♗e2 ♖fd8 21 ♖f2 ♕e7 22 ♕f2 cxd5 23 cxd5 ♖ac8 24 ♖f1 saw White go on to win in

V.Milov-V.Gashimov, Antalya 2004, I quite like the novel idea of 10 ♗d3 ♗c5 11 h3 ♗xf3 12 ♕xf3 c6 13 ♗g5 ♘bd7 14 0-0-0, which proved successful for another of the opening's leading exponents, Ukrainian GM Konstantin Lerner, back in 1990.

c) 8...a5 has the advantage of halting b2-b4 but, whilst it also provides Black's dark-squared bishop with a retreat along the c5-a7 diagonal, it does give White time to get his act together. The continuation 9 ♘f3 ♗g4 10 ♗e3 ♘a6 looks plausible, but in fact as far as I can see it has only ever occurred once in practice: 11 ♕a4+ ♗d7 12 ♕c2 ♘g4 13 ♗g1 ♗c5 14 ♗xc5 ♘xc5 15 h3 ♘f6 16 ♘xe5 ♕e7 17 ♘xd7 ♔xd7 18 ♗d3 and White went on to win in an endgame in D.Tyomkin-D.Contin, Saint Vincent 2002.

d) 8...♘g4 is the move that I had been ready to play when I first learnt of 4 f3, but in fact it is inaccurate. White obviously won't fall for 9 h3? ♗h4+, whilst 9 ♘f3 ♗c5 is merely a transposition to our main game. However, White can punish his opponent through 9 b4!. This keeps Black's bishop out of c5 and, try as he might, Black is unable gain that square back, for example 9...a5 10 ♖b1 axb4 11 axb4 ♘a6 12 c5!. Actually 12...♘xb4 is an interesting concept but, rather than 13 ♖xb4 ♘f2!?, White can keep the initiative via 13 d6!? cxd6 14 ♖xb4 dxc5 15 ♗b5+. Black will have three pawns for the piece, but with juicy squares such as d5 and f5 around, I prefer the pieces. Instead Black could settle for 9...♗g5, but even a trade of 'bad' for 'good' bishop doesn't disguise the fact that Black will at some stage have to come to terms with White's strong queenside pawns.

9 ♘f3 ♘g4

I'm giving this as the main line, but the alternative 9...♗g4 should be given respect. One particular game that has piqued my interest is: 10 h3 ♗h5 11 g4 ♗g6 12 b4 ♗e7 13 ♗d3 a5 14 b5 ♘bd7 15 ♗c2 ♗d6 16 ♕e2 ♕e7 17 ♗b2 ♘b6 18 ♘d1 ♘fd7 19 a4

♗b4+ 20 ♔f1 h5 21 g5 h4 22 ♘e3 0-0-0 23 ♘g2 ♗h5 24 ♘gxh4 g6 25 ♗d1 f6 26 gxf6 ♕xf6 27 ♕c2 ♕f8 28 ♖h2 ♗e7 29 ♖f2 ♗xh4 30 ♘xh4 ♗xd1 31 ♖xd1 ♕c5 32 ♘xg6 ♘xc4 33 ♖d3 ♖h7 34 ♗c1 ♖e8 35 d6 cxd6 36 ♖c3 ♘db6 37 ♗a3 ♕c7 38 ♕d3 ♔b8 39 ♖f6 ♖f7 40 ♖f5 ♖xf5+ 41 exf5 e4 42 ♕d4 ♕f7 43 ♗xd6+ ♔a8 44 ♘e7 ♖d8 45 ♘d5 ♕xd5 46 ♕xd5 ♘xd5 47 ♖xc4 ♘e3+ 48 ♔e2 ♘xc4 49 ♗e7 ♖d2+ 50 ♔e1 e3 51 f6 ♘e5 0-1 C.Garcia Palermo-L.Galego, Sao Paulo 2002. Talk about an exercise in controlling and giving away squares! Presumably 14 b5 would be the first move under the microscope as the c5-square is a nice prize.

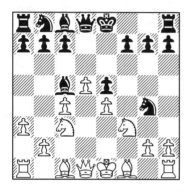

10 ♘a4

My first memory of this line was the thrilling 10 b4?! ♗f2+ (only the really materialistic would consider 10...♘f2? 11 ♕c2 ♘xh1 12 bxc5, and even then only until the penny dropped that the cornered knight probably wouldn't get out!) 11 ♔e2 c5! 12 ♘b5 (the escape plan is 12 h3 ♗d4!) 12...a6! 13 ♕a4 axb5!! 14 ♕xa8 ♗d4! 15 ♘xd4? cxd4 16 ♕xb8 0-0 (it's a whole rook but with the white queen caught offside and White's other bits at home, the white monarch is at Black's mercy) 17 ♔e1 ♕h4+! 18 g3 ♕f6 of V.Malaniuk-V.Ivanchuk, USSR Championship, Moscow 1988. Black went to win and I was all set to travel down this road if allowed. However, it never came up and since then 10 ♘a4 has become recognised as a significant

improvement.

10...♗f2+ 11 ♔e2

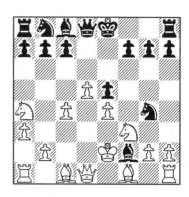

Frankly this is a ridiculous position for just a few moves into the game. White has a knight on the rim and his king looks silly on e2. On the other hand, Black's developed knight and bishop are precariously placed and he knows that the white pawns are already cramping him and have serious potential.

What would you do here?

11...f5

Well, I don't know whether or not you selected it, but arguably the most promising variation for Black is 11...b5!?, intending 12 cxb5 ♗d7. The point is that after 13 ♘c3 Black has safe retreats available (e.g. 13...♗b6), whilst 13 ♕b3 a6!? should see him not being afraid to make a permanent pawn sacrifice. Furthermore, Black has scored good results after 12 h3 bxa4 13 hxg4 ♗g3 14 ♖h3 ♗f4 15 ♗xf4 exf4 although objectively the position is rather unclear.

Theoretically speaking, alternatives are inferior. After 11...♗h4?! 12 g3 ♗e7 13 h3 ♘f6 14 ♕c2 0-0 15 ♔f2 (S.Ernst-J.Van der Wiel, Leeuwarden 2001) Black was obviously in the game but White's king had started to sort itself out and I like that queenside pawn majority. Another line is 11...♗d4?! 12 ♘xd4 exd4 13 ♕xd4 0-0 14 h3 ♕h4 15 g3! ♕h5 16 ♗g2 ♘e5+ 17 g4 (A.Shirov-R.Dautov, Daugavpils 1989) when Black was forced to sacrifice a piece on g4 but he didn't get enough for it.

12 h3 ♗g3

12...fxe4 13 hxg4 ♗g3 is simply a transposition.

13 hxg4 fxe4 14 ♕c2

With the black bishop having switched diagonals, it makes sense to reintroduce the queen's knight. However, although both 14 ♘c5 and 14 ♘c3 are reasonable, the text places the queen on a good square.

14...exf3+ 15 gxf3 ♕f6

Regarding my last comment, not now 15...0-0?? because of 16 ♕xh7+.

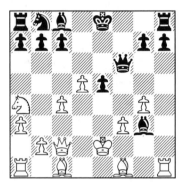

16 ♗e3

16 ♖xh7 was possible but ironically then 16...0-0!? provides good counterplay, e.g. 17 ♗g2? ♗xg4!.

16...h5 17 ♕e4

Possibly White could have done better than this, but it's harsh to criticise him for consolidating.

17...h4 18 ♔d2 0-0 19 ♗d3

Now it is Black's king that is the centre of attention.

19...g6 20 c5 ♔g7 21 ♘c3

White has the better pawn structure and the better pieces.

21...c6 22 ♖af1 ♘a6 23 f4!

This pawn is of course untouchable because of a ♗d4.

23...cxd5 24 ♘xd5 ♕c6 25 ♕xe5+ ♔h7

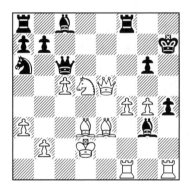

26 ♕h5+

Effectively terminating the proceedings, just as 26 ♗d4 would have too.

26...♔g8 27 ♘e7+ ♔g7 28 ♗d4+ 1-0

Summary

I don't like Game 12 for Black one bit, but I am willing to concede that there is method in Black's apparent positional madness in Game 13.

In theory, preserving the dark-squared bishop after 5...d5 6 a3 is very logical, but it seems now that White has fine-tuned his responses. An attractive centre is built up and Black's counterplay on and around f2 can probably be rebuffed. Definitely an area for future study though.

1 d4 ♘f6 2 c4 e6 3 ♘c3 ♗b4 4 f3 d5 5 a3 ♗e7

    5...♗xc3+ 6 bxc3 (D)

        6...0-0 – *Game 12*

        6...c6 – *Game 13*

    5...♗d6 – *Game 14*

6 e4 (D) dxe4

    6...c5 – *Game 15*

7 fxe4 e5 (D) – *Game 16*

    6...bxc3   *6 e4*   *7...e5*

CHAPTER THREE

4 f3: Others

1 d4 ♘f6 2 c4 e6 3 ♘c3 ♗b4 4 f3

In this chapter I take a look at some slightly more unusual black tries after 4 f3. The first two games feature 4...♘c6 – Black develops another piece and remains uncommitted for the moment about his central plans. After 5 a3 ♗xc3+ 6 bxc3, in Game 17 Black decides to erect a solid centre with the moves ...d7-d6 and ...e6-e5. In Game 18 White opts to play the immediate 5 e4 and Black replies by striking back in the centre with the sharp 5...d5!?.

Game 19 witnesses 4...0-0, which is arguably even more provocative than 4...♘c6. Black allows White to grab his big centre whilst simultaneously telegraphing his permanent king position. However, castling early does favour Black if the central situation becomes unstable because his king is safer than White's, which generally stays on e1 for a period of time while White completes his kingside development.

The final two games here concentrate on 4...c5. As White seems to be in the market for giving away dark squares, striking out in this manner is perfectly logical. Its obvious drawback though is that White is encouraged to cramp Black further with 5 d5. In Game 20 Black exchanges on c3 and follows up with a quick ...♘h5 and ...f7-f5, while in the

final game of this chapter Black adopts the ambitious pawn sacrifice 5...b5.

Game 17
S.Volkov-M.Bartel
playchess.com (blitz) 2004

1 d4 ♘f6 2 c4 e6 3 ♘c3 ♗b4 4 f3 ♘c6

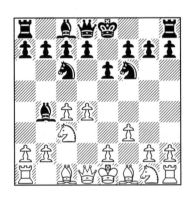

5 a3

Although it is quite possible that the same position will be reached via either 5 a3 or 5 e4, in fact both move orders have their upsides and their downsides. Regarding 5 e4, one drawback is that it encourages the complications of the next game (namely 5...d5!?). Also after 5...e5 (by the way I'd like to think that none of the readers would fall for 5...d6

6 ♘ge2 e5 7 d5 ♘e7?? 8 ♕a4+ although I can tell you that amazingly strong players have been known to drop pieces in this manner) 6 a3 Black does have the option of the intermezzo 6...exd4. However, the 7 axb4 dxc3 8 b5 ♘e5 9 f4 ♘g6 10 e5 ♘e4 11 ♘f3 ♕e7 12 bxc3 d6 13 ♗d3 ♘c5 14 0-0 dxe5 15 f5 ♘h4 16 ♗a3 ♘xf3+ 17 ♕xf3 ♕d6 18 ♕e3 ♕xd3 19 ♕xe5+ ♘e6 20 fxe6 ♗xe6 21 ♖ad1 1-0 of V.Moskalenko-R.Mateo, Sitges 2004 suggests that it is a risky policy. Black could have grabbed a hot pawn early on but I fancy those White bishops and that big pawn centre.

In my opinion the negative side of 5 a3 is that with 6...b6 Black can transpose back into the realms of a normal Sämisch and, specifically, to a line covered in the first game of the next chapter.

5...♗xc3+ 6 bxc3 e5

As Black's c-pawn is obstructed, now 6...d5 would be a positional error. However, as previously mentioned, 6...b6 7 e4 ♗a6 is a perfectly plausible continuation that comes under the microscope in the next chapter.

7 e4 d6

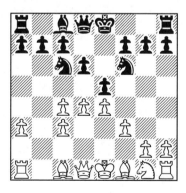

When I was a junior, playing the Nimzo against the likes of the Sämisch just seemed so easy. Swap off the bishop for the knight, block things up and let the steeds rule the world. Simplistic in the extreme, it was a surprisingly accurate outlook as my opponents would frequently concede great squares

to my knights and then suffer for having 'weak' pawns. Indeed, ironically I gave up the opening as White just for those reasons! However, the reality of the situation is that in those days I was competing at a much lower level. Stronger players tend not to play ball regarding conceding outposts; the truth is that actually it is the white pawn structure that tends to have the more dynamism.

8 ♗g5

This encounter is only a blitz game but nevertheless shows exactly the points that I want to make. However, a similar flow can be seen after 8 ♗e3 ♕e7 (incidentally 8...0-0 9 ♘e2 ♘a5 10 ♘g3 ♗e6 11 d5 ♗d7 12 c5 ♕e7 13 c6! bxc6 14 ♕a4 cxd5 15 ♕xa5 saw White convert his material advantage in A.Gorovets-V.Dydyshko, Minsk 2004) 9 ♗d3 ♘b8 10 ♘e2 c5 11 d5 ♘h5 12 g4 ♘f6 13 ♘g3; namely, White has expansion plans on the kingside and even the following steps to intercept those didn't disrupt the overall aim: 13...h5 14 g5 ♘h7 15 h4 g6 16 ♖a2 ♕c7 17 ♖f2 (clearly White is gearing up for the big f4 break when he'll have plenty of places to invade) 17...♕a5 18 ♕b3 ♘d7 19 0-0 f6 20 f4! fxg5 21 fxg5 ♖f8 22 ♗e2 a6 23 ♖xf8+ ♘hxf8 24 ♘xh5! (and then there's this sort of sacrifice, always in the offing when the opponent is operating under cramped conditions) 24...b5 25 ♘f6+ ♔e7 26 ♘g8+ ♔d8 27 h5 bxc4 28 ♕b2 gxh5 29 ♗xh5 ♘c7 30 ♘f6 ♘xf6 31 ♖xf6 ♗d7 32 g6 and White went on to win in C.Van Buskirk-R.Hermansen, Agoura Hills 2004.

8...h6

This is probably necessary sooner or later but, although back rank mates are prevented(!), this insertion is definitely a weakness. Whilst it's logical to put pawns on the opposite colour from the remaining bishop, this pawn is now a target itself. Also, if White's remaining knight makes it to f5, there will be no budging it via ...g7-g6.

9 ♗e3 ♕e7 10 ♗d3 0-0 11 ♘e2 b6

Black's main form of counterplay is going

to be the pressure that he can exert against the most forward of White's doubled c-pawns.

12 ♘g3 ♖e8 13 0-0

The key to handling these positions for White is to maintain the tension in the centre of the board for as long as possible. There is no need to make the c5-conceding advance d4-d5 sooner than is necessary.

13...♘a5 14 a4

Three typical ways for Black to attack the c4-pawn are via a knight on a5, a bishop on a6 and a queen on a4. The text prevents any possibility of the queen move.

14...♗a6 15 ♕e2 c5 16 ♘f5 ♕f8 17 g4

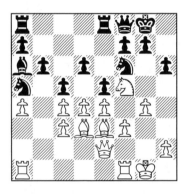

As the c5-square is now occupied by a black pawn, 17 d5 is possible too as Black no longer has the option of a later ...♘c5.

17...♖ac8

It could well be that even in this fast time limit the super-GM had observed 17...cxd4 18 cxd4 ♖ac8 19 c5!, which in the event of 19...♖xd3 20 ♕xd3 bxc5 21 dxc5 dxc5 22 ♕b5 would be completely winning.

18 d5

Making the rook on c8 look silly. Not only is it not going to get its c-file action, but it also blocks the retreat square of the bishop.

18...♖c7 19 ♔h1

Gearing up for g-file play!

19...♗c8 20 ♘g3

I could be slightly critical of specific elements of White's play, but it is the overall

direction that is so impressive and indeed instructive.

20...g6 21 ♖g1 ♘h7

The problem with this type of position for Black is finding anything constructive to do. Against a skilled opponent usually the only thing available is to sit back patiently and wait for an opportunity to block things up for a draw!

22 h4

Unfortunately there always seems to be one more available break or sacrifice that White can attempt. Anyway, enough of the abstract and back to the game! White continues with his kingside initiative.

22...♔h8 23 ♖g2 ♗d7 24 ♖a2 ♘b3 25 ♕b2 ♘a5 26 ♕d2!

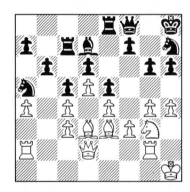

I told you that pawn on h6 would be a weakness and that, after it was placed there, ...g7-g6 would be impractical!

26...♘b3 27 ♗xh6 ♕e7

27...♘xd2 28 ♗xf8 is basically just a pawn; Black can't dabble in 28...♘xf3 because of 29 ♗xd6.

28 ♕f2 ♕xh4+

Black regains his pawn but an open h-file is a high price to pay.

29 ♖h2 ♕f6 30 ♕g2 ♔g8 31 ♗e3 ♘g5 32 ♘f5! ♖cc8 33 ♕g3

33 ♗xg5 ♕xg5 34 ♕h3 would have been immediately terminal as 34...♕f6 35 ♕h7+ ♔f8 36 ♕h8+ is mating and there is nothing but a spite check on c1. That said, White

remains in complete control as Black still can't capture the knight because of the g-file pin. That aside, her majesty is slowly (but not that slowly!) making her way across to the h-file.

33...♘h7 34 g5

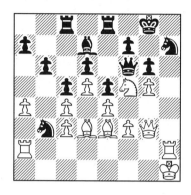

34...♕h8

Not the world's most attractive retreat, but 34...♕d8 35 ♖xh7 ♔xh7 36 ♖h2+ ♔g8 37 ♕h4 was hardly desirable either!

35 ♘xd6 ♔f8 36 ♖h6 ♖cd8 37 ♘xe8 1-0

Game 18
S.Volkov-S.Ionov
Russian Ch., St Petersburg 2004

---

1 d4 ♘f6 2 c4 e6 3 ♘c3 ♗b4 4 f3 ♘c6 5 e4 d5!?

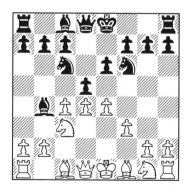

Striking out in the centre in this way is the most testing examination of White's big cen-

tre.

6 cxd5

Taking immediately forces Black to emerge with a pawn on d5. While I'm here though, observe the cheapo 6 e5 ♘g8 7 a3 ♗xc3+ 8 bxc3 dxc4 9 ♗xc4? ♘xe5! 10 dxe5 ♕h4+ 11 g3 ♕xc4.

6...exd5 7 e5 ♘g8 8 ♗e3!?

8 f4 ♘ge7 9 a3 ♗a5 10 b4 ♗b6 11 ♗b5 a5 12 bxa5 ♖xa5 13 ♘ge2 0-0 14 ♗e3 ♗g4 15 a4 ♘f5 16 ♕d2 ♘xe3 17 ♕xe3 ♘e7 felt very comfortable for Black in S.Volkov-A.Barsov, Panormo 2002, but this opening had some contentious points. White probably erred in chasing Black's dark-squared bishop to a different, useful diagonal and should have settled for 9 ♗e3! instead. Prior to that though, 8...♘h6!? is arguably more accurate as then 9 ♗e3?! can be met by 9...♘g4.

8...♘ge7

8...♘h6 could still be worth a whirl in view of 9 ♗xh6?! ♕h4+ 10 g3 ♕xh6. Of course White could try 9 g4 to keep the knight out of the action, but with 9...f5 available (amongst others) it all looks a bit random.

9 f4 ♗a5

9...0-0 10 ♗f2 f6 11 ♘f3 fxe5 12 fxe5 ♘g6 13 ♗e2 ♘f4 was fine for Black in S.Shkliar-M.Lushenkov, Samara 2003; I'm not sure what this apparent obsession is with this seemingly anticipatory ♗f2.

10 ♕d2

In my opinion the 10 ♗f2 0-0 11 ♗e2 f6 12 ♘f3 fxe5 13 fxe5 ♘g6 14 0-0 ♘f4 of S.Volkov-S.Ivanov, Krasnoyarsk 2003 is slightly better for White than the line given in the previous note as Black has used up a tempo on the move ....♗a5. Nevertheless Black didn't seem to have much trouble drawing.

10...0-0 11 0-0-0

Certainly an ambitious approach! White still has that strong pawn on e5 but Black has some handy squares.

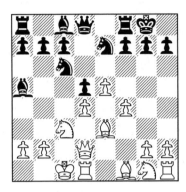

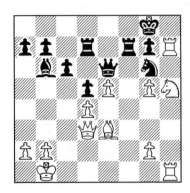

11...f6 12 ♗d3 fxe5 13 fxe5 ♗f5 14 ♘f3 ♕d7 15 ♗xf5 ♖xf5

I have a great deal of sympathy for Black in this game as he seems to be cruising along okay until, all of a sudden, wham and he's clearly worse! In retrospect I suspect that it's down to way he handles his knights. I like the repositioning of the queen's knight that Black soon engages in but it is his king's knight that becomes awkward. After 15...♘xf5 I don't believe that Black is worse.

16 ♔b1 ♘d8 17 ♖c1 ♘e6 18 ♕d3 c6 19 ♘e2 ♖af8 20 h4!?

One certainly can't be critical of White's aggressive play though.

20...♘g6?!

Presumably Black had always intended this when opting to recapture on f5 with the rook, but placed here this steed soon becomes a liability.

21 ♘g3 ♖5f7 22 ♘g5! ♘xg5 23 hxg5

And suddenly Black's h-pawn is a real cause for concern.

23...♕e6

Highlighting the danger, check out 23...♕g4 24 ♖xh7! ♔xh7 25 ♖h1+ ♔g8 26 ♕xg6 ♖e8 27 ♕h7+ ♔f8 28 g6 when White is surely winning.

24 ♖h3!

Now the plan is simple: target h7 with everything he's got!

24...♗b6 25 ♖ch1 ♖d7 26 ♖xh7 ♖ff7 27 ♘h5!!

Ruthless! White threatens ♘f6+ and if Black takes the rook that same move will be mate!

27...♖f5 28 g4 ♖f3 29 ♘f6+! ♔f7

After 29...gxf6 30 ♕xg6+ ♔f8 31 ♖h8+ ♔e7 White has a choice of mates.

30 ♕e2

30 ♖1h6! would have been bone crushing, but the text is also adequate to force the win.

30...♘xe5 31 ♘xd7 ♕xd7 32 g6+ ♔xg6 33 ♕c2+ ♔f7 34 dxe5 ♗xe3

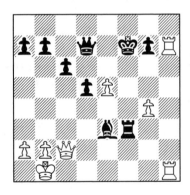

35 ♖xg7+!

A cute way to wrap things up!

35...♔xg7 36 ♕h7+ 1-0

Game 19
S.Volkov-N.Vekshenkov
Russian Team Ch., Togliatti 2003

1 d4 ♘f6 2 c4 e6 3 ♘c3 ♗b4 4 f3 0-0

5 e4

5 a3 is of course also possible and will transpose to variations considered in the next chapter.

5...d5

Of course Black can't take a back seat forever, and this challenging push is critical.

6 e5

Probably more accurate than 6 cxd5 exd5 7 e5 because then 7...♘e8 is an option too. Here 8 f4 c5 9 ♘f3 ♘c6 10 ♗e3 ♗g4 11 ♗e2 ♘c7 and a plan of parking the knight on e6 is an idea that has proven to be quite successful for Black.

6...♘fd7

With the e6-square currently occupied, now 6...♘e8 isn't as attractive.

7 cxd5

7 a3 ♗xc3+ 8 bxc3

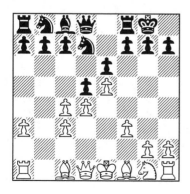

strikes me as being too slow, with three

different Black paths each looking reasonable:

a) 8...c5 9 cxd5 exd5 and now:

a1) 10 ♗d3 ♘c6 11 ♘e2 cxd4 12 cxd4 f6! 13 exf6 (the problem with 13 f4!? is that after 13...fxe5, if White recaptures with the d-pawn then 14...♘c5 brings Black a lot of action, whereas 14 fxe5 leaves White with difficulty castling; for example, 14...♘b6 15 ♘f4 ♘xd4 16 ♗xh7+ ♔xh7 17 ♕xd4 ♕h4+ 18 g3 ♕g4 and now if 19 0-0?! then 19...g5!) 13...♕xf6 14 0-0 ♘b6 15 ♗e3 ♗f5. Black has a slight edge which he was ultimately able to convert to the full point in J.Baron Rodriguez-I.Cheparinov, Zaragoza 2004: 16 ♖b1 ♕e7 17 ♗f4 ♕xa3 18 ♗xf5 ♖xf5 19 ♗c7 ♘c4 20 ♖xb7 ♘e3 21 ♕a1 ♕d3 22 ♘g3 ♖f7 23 ♖fb1 ♖c8 24 ♗e5 ♖xb7 25 ♖xb7 ♘xe5 26 dxe5 ♕d2 0-1.

a2) The position after 10 f4 has occurred surprisingly rarely. Upon reflection (and taking into account the previous note) it occurs to me that it could be critical. It's not too difficult to envisage White's position becoming enormous if he can get developed and ram his f-pawn down Black's throat. On the other hand, it's probably not that difficult for Black to erect a solid blockade or two on squares such as f5 and e6.

b) 8...dxc4 9 f4 (and not 9 ♗xc4? ♘xe5! 10 dxe5 ♕h4+ which is a trap that I'd like to think that you would have remembered!) 9...♘b6 10 a4!? (probably a better practical option than the 10 ♘f3 ♘c6 11 ♕c2 f5 12 a4 ♘a5 13 ♗a3 ♖e8 14 ♖a2 ♘d5 15 ♗c1 c5 16 ♗e2 ♕c7 17 0-0 b6 of A.De Santis-A.Rotstein, Arco 2003) 10...a5 11 ♘f3 ♗d7 12 ♗a3 ♖e8 13 ♗c5 when White had some but not a stunning amount of play for the pawn in A.Lauber-D.Lopushnoy, Budapest 1997.

c) 8...f6 9 exf6 ♘xf6 10 ♗d3 c5 11 ♘e2 b6 (initiating a familiar bishop-trading plan) 12 0-0 ♗a6 13 cxd5 ♗xd3 14 ♕xd3 exd5 15 ♗g5 c4 16 ♕c2 ♘c6 17 ♘g3 ♕d7 with approximate equality in D.Tyomkin-

D.Rogozenko, Internet 2001.

7...exd5

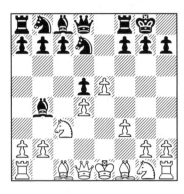

8 f4

As we soon see, the target in White's structure is his d-pawn. An obvious solution to bolstering it comes in the form of 8 a3 ♗xc3+ 9 bxc3. Then, however, Black may be able to transpose back into note 'a' to White's seventh move via 9...c5 10 ♗d3 ♘c6 11 ♘e2 cxd4 12 cxd4 f6!, although the immediate 9...f6!? also looks quite interesting. After 10 exf6 it is probably better to recapture with the knight rather than the queen, although the intermezzo 10...♖e8+!? looks like throwing a spanner in White's ♗d3 and ♘e2 works! Observe, also, how 10 f4 fxe5 11 dxe5 is punished by 11...♘xe5! 12 fxe5 ♕h4+ 13 ♔d2 ♕f4+. Well, what does White expect after wasting all his time moving pawns?

8...c5

This of course is the advantage of 4...0-0 over 4...♘c6: the c-pawn is free to put White's centre under pressure.

9 a3

Previously there has been quite a big debate over the likes of 9 ♘f3 ♘c6, in which Black is probably doing okay. After you've played over the main game though, return here and check out the possibility of 9...cxd4 10 ♘xd4 ♘xe5!? 11 fxe5 ♕h4+ 12 ♔e2 ♗c5 13 ♗e3 ♗g4+ 14 ♘f3 d4. Compared to the position with the white pawn on a3 and the bishop on b6, White does have available 15

♗g1 (note that 15 ♘a4 dxe3 16 ♘xc5 ♕f2+ 17 ♔d3 ♖d8+ is of no use), but I don't think I'd fancy White's defensive task after the simple 15...♖d8.

9...♗a5

9...♗xc3+ 10 bxc3 transposes to that rare but possibly critical position that I have previously mentioned. Here though Black takes advantage of the move order to preserve his bishop.

10 ♘f3

After 10 b4 cxb4 11 axb4 ♗xb4 12 ♗d2 ♘b6 13 ♗d3 ♘c6 the sacrifice of a pawn hadn't really aided White in the overall scheme of things – Black went on to win in J.Carleton-A.Corkett, British League 2000.

Although White can effectively force Black to part with his bishop via 10 dxc5, then 10...♗xc3+ 11 bxc3 ♘xc5 still leaves him with all of his pieces at home!

10...cxd4 11 ♘xd4

11 ♕xd4 is no better, with 11...♘c6 12 ♕xd5 walking into the tactic 12...♘dxe5!.

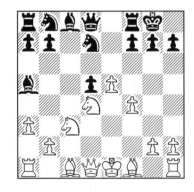

11...♘xe5!!

Given time to consolidate, positionally White would hold all of the cards. Right here and now, tactically he doesn't!

12 fxe5 ♕h4+ 13 ♔e2

13 g3? ♕e4+ is a simple fork.

13...♗b6!

Also quite conclusive was the 13...♗g4+ 14 ♘f3 ♘c6 15 h3 ♗xf3+ 16 gxf3 d4 17 ♘d5 ♖ad8 18 ♗g2 d3+ 19 ♕xd3 ♘d4+ 20

♔e3 ♖xd5 21 ♕e4 ♘f5+ 22 ♕xf5 ♗b6+ 23 ♔e2 ♕f2 mate of D.Palo-A.Maksimenko, Germany 2004! I'm sticking with the main game as there are no obvious improvements for White but, as this recent encounter proves, Black could be spoilt for choice.

14 ♗e3

If the d4-knight moves then the queen check on f2 is a killer.

14...♗g4+ 15 ♘f3 d4!

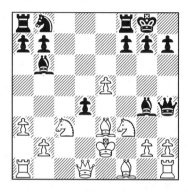

Black is relentless and rightly so as the text recoups the sacrificed material.

16 ♗xd4 ♗xf3+ 17 ♔xf3 ♗xd4

Yes, the material situation is now level but the e5-pawn looks set to drop off and the less said about the white king's positioning the better!

18 g3 ♕h5+ 19 ♔g2 ♕xe5 20 ♕f3 ♘c6 21 ♗b5 ♗xc3

Simple chess! Black has done all the hard work and now there's no need to be flashy.

22 ♗xc6 bxc6 23 ♕xc3 ♕e2+

That said, given the exposed nature of the white monarch, Black still retains more winning chances by preserving the queens.

24 ♔h3 ♖ab8 25 ♖he1 ♕h5+ 26 ♔g2 ♕d5+ 27 ♔h3 ♕h5+ 28 ♔g2 ♕d5+ 29 ♔h3 ♖b3 30 ♕e5 ♕d7+ 31 ♔g2 ♖fb8 32 ♖e2 ♖3b5 33 ♕e7 ♕d5+ 34 ♔h3 ♕h5+ 35 ♔g2 ♕xe2+ 36 ♕xe2 ♖xb2 37 ♖e1 h5

Two extra pawns will be enough to win the rook ending (although I think Black

could have handled it better!).

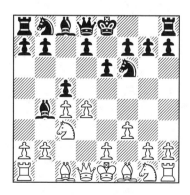

38 ♔h3 ♖xe2 39 ♖xe2 ♖b3 40 ♖e4 ♔h7 41 ♖e7 ♖xa3 42 ♖xf7 ♔g6 43 ♖d7 ♖a6 44 ♖c7 ♔f6 45 ♔h4 g6 46 h3 ♔f5 47 ♖f7+ ♔e5 48 ♖e7+ ♔f5 49 ♖f7+ ♔e5 50 ♖e7+ ♔f6 51 ♖c7 ♖b6 52 ♖xa7 ♖b4+ 53 g4 g5+ 54 ♔g3 h4+ 55 ♔g2 ♖b2+ 56 ♔f1 ♔e5 57 ♖c7 ♖c2 58 ♖f7 ♔d4 59 ♖e7 ♖c5 60 ♖e6 ♔d5 61 ♖f6 ♔e4 62 ♔f2 ♖c2+ 63 ♔e1 ♔e3 64 ♔d1 ♖c5 65 ♖f7 ♖d5+ 66 ♔c2 ♖d2+ 67 ♔c1 ♖h2 68 ♖f5 ♖xh3 69 ♖xg5 ♖g3 70 ♖h5 h3 71 g5 ♔f2 72 g6 ♔g2 0-1

Game 20
V.Ivanchuk-I.Csom
Yerevan 1989

---

1 d4 ♘f6 2 c4 e6 3 ♘c3 ♗b4 4 f3 c5

5 d5 ♗xc3+

Given that Black intends ...♘h5 anyway he can make this trade almost at any stage. On the other hand, if he wanted to strike out with ...b7-b5 (as in the next game) then of course showing his cards by given up the bishop now would be silly.

Irrespective of Black's decision to delay or not to delay ...♗xc3+, after 5...♘h5 the main alternative to the cautious g3 seen in the main game is 6 ♘h3!?. I can remember analysing the likes of 6...♗xc3+ 7 bxc3 ♕h4+ 8 ♘f2 ♕xc4 9 e4 ♕xc3+ 10 ♗d2

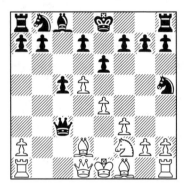

when I was coaching the Barbados national men's team. In all fairness I didn't appreciate that the simple 6 g3 was good for White and was trying to make greed pay for Black in what I thought was the critical 6 ♘h3!?. In fact it's irrelevant what I had previously thought because then and indeed now I understand that the pawns aren't worth the suffering for Black. Three practical examples demonstrate this:

a) 10...♕e5 (the line I'd fruitlessly spent most of my time on) 11 ♖c1! b6 (and specifically 11...d6 but my advice is don't waste your energy!) 12 g4 ♘f6 13 f4 ♕c7 14 g5 ♘g8 15 ♗c3 ♔f8 16 d6 ♕d8 17 ♕d2 h6 18 ♕b2 ♖h7 19 g6 fxg6 20 ♖g1 ♘f6 21 ♖xg6 ♕c8 22 ♖g1 ♕f7 23 ♗d3 ♗a6 24 ♗b1 ♘e8 25 e5 ♕xf4 26 ♗xh7 ♕e3+ 27 ♔d1 ♕f3+ 28 ♔e1 ♕e3+ 29 ♔d1 ♕f3+ 30 ♔c2 ♕xf2+ 31 ♔b1 ♕xb2+ 32 ♔xb2 g5 33 h4! ♘g7 34 hxg5 h5 35 ♖c2 ♘f5 36 ♗xf5 exf5 37 ♖h2

♘c6 38 ♖xh5 ♗c4 39 g6 ♗e6 40 ♖h8+ ♗g8 41 e6 dxe6 42 ♗f6 e5 43 ♖xg8+ ♔xg8 44 ♖h1 1-0 I.Khenkin-R.Kholmov, Voskresensk 1990.

b) 10...♕f6 11 g4 exd5 12 gxh5 d4 13 ♗g2 ♘c6 14 0-0 h6 15 e5 ♕e6 16 f4 0-0 17 ♘e4 b6 18 f5 ♕xe5 19 ♗f4 ♕xf5 20 ♗xh6 ♕e6 21 ♘f6+! gxf6 22 ♗d5 1-0 M.Montroig-E.Chery, correspondence 1997.

c) 10...♕d4 11 ♕c1 (to show the sort of uphill struggle Black faces, he is currently two pawns up but even Fritz prefers White!) 11...exd5 12 ♗c3 ♕a4 13 ♕g5 d6 14 ♕xh5 d4 15 ♗d2 ♗e6 16 ♗e2 ♘c6 17 0-0 0-0-0 18 ♖fc1 c4 19 f4 f6 20 ♗d1 ♕a3 21 ♗g4 1-0 M.Marin-V.Vehi Bach, Roses 1992. When push comes to shove, the pawns never seem to match up to the pieces when so much is going on.

6 bxc3 ♘h5

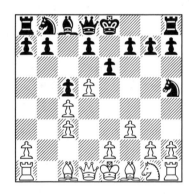

The purpose of this move is twofold: firstly, to set up a nifty check on h4 (that can't be stopped by g2-g3 because of ...♘xg3) and, secondly, to free up the f-pawn so that it can have a say in the centre.

7 g3 f5

This doesn't appear to work, but regarding something like 7...d6 8 e4 e5 9 ♗d3 0-0, the reader will already know my reservations about this sort of position. Black can't easily play ...f7-f5 because of the eventual fork g2-g4. On the other hand, although this is a semi-closed position White always seems to have something to play with. He may arrange the break f3-f4 or manoeuvre his knight to f5 via g3. Still, there may be one or two technical problems (for example checks on h4, a bishop to h3, a knight to f4) that will mean that White has his work cut out, and there may be the odd individual out there who would try to defend Black's position.

8 e4

8 ♘h3 is by no means ridiculous but the text gets straight to the point.

8...f4

The variations after 8...♕f6 9 f4! are not very appetising for Black:

a) 9...♕xc3+ 10 ♗d2 ♕d4 when both 11 ♘f3 ♕xe4+ 12 ♔f2 and 11 ♗g2 ♘f6 12 ♘e2 ♕xc4 13 ♖c1 ♕xa2 14 ♖xc5 0-0 15 e5 ♘e4 (or 15...♘xd5 16 ♖xd5 exd5 17 ♗b4) 16 ♘c3 ♘xc3 17 ♖xc3 leave Black's queen out in the cold and White's pieces looking dominant.

b) 9...♘xg3 10 hxg3 ♕xc3+ 11 ♗d2 ♕xg3+ 12 ♔e2 fxe4 13 ♕b3, as seen in J.Nogueiras-S.Kindermann, Dubai Olympiad 1986, again sees a piece preferable to pawns, particularly as Black has difficulty developing his queenside.

Incidentally, the position after 8...0-0 could be reached in a few different ways but the outcome is the same. Namely 9 e5!, leaving both of Black's knights looking dumb.

9 dxe6!

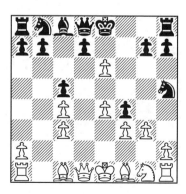

Unfortunately (that is for Black!) this ap-

pears to be the refutation of his audacious opening play. The first thing to note is that recapturing on e6 leads to a grim ending via a queen trade and g3-g4, netting the f4-pawn.

9...fxg3

The f4-bolstering 9...♕f6 is the main alternative but after 10 ♘e2 fxg3 11 ♗g2 Black is clearly worse if he lets White recapture on g3; for example, 11...♕xe6 12 hxg3 ♘f6 13 g4 0-0 14 g5 ♘e8 15 ♘f4 ♕e5 which, in Silman-Kane, San Francisco 1982, White went on to win, though not via the fairly straightforward 16 ♕d5+.

On the other hand, 11...gxh2 12 ♖xh2 g6 13 exd7+ still favours White as whichever way Black recaptures, White can park the queen on d5 when moves such as ♗g5 and ♖d1 or 0-0-0 will flow.

10 ♕d5!

The d5-square is a great square for White, and on here the white queen is a monster.

10...g2

10...♘h4 11 ♗g5! g2+ 12 ♗xh4 gxh1♕ 13 ♕xh5+ g6 14 ♕e5 is game over, but in my opinion 10...♘f6!? 11 exd7+ ♗xd7 12 ♕e5+ ♔f7 13 hxg3 ♕a5 poses more problems; White is a pawn up and has a strong kingside structure, but Black's lead in development offers him at least some chances.

11 ♕xh5+ g6 12 ♕e5 ♕h4+

Of course not 12...gxh1♕? 13 ♕xh8+ ♔e7 14 ♗g5+.

13 ♔e2 gxh1♕

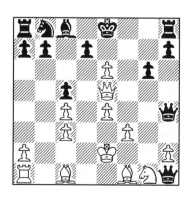

14 ♕xh8+ ♔e7 15 ♕g7+ ♔xe6 16 ♗h3+ ♔d6 17 ♕f8+ ♔c7

Also visual is 17...♔e5 18 ♗f4+! ♕xf4 19 ♕e7 mate – Ivanchuk has calculated perfectly.

18 ♗f4+ ♕xf4

After 18...♔b6 19 ♖b1+ ♔a6 20 ♕xc8 the two black queens are powerless to stop White's mating threats. Hence Black's decision to give up one of them.

19 ♕xf4+ d6 20 ♖d1 ♘c6 21 ♕xd6+ ♔b6 22 ♕g3!

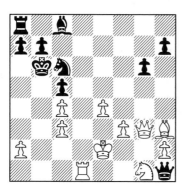

Black's remaining queen is trapped.

22...h5 23 ♗xc8 ♖xc8 24 ♘h3 h4 25 ♕f2 1-0

Game 21
F.Berkes-Cao Sang
Hungarian Ch., Budapest 2004

---

1 d4 ♘f6 2 c4 e6 3 ♘c3 ♗b4 4 f3 c5 5 d5 b5

A bold move that I would really like to see working. Unfortunately, just like so many opening variations these days, it seems to lead to a relatively forced sequence that ultimately favours White.

Regarding 5...0-0 6 e4 I can only reiterate that I don't like the idea of trying to block things up (e.g. 6...♗xc3+ 7 bxc3 d6 8 ♗d3 e5 9 ♘e2). Meanwhile, 6...♘h5 at best transposes to a bad line of our previous game (mind you, most of them were bad!) after 7

g3 f5 8 e5!, whilst the delayed pawn sacrifice 6...b5 is discussed in the notes to Black's next move.

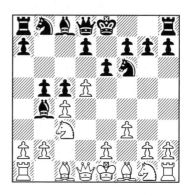

6 e4

Black is trying to undermine d5 and so White rightly ignores the offered pawn in order to bolster his centre. On occasion as Black I have been known to wheel out the Blumenfeld Counter Gambit (1 d4 ♘f6 2 c4 e6 3 ♘f3 c5 4 d5 b5) and I can tell you that in comparison 6 dxe6?! fxe6 7 cxb5 d5 would be like a dream! The bishop is active on b4 whilst White's pawn is blatantly detrimentally placed on f3.

6...bxc4

Having now studied all the available data it seems to me as though Black may find more joy in the '...b5 gambit delayed'. In other words, castling earlier and then playing ...b5 or reaching the same position via 6...0-0 now.

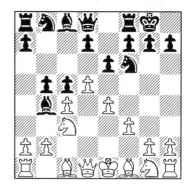

It is still a pawn offering and that's where we start covering some of White's options:

a) 7 cxb5?! exd5 8 exd5 ♖e8+. I can't believe any self-respecting 1 d4 player would really want to travel this road and a rare example shows why: 9 ♔f2 d6 10 ♗c4 ♘fd7 11 ♗f4 ♘b6 12 ♗b3 a6 13 ♘ge2 c4 14 ♗c2 ♗c5+ 15 ♔f1 axb5 16 ♘xb5 ♘a6 17 a3 ♗b7 18 ♘bc3 ♘c7 19 ♗e4 f5 20 ♗xf5 ♘cxd5 21 ♕c2 ♕h4 22 g3 ♕h5 23 ♗g4 ♕f7 24 ♘xd5 ♘xd5 25 ♔g2 ♕xf4! (I can see you are tempted by the delayed gambit already!) 26 ♘xf4 ♘e3+ 27 ♔h3 ♘xc2 28 ♖ac1 ♘d4 29 ♖xc4 ♘xf3 30 ♘d3 ♘g5+ 0-1 A.Vlaskov-V.Timofeev, Smolensk 1992.

b) 7 ♗d2 (solid but hardly inspirational!) 7...bxc4 8 ♗xc4 ♗a6 9 b3 exd5 10 ♘xd5 ♘xd5 11 ♗xd5 ♕g5!? (dynamic but unfortunately only really forcing a draw) 12 ♗xb4 ♕xg2 13 ♗xc5 ♕f1+ 14 ♔d2 ♕d3+ 15 ♔e1 ♕f1+ 16 ♔d2 ♕d3+ 17 ♔e1 ½-½ S.Volkov-A.Gershon, Halkidiki 2002.

c) 7 ♗g5 h6 8 ♗h4 ♖e8!? (not forced but there is an interesting appeal to maintaining and indeed even building up the tension in the centre) 9 dxe6 ♖xe6 when the position is double-edged and surely offers Black more chances than in our main game.

d) 7 e5 exd5 8 exf6 d4 9 a3 ♗a5 10 b4 dxc3 11 bxa5 ♕xf6 12 ♕d5. If I were consistent about my piece versus pawns comments then I would have to favour White (though admittedly things are a bit different here). Although the 12...b4 13 ♗g5 ♕e6+ 14 ♕xe6 fxe6 15 ♗e7 ♘a6 16 ♗xf8 ♔xf8 17 ♗d3 ♖b8 18 ♘e2 d5 19 ♔f2 d4 20 axb4 ♘xb4 21 ♗xh7 ♗a6 22 ♖hc1 ♗xc4 23 ♘xc3 dxc3 24 ♖xc3 ♗a6 25 ♖xc5 ♗d3 26 ♖h5 g6 1-0 (because of the check on h8, White can just take this pawn on g6) of N.Legky-D.Levacic, Cannes 1993 would appear to justify that assessment, Black isn't actually compelled to sacrifice the piece. Instead both 7...♘h5 and 7...♘e8 encourage White to overplay his hand.

e) 7 ♘h3 bxc4 8 ♗xc4 ♘xd5 9 ♗xd5

exd5 10 ♕xd5 ♘c6 11 0-0 ♗a6 12 ♖f2 was played in M.Simantsev-G.Golovchenko, Serpukhov 2004. Although Black wasn't compelled to play in this way a clear comparison can now be made with our main game. White has managed to castle and has been able to protect his b-pawn along the second rank with his rook. His knight, however, is placed in a worse position as on h3 it neither supports its partner on c3 nor controls the d4-square.

Aside from 6...0-0 there are no sensible alternatives with, for example, 6...♗b7?! (fianchettoing against a wall of pawns is at this moment definitely too committal) 7 ♗g5 h6 8 ♗h4 bxc4 9 ♗xc4 exd5 10 exd5 ♗xc3+ 11 bxc3 0-0 12 ♘e2 d6 13 ♖b1 leaving White with a simple bishop-pair advantage and Black's remaining bishop looking silly in I.Khenkin-P.Eljanov, Andorra 2003.

7 ♗xc4 ♘xd5

Restricting White's responses to one (i.e. White can't now recapture with the pawn because of ...♕h4+).

8 ♗xd5 exd5 9 ♕xd5 ♘c6

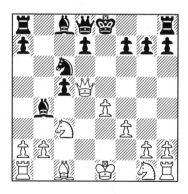

10 ♘ge2

The recent try 10 ♗f4 0-0 11 ♗d6 is, if anything, worse because after 11...♖e8 White can't take the pawn on c5 anyway due to ...♗xc3+ and ...♕a5. Hence 12 ♘ge2, when 12...♗a6 13 ♔f2 ♕f6 14 a3 ♗a5 15 b4?! cxb4 16 axb4 ♗b6+ 17 ♗c5 ♘xb4 18 ♗xb6 ♘xd5 19 ♘xd5 ♕b2 20 ♖xa6 axb6 21 ♖xb6

♕d2 was certainly entertaining, with Black eventually grinding out the win in I.Spiric-C.Nanu, Obrenovac 2004.

10...♗a6 11 ♔f2 0-0 12 ♖d1 ♗a5

Just as in the game, 12...♕b6 is well met by 13 ♗e3 when the threat of a2-a3 is embarrassing for the black bishop. The c-pawn is pinned and a target.

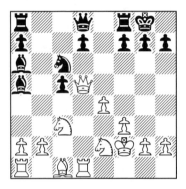

13 ♗g5!?

13 a3 (to eliminate ...♘b4) 13...♖b8 14 ♗g5 is similar, and after 14...♕c8 15 ♖ab1 ♖e8 (S.Volkov-M.Sorokin, Ekaterinburg 2002) there is no obvious reason why White can't just grab a pawn. Indeed 16 ♕xd7 (rather than the actually played 16 ♗f4 ♖b7) 16...♘e5 17 ♕xc8 ♖exc8 18 ♘d5 ♔h8 19 ♘c1 seems to consolidate White's position, with 19...c4 only offering some sort of Benko Gambit style compensation.

I have mentioned before that Tiger's ideas are often worth taking on board, but possibly 13 ♕h5 ♖b8 14 ♘g3 ♗c7 15 f4 ♘b4 16 ♘f5 ♘d3+ 17 ♖xd3 ♗xd3 18 ♕g4 g6 19 ♘d5 ♗xe4! was pushing the boat out a tad too far in T.Hillarp Persson-B.Ahlander, Skara 2002. It looked like interesting stuff though, and at the end of the day he emerged with a draw.

Most humans would be uncomfortable dealing with 13 ♕xd7 ♘b4 as Black has some good minor pieces.

13...♕b6

Now though White should have no

qualms about meeting 13...♕c8 with 14 ♕xd7! as his rooks are connected and Black can't avoid a trade of queens.

14 ♗e3

This transposes to the note to Black's 12th move, but with ...♗a5 thrown in for free. As the c5-pawn is hanging, though, it isn't much of a gain.

14...♖fb8 15 ♗xc5!

If I wasn't so impressed with the game continuation I would also suggest that there is an argument for defending the b-pawn.

15...♕xb2 16 ♖ab1 ♗xc3

16...♕c2? 17 ♖xb8+ ♖xb8 18 ♖d2 is a significantly inferior way of parting with the queen.

17 ♖xb2 ♖xb2

Black only has a rook and a piece for the queen at the moment but, because of the attack on the white knight he is destined to secure some more material. However, White has factored all of this into the equation.

18 ♖d3 ♗xd3 19 ♕xd3 ♗f6 20 f4!

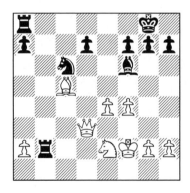

White is not interested in the d-pawn right now. Black may have two rooks for the queen but White's promising kingside pawn structure and better pieces tip things in his favour.

20...♘b4 21 ♗xb4 ♖xb4 22 ♔f3 ♖b2 23 e5

Queen and knight are a deadly combination and this duo is about to weave its magic.

23...♗d8 24 f5

I like this continuation although it is difficult to find fault with 24 ♕d5! ♖ab8 25 ♕xd7 as Black's pieces coordinate poorly.

24...♗b6 25 f6

Yes, White is getting straight to the point; namely the defenceless black king.

25...gxf6 26 exf6 ♖e8 27 ♕xd7 ♖e3+ 28 ♔f4 ♖b4+

The knight was not really en prise as 28...♖bxe2 29 ♕c8+! ♖e8 (or 29...♗d8 30 ♕xd8+ ♖e8 31 ♕d5 with complete control and a continued attack) 30 ♕g4+ ♔f8 31 ♕g7 is of course mate!

29 ♔f5 ♖be4 30 ♘f4 ♖e5+ 31 ♔g4 ♖3e4 32 ♔h3

Again the knight is immune to capture because of the back rank threats.

32...h5

33 ♘g6

33 ♘d5 is less visual but should also do

the trick. On g6 the knight attacks the rook and threatens ♘e7+. In case it had escaped your attention, the troublesome steed can't be taken because of ♕g7 mate!

33...♖e6 34 ♕c8+ ♖e8 35 ♕f5

White appears to be toying with his opponent. I suppose he is but nevertheless he has a clear plan of progression.

35...♗d8 36 ♕g5 ♗xf6 37 ♘e7+ ♔h7 38 ♕xh5+ ♔g7 39 ♘f5+ ♔g8 40 ♘h6+ ♔g7 41 ♕xf7+ ♔xh6 42 ♕xf6+

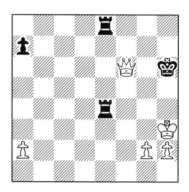

After a wonderful demonstration of handling the deadly queen and knight duo, the rest is like a walk in the park!

42...♔h7 43 ♕f7+ ♔h6 44 g4 ♖e2 45 ♕f6+ ♔h7 46 g5 ♖8e7 47 ♔g4 ♖g2+ 48 ♔f3 ♖ge2 49 h4 ♖2e6 50 ♕f5+ ♔g8 51 ♕d5 ♔g7 52 ♔f4 ♖e1 53 ♕d4+ ♔g8 54 h5 ♖f7+ 55 ♔g4 ♖fe7 56 ♕d5+ ♔f8 57 h6 ♖1e5 58 ♕d8+ ♔f7 59 h7 1-0

Summary

An important conclusion to come from this chapter is that blocked positions aren't actually that attractive a prospect for Black because White can always drum something up on the king-side, and often play against the c4-pawn is all that the second player has. I never used to like the concept myself, but upon reflection (and the study of numerous games) instead I recommend to Black employing the challenging ...d7-d5 in some form or other.

The 4...c5 5 d5 lines are quite exciting, but it looks as though White has them reasonably well under control.

1 d4 ♘f6 2 c4 e6 3 ♘c3 ♗b4 4 f3 c5

    4...0-0 (D) – *Game 19*

    4...♘c6 (D)

        5 a3 – *Game 17*

        5 e4 – *Game 18*

5 d5 b5 (D) – *Game 21*

    5...♗xc3+ – *Game 20*

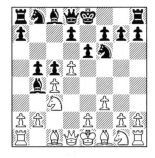

4...0-0   *4...♘c6*   *5...b5*

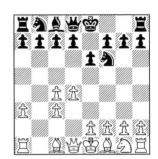

CHAPTER FOUR

The Stand-alone Sämisch
(4 a3 ♗xc3+ 5 bxc3)

1 d4 ♘f6 2 c4 e6 3 ♘c3 ♗b4 4 a3 ♗xc3+ 5 bxc3

In this chapter we look at positions that can either only be reached via 4 a3 or ones where White plays 4 f3 but then forgoes the opportunity to play an early e2-e4 in favour of a quick a2-a3.

After 4 a3 ♗xc3+ 5 bxc3, Black has quite a few reasonable options. In Game 22, for example, Black chooses 5...♘c6 followed by a quick-fire attack on the c4-pawn with ...b7-b6, ...♗a6 and ...♘a5. Game 23 features a game of my own where I employ the move 5...♘e4!?. I must confess that originally I adopted this move against the Sämisch because there seemed to be hardly any theory on it; now it could well be one of the main contributing factors to 4 f3 being much more popular these days than 4 a3. In Game 24 I take a look at Black's less testing ideas; in other words, lines where Black just tries to achieve a blocked position and shows no urgency to attack White's c4-pawn.

In the last three games of the chapter I consider more mainstream options for Black. His choice in Game 25 is perfectly logical – Black castles before deciding on his approach in the centre. The only downside is that, as we have seen before, there are certain dangers to committing the king so early. Games

26-27 feature the most popular move 5...c5, although you will see that there is more than one move order to reach the traditional main line 4 a3 ♗xc3+ 5 bxc3 c5 6 e3 0-0.

Game 22
Z.Martic-A.Jankovic
Zadar 2004

---

1 d4 ♘f6 2 c4 e6 3 ♘c3 ♗b4 4 f3 ♘c6 5 a3

Yes, it doesn't seem clever to be kicking off a chapter entitled 'The stand alone Sämisch' with a 4 f3 encounter, but I mentioned in the previous chapter that this game sort of belongs here because White has eschewed the chance to flick in 5 e4. Of course there are going to be several similarities and possible transpositions/overlaps between 4 a3 and 4 f3, but the bottom line is that in the former White doesn't have to go for a quick f2-f3 – the slower e2-e3 was the main line when I was a junior (see Game 27). Anyway I'm getting ahead of myself!

5...♗xc3+ 6 bxc3

The strict 'stand-alone Sämisch' move order to reach this position would be 4 a3 ♗xc3+ 5 bxc3 ♘c6 6 f3.

6...b6!?

There is an obvious weak point in White's

position and Black intends to pressurise it *asap*!

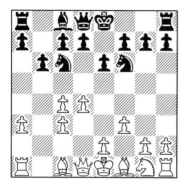

7 e4 ♗a6

The added bonus of being able to capture the c4-pawn is that it often entails eliminating White's bishop-pair advantage at the same time.

8 e5

Though it is to the point, clearly Black's approach is very provocative. On the face of it this would appear to be the acid test, but the reality is that White scores poorly with 8 e5. That said, even reflecting upon the alternatives, results in general don't look that great for White:

a) 8 ♗d3 is obviously possible, but after 8...♘a5 9 ♕e2 d6 10 ♗g5 h6 11 ♗h4 one simple plan is 11...♕d7!? aiming for ...♕a4 and further pressurisation of the c4-pawn.

This is a very instructive set-up of black

pieces and is worth remembering. A knight on the rim is not dim when kept company by a queen and bishop!

b) As Sergey Volkov featured heavily as White in the previous chapter, it also makes sense to check out what he does here. Well, in the last couple of years he has tried 8 ♗g5 h6 (8...♕c8 9 ♗d3 ♘a5 10 ♕e2 d6 has scored quite well for Black too) 9 ♗h4 ♘a5 10 e5 g5 11 ♗f2 ♘h5 12 c5 ♗xf1 13 ♔xf1 f5 14 ♘e2 ♕e7 15 g3 bxc5 16 ♔g2 ♘c6, which eventually led to a draw in S.Volkov-M.Brodsky, Dubai 2003

c) Another Volkov game went 8 ♘h3 ♘a5 9 c5 ♗xf1 10 ♖xf1 d6 11 ♗g5 ♕d7 12 cxd6 cxd6 13 ♔f2 ♖c8 14 ♔g1 ♖xc3 15 ♗xf6 gxf6, which also eventually led to a draw in S.Volkov-E.Shaposhnikov, St Petersburg 2004.

Nothing terribly convincing then, and I'm forced to conclude that overall the chances are about level but White must play actively to prevent Black from simply exploiting those weaknesses.

8...♘g8

Yes, Black can afford to return home and still have a two-piece lead in development! Note the alternative rim is much worse as after 8...♘h5? 9 ♘h3, g2-g4 is a very awkward threat.

9 f4

Perhaps I'm sounding a little bit negative regarding White's chances, but on the plus side 9 ♘h3!? ♘a5 10 ♕a4 is perfectly plausible. White does have his space advantage and the two bishops but it just seems to be a bit of a drag to have to defend the c4-pawn in this manner. Now a particularly interesting nugget of information is that GM Vladimir Tukmakov has twice played 10...♕e7!? against the same opponent!:

a) 11 ♗d3 0-0-0 12 ♗g5 f6 13 ♗h4 ♕f7 14 0-0 ♘e7 15 f4 ♘f5 16 ♗f2 d5! 17 exd6 ♘xd6 18 f5 exf5 19 ♗g3 ♗xc4 20 ♗xf5+ ♔b8 with a better pawn structure and an extra pawn, F.Liardet-V.Tukmakov, Geneva 1997.

b) 11 c5 ♗xf1 12 ♖xf1 f6 (incidentally 12...♕h4+ 13 ♖f2 ♘e7 14 ♗g5 ♕h5 15 cxb6 axb6 16 ♗xe7 ♔xe7 17 ♕b4+ ♔e8 18 ♔f1 ♘c6 19 ♕c4 ♖a5 eventually turned out well for Black in G.Puyou-O.Panno, Olavarria Azul 2001; I'm certainly not claiming that Black is winning here or in such positions, but he always has a structural advantage to work with as even if White gets in c4-c5xb6, after ...axb6 White is still saddled with what will be a target a-pawn isolani) 13 f4 ♘h6 14 ♗e3 ♘g4 15 ♗g1 0-0 16 0-0-0 ♘c6 17 ♖fe1 fxe5 18 dxe5 ♘h6 19 g3 ♖ab8 20 ♘g5 ♘f5 21 ♖d3 bxc5 22 ♘e4 c4 23 ♗c5 d6 24 ♕xc6 cxd3 25 ♗b4 ♖b6 26 ♕c4 ♖fb8 27 ♕xd3 a5 28 ♗xa5 d5 0-1 F.Liardet-V.Tukmakov, Geneva 1996.

Incidentally, after 9 ♗d3 ♘a5 10 ♕a4 another idea worth remembering is 10...♕c8!? possibly intending ...♕b7-c6.

Regarding White's ninth move selection in our main game, I'm sure this push would be the choice of a many club players, who would be eager to bring their knight out to a more natural square. The problem is of course that, as things stand right now, White is lacking somewhat in the development department!

9...♘a5 10 ♕g4

10 ♕a4 does look after the pawn but is debatable whether the queen has a big future there. The text is more ambitious as White

tries to punish Black's lack of a dark-squared bishop.

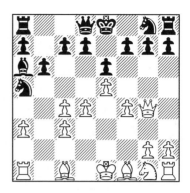

10...g6 11 f5

Rather than grovel with 11 c5, White goes all in.

11...exf5 12 ♕g3 ♗xc4 13 ♗g5 f6

Unfortunately for White, Black's dark-squared suffering is only going to be minimal.

14 exf6 ♘xf6 15 ♗xc4

15 ♕e5+ is of course met by the simple 15...♔f7.

15...♘xc4 16 ♕h4 0-0 17 ♘f3

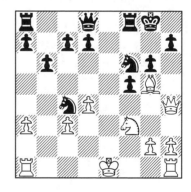

17...♕e8+

White couldn't gang up on f6 with anything else and now Black uses this check to escape the pin.

18 ♔f1 ♕f7

This has all been fairly effortless for Black, who has basically just found himself two pawns up for nothing. It's effectively all over now but the rest of the game is worth viewing.

19 ♖e1 ♘d5 20 ♔f2 ♖fe8 21 ♗f4 ♘b2 22 ♘g5 ♘d3+ 23 ♔g3 ♕g7 24 ♗e5 ♘xe5 25 dxe5 ♖xe5 26 ♕c4 f4+ 27 ♔g4 h5+ 28 ♔h4 ♖xg5 29 ♔xg5 ♕f6+ 30 ♔h6

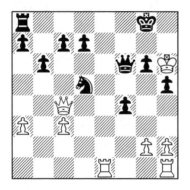

There is no diagram error – the white king really is on the h6-square, and amazingly there are still nearly twenty more moves to go!

30...c6 31 ♕d4 ♔f7 32 ♕xf6+ ♔xf6 33 ♔h7 ♘xc3 34 g3 g5 35 h4 gxh4 36 gxf4 ♘d5 37 ♖xh4 ♔f7 38 ♖hh1 ♘f6+ 39 ♔h6 ♖h8+ 40 ♔g5 ♖g8+ 41 ♔f5 ♖g3 42 ♖e5 ♖xa3 43 ♖he1 ♘d5 44 ♔g5 ♖g3+ 45 ♔xh5 ♘f6+ 46 ♔h4 ♖g4+ 47 ♔h3 ♖xf4 48 ♖e7+ ♔g6 0-1

Game 23
G.House-C.Ward
Jersey 2002

---

1 d4 ♘f6 2 c4 e6 3 ♘c3 ♗b4 4 a3 ♗xc3+ 5 bxc3 ♘e4!?

This knight isn't actually threatening to take the c3-pawn because of ♕c2 but White can't budge it just yet with 6 f3? because of 6...♕h4+. Thus Black makes it difficult for White to arrange f2-f3, whereas he will be able to employ his own f-pawn relatively quickly.

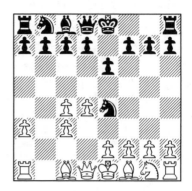

6 ♕c2

In case you'd overlooked my introduction to 5...♘e4!?, I will say again that Black isn't threatening to take on c3 just yet because of the knight-trapping ♕c2. Hence there is actually no compulsion for White to defend his pawn just yet. The text therefore is mainly to force Black to make a decision about his knight.

Clearly 6 e3 is the main alternative. Then White players trying to get an opening edge should probably take a closer look at 6...0-0 7 ♗d3 f5 8 ♘e2 ♘f6 (also of interest is 8...b6 9 0-0 ♗a6 10 a4 c5 11 ♘g3 ♘xg3 12 fxg3 ♘c6 13 ♖a2 ♘a5 14 ♖af2 d5, which Black went on to win in T.Taylor-S.Sulskis, Los Angeles 2003; of course things are never simply black and white(!), but often Black has a choice of whether to adopt a ...d7-d6 and ...e6-e5 plan or to go with the ...b7-b6 that facilitates either ...♗b7 or ...♗a6)

9 0-0 d6 10 ♘g3 ♘c6 11 e4 ♘e7 12 ♖a2 c5 13 ♖e2 ♗d7 14 ♖fe1 ♖c8 15 exf5 ♘xf5 16 ♘xf5 exf5 17 d5 ♖c7 18 ♕c2 ♘h5 19 ♗d2 h6 20 f3 b6 21 a4 ♕f6 22 ♕a2 a5 23 ♕b1 ♖b7 24 ♖e7 ♖f7 25 ♖xf7 ♕xf7 26 g4 ♘f6 27 ♗xf5 ♗xf5 28 ♕xf5 ♖e7 29 ♖xe7 ♕xe7 30 ♔f2 ♕e8 31 g5 hxg5 32 ♗xg5 ♕xa4 33 ♗xf6 gxf6 34 ♕g6+ ♔h8 35 ♕xf6+ ♔h7 36 ♕e7+ ♔h8 37 ♕d6 ♕c2+ 38 ♔g3 ♕xc3 39 ♕f8+ ♔h7 40 d6 ♕e5+ 41 ♔g4 ♕d4+ 42 f4 a4 43 ♕f7+ ♔h6 44 d7 a3 45 ♕f8+ ♔g6 46 ♕g8+ ♔h6 47 ♕g5+ ♔h7 48

d8♕ ♕g1+ 49 ♔f5 ♕b1+ 50 ♔f6 1-0 I.Sokolov-M.Adams, Reykjavik (rapid) 2003. Mickey is a fantastic player and in my opinion the best handler of the Nimzo-Indian around; hence this victory should carry some weight! However, it was a rapidplay game, and besides Black has two other sensible alternatives to consider.

Firstly, 6...c5 has the idea of a swift ...♕a5, but 6...f5 must also figure highly in the reckoning. Certainly 7 ♕h5+ g6 8 ♕h6 ♕g5 9 ♕xg5 ♘xg5 10 f3 ♘f7 11 a4 d6 12 a5 e5 13 ♗d3 c5 14 ♘e2 ♘c6 15 d5 ♘e7 16 ♗d2 ♗d7 17 0-0 ♔d8!? (the 'Levenfish' style king manoeuvre to protect the queenside that we will soon see more of) 18 ♗c2 ♔c7 was fine for Black in G.Pieterse-A.Miles, Amsterdam 1988. White doesn't gain from a queen trade and instead 7 ♕c2 would transpose back into our main game.

6...f5

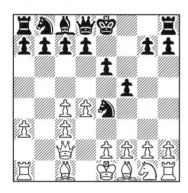

7 e3

7 ♘f3 0-0 8 e3 b6 9 ♗d3 ♗b7 leaves Black with a very comfortable game, and attempts to spice things up via 10 ♘d2 ♘xd2 11 ♗xd2 ♗xg2 12 ♖g1 ♗f3 13 ♖g3 ♗h5 14 e4 ultimately backfired after 14...f4 15 ♖g1 e5 16 dxe5 ♕e7 17 ♕c1 ♕xe5 in V.Zilberman-V.Andreev, Dniepropetrovsk 2003.

Perhaps the sharpest continuation is 7 ♘h3!? when 7...b6 8 f3 ♘f6 9 e4 fxe4 10 fxe4 ♗b7 11 ♗d3 saw White close to obtaining a very big position already in Dao Thien

Hai-Nguyen Thanh Binh, Vietnamese Championship, Thua Thien Hue 2000. Black probably has to play 11...e5 now or else reconsider his set-up and revert to 7...0-0, intending ...d7-d6 and ...e6-e5 instead.

7...b6

As we know, offering that choice: either the simple fianchetto or the pressurisation of c4 via ...♗a6.

8 f3

Far from forced, the interesting sequence 8 ♗d3 ♗b7 9 ♘e2 ♕g5 10 ♘f4 ♕h4 11 0-0 g5 12 ♘e2 g4 13 d5 was double-edged in V.Feldman-L.Jones, Warwick Fiji 2002. Though outside the realms of this book, this is reminiscent of the 4 e3 b6 variation in which I have had a lot of experience. My personal preference is for Black.

8...♕h4+!

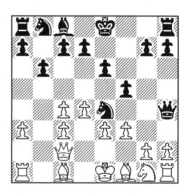

9 g3 ♘xg3 10 ♕f2 f4 11 ♘h3

Upon 11 exf4 the knight can escape via f5 with White's pawn structure having been shot to bits.

I suppose White has a little compensation for the exchange after 11 hxg3 ♕xh1 or 11 e4 g5 12 hxg3 ♕xh1, but there is no realistic chance of the black queen being trapped.

11...♘f5 12 ♘xf4 ♕xf2+ 13 ♔xf2

White has regained his pawn but the presence of two isolated rooks' pawns and a set of doubled c-pawns mean that he is definitely worse off in the structure stakes.

13...0-0

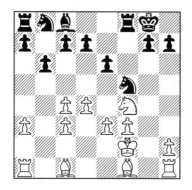

During this game I had it in mind to ultimately hit White's f-pawn although, as is usual for such positions, c4 is a target too.

14 ♗d3 ♘c6 15 ♖g1 ♗a6 16 c5

The advantage of a c4-c5xb6 is that it undoubles the pawns and thus eliminates a weakness. The disadvantage is that an ...axb6 leaves Black with a half-open file for which to pressurise White's a-pawn.

16...♗xd3 17 ♘xd3 d6 18 cxd6

A lesser evil than 18 cxb6 axb6!.

18...cxd6 19 e4 ♘h4 20 ♖g3 e5

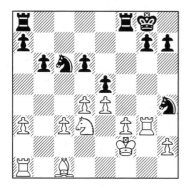

Ideally Black should be trying to fix his opponent's pawns on dark squares, but with a well-supported centre there is no need for White to oblige.

21 ♗e3 ♖f7 22 ♔e2 ♖e8 23 ♘b4 ♘xb4

I didn't really want to help iron out White's pawns like this, but on the other hand I didn't want the white knight setting

up camp on d5 either.

24 axb4 d5!?

This 'mixing things up' move was what I had been planning. The idea is to try and make White's centralised king out as a weakness rather than the strength that it would be in most endgames.

25 dxe5 dxe4 26 fxe4

This leaves the e-pawn(s) isolated, but 26 f4 ♘f5 would see the black knight and pawn combine well to deprive White of squares.

26...♖xe5 27 ♖g4 ♘g6 28 ♖d1 ♖fe7 29 ♖d4 ♖h5 30 ♗g1

30 h4 looks like a better defence. Although I was trying to win throughout, it's only now that Fritz starts to believe that Black might have the upper hand!

30...♖c7 31 ♔d2 ♔f7

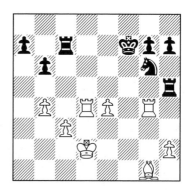

Initially in this endgame I had been a little nervous that, rather than merely placing the king and rooks to avoid forks, White might somehow be able to activate them so as to create a passed pawn or attack my queenside. I knew, however, that the danger of that would pretty much be averted once my king was centralised.

32 ♖g3 ♘e5 33 ♖d5?!

Probably White should have been able to get a draw, but his passive defence doesn't quite cut it.

33...♔e6 34 ♖d4 ♖h4 35 ♔c2 ♖f4

Infiltrating with the rook makes sense, although 35...♘c6 looks quite strong too.

36 ♔b3 g6 37 ♗e3 ♖f1 38 ♖d8 ♖b1+ 39 ♔c2 ♖h1 40 ♖e8+ ♖e7 41 ♖xe7+ ♔xe7 42 ♗g1 b5

This is the move that White so dearly would have loved to achieve himself. Although the black rook looks funny in the corner, White uses plenty of resources to keep it jailed, and in all fairness I had calculated that White wouldn't be able to win it.

43 h3

To illustrate the significance of Black's last move, note that 43 ♗xa7 ♖xh2+ 44 ♔b3?? ♘c4 would have seen White walking into a mating net.

43...a6 44 ♔d1 h5 45 ♔e2 h4 46 ♗c5+ ♔e6 47 ♖g2 ♖xh3 48 ♗d4 ♖g3 49 ♖xg3 hxg3 50 ♔f1 ♘c4 51 ♔g2 ♘d2 52 ♔xg3 ♘xe4+ 53 ♔f4 ♔d5 0-1

Game 24
V.Moskalenko-J.Gonzalez Rodriguez
Barcelona 2003

---

1 d4 e6 2 c4 ♘f6 3 ♘c3 ♗b4 4 a3 ♗xc3+ 5 bxc3 d6 6 e3

Presumably White was intending to meet 5...0-0 with 6 e3 when 6...d6 would have transposed to this game. Given the move order that occurred here though, White could certainly have opted for 6 f3 too.

6...0-0 7 ♗d3

A similar occurrence to the main game is 7 ♘e2 e5 8 ♘g3 ♖e8 9 ♗d3 e4 10 ♗b1. The

tussle over e4 is now the critical theme in the position: 10...b6 11 f3 ♗a6 12 fxe4! (an improvement over 12 ♘xe4 ♘xe4 13 ♗xe4 ♖xe4!? 14 fxe4 ♕h4+, which would offer Black compensation for the exchange) 12...♗xc4 13 ♕f3 ♘bd7

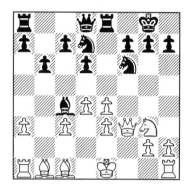

and now there's the amazingly cheeky 14 ♖a2!?, as seen in G.Kaidanov-A.Onischuk, Chicago 2002. The premise of this outwardly shocking move is that the likes of 14...♗xa2 15 ♗xa2 ♘f8 16 0-0 this time offers White excellent piece play for the exchange. Indeed, aside from the dark-squared bishop, all of White's pieces are well placed.

7...e5

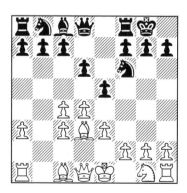

Although after trading his dark-squared bishop it is logical for Black to place his pawns on dark squares, this whole plan is a little slow for my liking. Indeed, in my opinion both the 7...♘bd7 8 e4 b6 9 ♘e2 c5 10 0-0 of

P.Bergen-D.Zoler, Graz 2002 and the 7...♘c6
8 ♘e2 e5 9 e4 ♖e8 10 f3 ♘e7 11 0-0 ♘g6 12
♗e3 ♕e7 13 ♕d2 of C.Minzer-G.Gonzalez,
La Coruna 1995 favour White because he has
clear-cut play on the kingside. I have spoken
previously about the dynamism in White's
structure in these semi-closed positions and
no doubt I will do so again!

8 ♘e2

One advantage of not taking time out with
f2-f3 is that White can prepare to make the
aggressive lunge f2-f4 in one turn.

8...e4

If Black could maintain this pawn here
then things would actually look quite rosy for
him as White's c4-pawn would remain a target. Unfortunately, White is quick to challenge it.

9 ♗c2

9 ♗b1 is also possible, and indeed 9...♗e6
10 ♘g3 ♗xc4 11 ♘xe4 ♘xe4 12 ♗xe4
could easily be a variant of our main game.
Now 12...d5 13 ♗d3 ♗xd3 14 ♕xd3 c5 15
0-0 c4 16 ♕b1 ♕d7 17 f3 ♘c6 18 e4 is a
similar type of position to the one we encountered in Chapter 1. I like White's centre
and clearly it has potential: 18...f5 19 e5 ♘a5
20 a4 ♘b3 21 ♖a2 ♖f7 22 ♗a3 ♖e8 23 ♗d6
f4 24 g4 fxg3 25 hxg3 ♕h3 26 ♕e1 ♖e6 27
♖h2 ♕f5 28 g4 ♕d3 29 f4 ♖d7 30 f5 gave
White a powerful attack in A.Cherniack-
J.Rasin, Boylston 1995.

9...♗e6 10 ♘g3 ♗xc4 11 ♘xe4

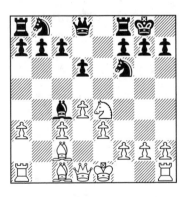

11...♘bd7

11...♘xe4 12 ♗xe4 d5 transposes to the
previous note.

12 ♘g3

Preserving the knight with a view to a
timely invasion of Black's kingside.

12...d5 13 f3 ♖e8 14 ♗d3

White could also have considered preserving the bishop pair and castling by hand via
14 ♔f2. However, as White's central pawn
push is inevitable, he has something concrete
to work with anyway.

14...♗xd3 15 ♕xd3 c5

Black does his best to dissuade e3-e4, but
White is in no hurry and the dark-squared
bishop is happy to bide its time.

16 0-0 ♖c8 17 ♖b1 b6 18 ♗b2

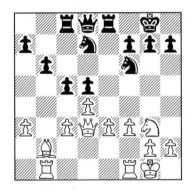

It took me a long while to understand this
type of position. Originally I thought that
Black had to be fine but now I appreciate
that White's position has all the potential.
Still, accuracy is required as a premature
queen trade, for example, could leave White
with a duff bishop in an ending.

18...♕c7 19 e4!

There is no time like the present!

19...dxe4 20 fxe4 cxd4 21 cxd4

Suddenly White has ferocious attacking
possibilities, with one simple threat being e4-
e5 and ♕f3.

21...♘f8 22 ♖xf6

This sacrifice was always going to tempting, but if truth be told perhaps both 22 e5

♘d5 23 ♘f5 and 22 d5 were better.

22...gxf6 23 ♘h5 ♘d7 24 d5

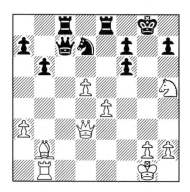

The bishop finally says 'hello' but all may not be as it seems.

24...f5 25 ♕f3 ♕d6

25...♖xe4!, intending to meet 26 ♕xf5? with 26...♕c5+ 27 ♔h1 ♕e3!, is a far better defence but it doesn't change my opening assessment!

26 ♖f1 ♖c2 27 ♕b3

27 ♗f6!, threatening amongst other things e4-e5, would have secured the point smoothly. The less said about what occurs now the better!

27...♖xb2?

27...♕c5+! 28 ♔h1 ♖xe4 could well have been very bad news for White.

28 ♕xb2 ♕e5 29 ♕b5 1-0

Game 25
H.Hofstra-V.Ikonnikov
Vlissingen 2000

---

1 d4 ♘f6 2 c4 e6 3 ♘c3 ♗b4 4 a3 ♗xc3+ 5 bxc3 0-0 6 ♘f3?!

The fact is that after the move order 1 d4 ♘f6 2 c4 e6 3 ♘c3 ♗b4 4 ♘f3 0-0, theory doesn't even consider 5 a3 as it is far too slow. Hence obviously 6 ♘f3, as played here (reaching the same position), is not remotely threatening either.

White should choose either 'a' or 'b' in the following alternatives:

a) 6 e3 c5 transposes to Game 27, although Black could also consider forgoing 6...c5, instead concentrating on a quick ...b7-b6 and ...♗a6 etc.

b) 6 f3, reaching a position I have previously alluded to, has been White's most popular choice in practice. Recently 6...♘e8!? has been scoring rather well in practice.

Black avoids an awkward ♗g5 pin and facilitates a possible ...♘e8-d6 relocation to add further pressure to c4. Now 7 e4 b6 is standard, when divisions appear:

b1) 8 a4 ♘c6 9 ♗a3 d6 when both 10 ♗d3 (10 f4 ♗a6 11 ♘f3 ♘a5 12 ♘d2 c5 13 ♗d3 cxd4 14 cxd4 ♕f6 15 ♗b2 ♕xf4 clearly saw White's dark-squared bishop misplaced on a3 in M.Cebalo-M.Palac, Zagreb 2004) 10...♗a6 11 ♘h3 ♘a5 12 ♕e2 c5 13 d5 ♕h4+ 14 ♘f2 exd5 15 cxd5 ♗xd3 16 ♕xd3 f5!, A.Kretchetov-I.Ibragimov, Las Vegas 2004.

b2) 8 ♘h3 ♗a6 9 ♗g5 (or 9 e5 ♘c6 10 ♗g5 f6 11 exf6 ♘xf6 12 ♗d3 e5 with more life in the position; it is a fairly open one and White has the two bishops, but he also has an inferior pawn structure that Black intends to exploit) 9...f6 10 ♗e3 ♘c6 11 ♗d3 ♘a5 12 c5 ♗xd3 13 ♕xd3 d5 14 cxd6 ♘xd6 15 ♘f4 ♕d7 16 d5 exd5 17 ♕xd5+ ♕f7 18 ♔f2 ♕xd5 19 exd5 c6 ½-½ S.Volkov-G.Timoshenko, Tusnad 2000.

b3) 8 ♗d3 ♗a6 9 f4 ♘c6 10 ♘f3 ♘a5 11 ♕e2 (or 11 e5 f5 12 ♕e2 d5 13 a4 c5 with similar complex play in M.Cebalo-

B.Chatalbashev, Reggio Emilia 2005, which incidentally Black went on to win) 11...c5 12 d5 f5 13 e5 d6.

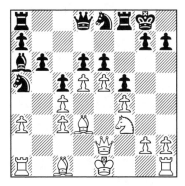

Tension in the centre is a common theme in this line, and it's probably fair to say that there were equal chances in P.Acs-Z.Almasi, Hungarian Championship, Budapest 2004.

Frankly, the alternatives to 6 f3 and 6 e3 aren't much cop, but I thought that I would include them for purpose of completion. So, other moves seen before are:

c) 6 ♗g5 c5!? (by no means the only move but I like this attempt to punish White's non-existent kingside development) 7 e3 ♕a5! (unpinning and pinning! White's next move is a mistake but ...♘e4 was coming otherwise) 8 ♗xf6 ♕xc3+ 9 ♔e2 ♕xc4+?? (this was a bit of overkill though!) 10 ♔e1?? (luckily White returns the error; 10 ♔d2 was a significantly better move!) 10...♕c3+ 11 ♔e2 gxf6 12 ♘f3 ♘c6 13 dxc5 ♕xc5 14 ♘d2 b6 15 ♔e1 ♘e5 16 g4 ♗b7 17 ♖g1 ♕c3 18 g5 ♘f3+ 19 ♔e2 ♘xg1+ 20 ♔e1 ♘f3+ 0-1 M.Barahona-E.Bastidas Rodriguez, Guayaquil 2003.

d) 6 ♕c2 c5 7 ♘f3 d6 8 ♗g5 h6 9 ♗h4 ♘bd7 10 e4 e5 11 ♖d1 ♕e7 12 d5 ♖e8 13 ♗d3 ♘f8 14 0-0 ♘g6 15 ♗g3 ♘h5 reached a closed position that does favour Black in C.Sallfert-T.Polak, Aschach 1993 as White has few prospects of getting his f-pawn into gear; indeed it is his opponent who has all the kingside play.

6...b6 7 ♗g5 ♗b7 8 e3 d6

Having not long ago written *Nimzo-Indian Kasparov Variation*, which heavily featured 1 d4 ♘f6 2 c4 e6 3 ♘c3 ♗b4 4 ♘f3 b6 5 ♗g5, I can also tell you that a3 is a waste of time. Indeed, in one of the main lines Black even opts to voluntarily concede his dark-squared bishop without any provocation.

9 ♗d3 ♘bd7 10 ♘d2

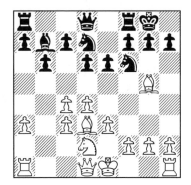

White is really mixing his plans. Typically this retreat is made with the bishop still on f1 as White prepares f2-f3 and e3-e4 (note, without having wasted time on a2-a3). Here we also have to factor into the equation the hanging pawn on g2.

10...h6 11 ♗xf6

Given that he's started, frankly he may as well have finished (i.e. 11 ♗h4!? would have been more in the spirit of things). With the text, out of the window goes the bishop-pair advantage and all that remains is an inferior pawn structure!

11...♘xf6 12 f3 e5 13 0-0 ♖e8 14 ♖e1 e4! 15 ♗b1

The likes of 15 fxe4 ♘xe4 16 ♘xe4 ♗xe4 17 ♗xe4 ♖xe4 are too ugly to contemplate but the text fares no better.

15...exf3 16 gxf3 ♘h5!

Preparing to make White suffer down the g-file.

17 ♘f1 ♕h4 18 ♗c2 ♖e6 19 d5 ♖f6 20 ♕e2 ♖e8

The pressure mounts and White cracks.

21 ♝e4??

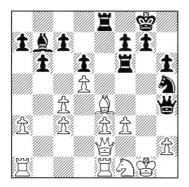

21...♜xe4! 0-1

Oops! The check on g6 and the 'big one' on e4 will terminate the proceedings.

Game 26
I.Saric-J.Nikolac
Pula 2001

1 d4 ♞f6 2 c4 e6 3 ♞c3 ♝b4 4 f3 c5 5 a3 ♝xc3+ 6 bxc3

The typical stand-alone Sämisch move order would be 4 a3 ♝xc3 5 bxc3 c5 6 f3, reaching the same position.

6...♞c6 7 e3?!

Given that White made the preparatory 4 f3 this seems kind of pointless. It just doesn't make any sense here not to play 7 e4 as after all that is what this Sämisch system is all about.

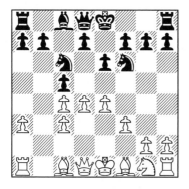

That said, surprisingly the above position is seen very rarely these days. Basically the story seems to be that Black decides whether or not to allow a further incursion by the e-pawn but, that aside, gets on with the usual pressurisation of the c4-pawn. A couple of notable examples are:

a) 7...0-0 8 e5 ♞e8 9 f4 b6 10 ♞f3 ♝a6 11 ♝d3 f5 12 d5 ♞a5 13 ♕e2 d6 14 dxe6 dxe5 15 fxe5 ♕e7 16 g4!? with an extremely double-edged game in P.Harikrishna-J.Werle, Nakhchivan 2003.

b) 7...d6 8 ♞e2 (8 ♝e3 b6 9 ♝d3 ♕d7 10 ♞e2 ♝a6 11 0-0 ♞a5 12 e5 dxe5 13 dxe5 ♝xc4! 14 ♝xc4 ♞xc4 15 ♝xc5 ♕xd1 16 ♜fxd1 ♞xe5 saw Black stick impressively to a simple plan and then easily go on to convert the full point in M.Sadler-J.Howell, London 1988) 8...b6 9 ♞g3 ♞a5 10 f4 0-0 11 e5 ♞e8 12 ♝e3 ♝a6 13 ♝d3 ♝xc4 14 0-0 f5 15 exf6 ♞xf6 16 ♕e2 ♝xd3 17 ♕xd3 ♕d7 18 ♜ae1 ♜ae8 was essentially just an extra pawn for Black in B.Spassky-R.Hübner Turin 1982.

7...b6

Surely meat and potatoes for the reader by now! Black is not fianchettoing his bishop, but rather playing it to a6 where, combined with ...♞a5, he can pressurise the weaker of White's doubled c-pawns.

8 ♝d3 0-0 9 ♞e2 ♝a6

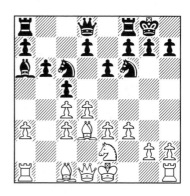

10 e4

White has effectively lost a tempo with the

way he has handled the position, and now his kingside play should surely be too slow.

10...♘e8

10...d6 looks very sensible but this is another move that we have already seen employed before; with this retreat Black prevents ♗g5 from being an awkward pin.

11 f4 f5

11...♕h4+!? 12 g3 ♕h3 would interfere with White's kingside intentions and 11...♘a5 gets straight to the point, but it is difficult to criticise the text.

12 ♘g3

Or 12 e5 ♘a5 when White isn't really going anywhere.

12...♘d6 13 0-0 cxd4 14 cxd4 fxe4 15 ♘xe4 ♘xe4 16 ♗xe4

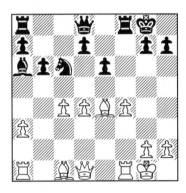

16...d5!

16...♗xc4 17 ♗xh7+ ♔xh7 18 ♕c2+ is less clear, and the text keeps on top of the tactics.

17 cxd5 exd5!

17...♗xf1 18 dxc6 would be a silly exchange to take, even with the possibility of 18...♗e2.

18 ♗b1

Clearly 18 ♗d3 ♗xd3 19 ♕xd3 ♕f6 20 ♗b2 ♘a5 is a simple bad bishop versus good knight scenario and so White tries to keep some tricks going instead.

18...♗xf1 19 ♕h5 g6 20 ♗xg6 ♕d7!

Black keeps his cool. Taking the bishop here would have conceded a perpetual check

draw.

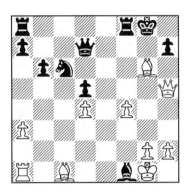

21 ♔xf1 hxg6 22 ♕xg6+ ♔h8 23 a4

23 ♕h6+ ♕h7 24 ♕xc6 ♕d3+ 25 ♔f2 ♕xd4+ allows Black to pick up the rook in the corner and still return for check-blocking duties.

23...♕h7 24 ♕xc6 ♖ac8

Winning, just as 24...♕d3+ would have been.

25 ♕b5 ♕xh2 26 ♕xd5 ♖xc1+! 27 ♖xc1 ♕xf4+ 0-1

Black picks up the rook and White doesn't get a perpetual.

Game 27
V.Milov-J.Polgar
FIDE World Ch., Moscow 2001

---

1 d4 ♘f6 2 c4 e6 3 ♘c3 ♗b4 4 e3

Here we have the Sämisch coming via a 4 e3 Nimzo. Regarding the traditional move order 4 a3 ♗xc3+ 5 bxc3 c5 6 e3, another thought that occurs to me is the idea of delaying ...0-0, for example 6...b6 7 ♗d3. Now 7...♗b7 8 f3 ♘c6 9 ♘e2 ♖c8 has been seen before but surely it would make more sense to hurry into a ....♗a6 and ...♘a5 plan instead. The disadvantage, however, of leaving the king on e8 is that after, say, 7...♘c6 White can play 8 e4!? when a further advance of the e-pawn will embarrass the knight. Compared to the first game of this chapter the retreat ...♘g8 doesn't really appeal!

4...0-0 5 a3 ♗xc3+ 6 bxc3 c5

I suppose that this was the old main line of the Sämisch. Playing ...c7-c5 at this point offers Black the chance of getting the queen out, but as that is a rare occurrence I would also go along with the immediate 6...b6. The intention though is not to meet 7 ♗d3 with 7...♗b7 because 8 f3 d6 9 ♘e2 c5 10 e4 ♘fd7 11 0-0, as seen in C.Minzer-R.Kasimdzhanov, Benidorm 2004, to my mind sees the bishop misplaced. No, instead Black's idea is 7...♘c6 8 ♘e2 ♗a6 9 0-0 ♘a5 10 e4 ♘e8 with similar ideas to the main game but without ...c7-c5. There are clearly chances for both sides, but the 11 f4 f5 12 exf5 exf5 13 ♘g3 g6 14 c5 ♗xd3 15 ♕xd3 d5 16 cxd6 ♘xd6 17 a4 ♘dc4 18 ♗a3 ♖e8 19 ♗b4 ♕d5 of H.Pecorelli Garcia-I.Csom, Cienfuegos 1985 should be a warning to White of how things can go positionally downhill.

7 ♗d3

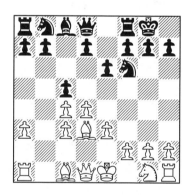

7...♘c6 8 ♘e2 b6 9 e4

Getting straight to the point. Instead 9 ♘g3 commits the knight a little prematurely and 9...♗a6 10 e4 ♘e8 11 ♕h5 f6 12 e5 f5 13 ♗g5 ♕c7 14 ♘e2 d6! 15 ♘f4 ♕d7 16 ♖d1 cxd4 17 cxd4 ♘xd4 18 exd6 ♕xd6 19 0-0 ♘f6 20 ♕h3 ♖ac8 21 ♖fe1 ♗xc4 22 ♗xc4 ♖xc4 23 ♘xe6 ♘e2+ 24 ♔f1 ♕xe6 25 ♖xe2 ♖e4 saw White successfully rebuffed in I.Bern-S.Busemann, correspondence 1993.

Needless to say, 9 f3?! is redundant now,

although the position reached transposes to the instructive previous game.

9...♘e8

A standard retreat; its primary aim is to avoid the annoying pin ♗g5, but Black can also now deploy his f-pawn whenever he might want.

10 0-0 ♗a6 11 f4 f5

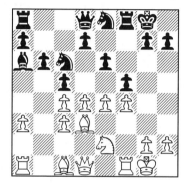

This position has occurred many times in practice, and very often Black players have allowed White's f-pawn to progress further in favour of going after the c-pawn. I know I wouldn't!

12 d5!?

With this move White is basically sacrificing a pawn for more space. Certainly, neither 12 exf5 exf5 13 dxc5 bxc5 14 ♗e3 ♕a5 nor 12 ♘g3 g6!? have previously given White any advantage in practice.

12...♘a5 13 e5

All part of White's master plan.

13...♗xc4

Black has nothing better to do than accept the pawn, and the greatest ever female player takes up the challenge.

14 ♗xc4 ♘xc4 15 d6

Not only has White jettisoned a pawn but now he closes off the position. Usually that would be good news for knights but the one on e8 isn't so sure!

15...b5

If Black had her time again (and perhaps she will!?) this move might be changed as the queenside soon gets opened up to Black's detriment. 15...g6!? has been suggested as an improvement to give the king's knight some breathing space but the key idea is to keep the queen's knight as a blocker by retreating it via a5 to c6.

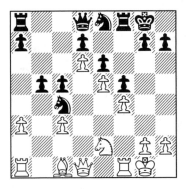

16 a4! a6 17 ♕d3 g6

17...♕c8 18 ♖a2 ♖b8 19 ♗e3 ♖b6 20 ♘c1 ♘cxd6!? 21 exd6 ♘xd6 is a possible solution to Black's cramped position but after 22 axb5 axb5 23 ♖a7 the piece is probably preferable to the pawns.

18 axb5 axb5 19 ♗e3 ♖xa1 20 ♖xa1

The more pieces that are swapped off, the more noticeable Black's 'out of the game' kingside pieces become.

20...♕b6 21 ♘c1

Continuing the quest to pound the c5-pawn.

21...♘g7

After 21...♕c6 22 ♘b3 the tactic 22...♘xe5? 23 fxe5 c4 fails miserably to 24 ♘d4 cxd3 25 ♘xc6 dxc6 26 ♗g5. However, 22...g5!? might be worth a punt.

22 ♘b3 ♖c8 23 ♗f2 ♘b2?

In view of the visual sequence 23...h6 24 ♕f3 ♔h7 25 ♖a8 ♖c6 26 ♕h3! b4 27 ♕xh6+!! ♔xh6 28 ♖h8 mate, one can see why Black is eager to try and seal off the a-file. Alas, the text ultimately doesn't achieve its aim.

24 ♕c2 ♘a4

24...♘c4 25 ♕a2 b4 26 ♕a4! shows how

White can sneak his way in!

25 c4! ♕b8

Black dare not allow something like 25...bxc4 26 ♕xc4 ♖b8 27 ♕xa4 ♕xb3 28 ♕xd7 but she is struggling to keep all ends covered.

26 ♘d2

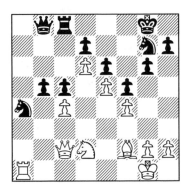

26...♘b6

This appears to give the pawn back cheaply, but ♖b1 was on its way.

27 cxb5 c4 28 ♘f3 ♘h5 29 g3

'Knights on the rim are dim', and this one has gone from one rim to another!

29...♕b7 30 ♖a3 ♔g7 31 ♘d4 ♔f7 32 ♕a2

No prizes for guessing where White intends to invade now!

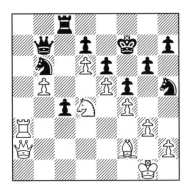

32...♕e4 33 ♖a7 g5

Finally Black tries to break out of the bind. In case you hadn't noticed, 33...c3? is flattened by White taking with something on e6.

34 ♕e2 ♕b1+

There is no solace in the endgame as after 34...♕xe2 35 ♘xe2, because of the attack on the b6-knight, the d7-pawn is doomed.

35 ♕f1 ♕e4

35...♕xf1+ 36 ♔xf1 gxf4 37 ♘e2! is still a problem.

36 ♕e2 ♕b1+ 37 ♔g2

White had repeated moves to help reach the time control – he never intended succumbing to the draw.

37...♔g6 38 fxg5 c3 39 ♕c2 ♕b4 40 ♖b7

In view of the outrageous missed opportunity for Black that this game throws up, 40 ♖c7! may have been more accurate.

40...♖c4 41 ♘xe6 dxe6 42 ♖xb6 ♕b2 43 ♕d3 ♖f4

Now things get crazy. Whilst 43...c2 loses to 44 ♕xc4 c1♕ 45 ♕xe6+ ♔xg5 46 h4+ ♔g4 47 ♕g8+ ♘g7 48 ♕xg7+ ♔h5 49 ♕xh7+ ♕h6 50 ♕xf5+ ♔g5 51 ♕xg5 mate, any old computer(!) would spot 43...♖g4!! 44 ♔f3 ♘f4! 45 gxf4 ♖xf4+! 46 ♔xf4 ♕xf2+! 47 ♕f3 ♕xb6 48 ♕xc3 ♕f2+ 49 ♕f3 ♕xh2+ with a drawn queen ending!

44 ♕e3 c2 45 d7 c1♕ 46 d8♕

Black has two queens and is on the move,

yet he can do nothing.

46...♖xf2+

Upon 46...♕xe3 47 ♖xe6+ ♘f6 48 ♕xf6+, mate follows shortly with Black's major pieces powerless to help.

47 ♕xf2 ♕xe5

47...♕xf2+ 48 ♔xf2 ♕c2+ 49 ♔e3 ♕e4+ 50 ♔d2 doesn't generate a perpetual check as the white king is able to run for the hills.

48 ♕e8+! ♔xg5 49 ♕xe6

This eliminates Black's checks, although 49 h4+ ♔h6 (or 49...♔g4 50 ♕f3 mate) 50 ♖xe6+ looked more impressive.

49...♕xe6 50 ♖xe6 f4 51 ♖e5+ ♔g6 52 ♖c5 f3+ 53 ♔xf3 ♕h1+ 54 ♔e3 1-0

The checks have dried up and Black is the exchange and two pawns down.

Summary

At top level tournament chess these days 4 a3 is significantly less popular than 4 f3, and I guess the main reason is that the a-pawn advance could be seen as a waste of time whereas preparing the central push e2-e4 is much more constructive. However, the chapters up to now have shown that Black has other options when not immediately forced to concede his bishop, so obviously the story is not that straightforward. One clear difference is that in the (original) Sämisch variation Black has the option of 5...♞e4!?, and that is yet to be refuted. Whilst the Milov-Polgar encounter (Game 27) understandably generated a lot of interest, whether Black's knight ends up back on e8 or g8, I quite like the idea of a quick pressurisation of the vulnerable c4-pawn even without the inclusion of ...c7-c5.

1 d4 ♞f6 2 c4 e6 3 ♞c3 ♝b4 4 a3 ♝xc3+ 5 bxc3 (D) c5

      5...♞c6 6 f3 b6 – *Game 22*
      5...♞e4 – *Game 23*
      5...d6 – *Game 24*
      5...0-0 – *Game 25*

6 e3

      6 f3 ♞c6 (D)
            7 e3 – *Game 26*
            7 e4 – *Game 26* (notes)

6...0-0 (D) 7 ♝d3 – *Game 27*

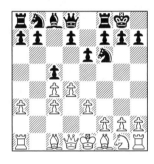

    5 bxc3   *6...♞c6*   *6...0-0*

CHAPTER FIVE

4 ♗g5 (The Leningrad Variation)

1 d4 ♘f6 2 c4 e6 3 ♘c3 ♗b4 4 ♗g5

The idea of 4 ♗g5 always appealed to me as a junior, although ironically I enjoyed facing it as Black too! It's definitely an ambitious variation as White ignores the pin on his own knight and instead pins Black's. The kingside development is temporarily neglected, although White might argue that's because he hasn't yet decided where those pieces want to go, whereas he wants his bishop outside the pawn chain before playing e2-e3. Compared to the Nimzo/Queen's Indian Hybrid of 4 ♘f3 b6 5 ♗g5, White may prefer to place a pawn on f3 but, on the other hand, Black is not committed to a queenside fianchetto.

There are two truths that I want to share with you. The first is that this book was a very ambitious project. Just as with the Sämisch, whole books have been written on 4 ♗g5 (well, actually not that many) and so it is inevitable that I will be criticised for covering this whole variation in just one (albeit long) chapter. However, coming to my rescue is the second truth, which is that the Leningrad's popularity has dwindled in recent years. I emphasised in the Introduction that my focus is on more recent games and modern approaches, and the fact is that these days the Leningrad is rarely employed at the highest levels. You will notice that even as a

grandmaster, I myself have employed it a few times and I probably will do again. Nevertheless, it is more likely to be used as a surprise weapon (not that it's going to be much of a surprise now) than as a permanent main line.

I like the aggressive attitude of 4 ♗g5, but it could be argued that the move itself is a bit premature. The main problem that you will discover by reading this chapter is that Black has a variety of ways to meet it and it is far from clear that any of them is particularly bad.

> *Game 28*
> **V.Danilov-H.Hernandez**
> Pedrido 2004

1 d4 ♘f6 2 c4 e6 3 ♘c3 ♗b4 4 ♗g5 c5

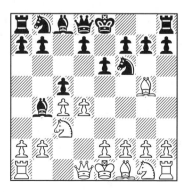

Some opt to play 4...h6 now and some don't. More often than not, positions transpose at some stage but as the reader will soon appreciate playing through this chapter's games, there are advantages and disadvantages of moving the h-pawn.

5 d5

First up, it should be understood that the text advance is necessary and that 5 e3? is a mistake in view of the simultaneously pinning and unpinning 5...♕a5!. A recent encounter saw 6 ♗xf6 (there's no prizes for guessing what Black intended next, and indeed 6 ♘ge2 ♘e4 would be very awkward for White) 6...♗xc3+ 7 bxc3 ♕xc3+ (comparing this to the similar – but with key differences! – Kasparov Nimzo line 1 d4 ♘f6 2 c4 e6 3 ♘c3 ♗b4 4 ♘f3 0-0 5 ♗g5 c5 6 e3 ♕a5 7 ♗xf6 ♗xc3+ 8 bxc3 ♕xc3+, here there is now no knight to block the check; as ♕d2 leaves the rook hanging, White's next move is forced) 8 ♔e2 ♕b2+ 9 ♔e1 (actually for harmonious kingside development reasons, I think that I would have preferred 9 ♔f3; it's fair to say though that White's opening hasn't been a raging success!) 9...gxf6 10 ♘f3 ♕c3+ 11 ♘d2 cxd4 12 ♖c1 ♕a5 (M.Keiser-D.Saiboulatov, Charleroi 2004). Clearly worse here, White actually got back into the game before losing anyway!

5...h6

Other than gaining more space, an important point behind White's last move is that 5...♕a5?! can now be met by 6 ♗xf6 as the bishop protects the knight on c3 (although with the bishop on g5 instead of h4, 6 ♗d2 with 7 a3 to follow may also be good). Regarding the trade on f6, the recent 6 ♗xf6 gxf6 7 ♕c2 d6 8 e4 e5 9 ♗d3 ♘d7 10 ♘ge2 f5 11 exf5 ♘f6 12 0-0 ♕d8 13 ♘g3 ♗xc3 14 ♕xc3 0-0 15 ♖ae1 b5 16 b3 b4 17 ♕d2 ♔h8 18 f4 ♘g4 19 h3 exf4 20 ♖xg4 fxg3 21 f6 1-0 (E.Julia-F.Benko, Buenos Aires 2004) was very impressive from White's point of view.

Just so that it doesn't come as a shock, still rearing its dubious ugly head from time to time is 5...♘xd5?! 6 ♗xd8 ♘xc3 7 ♕b3 ♘e4+ 8 ♔d1 ♘xf2+. Black gets a bit of material but the likes of 9 ♔c1 ♔xd8 10 ♕g3! ♘xh1 11 ♕xg7 ♖e8 12 g4 d5 13 ♗g2 ♘f2 14 ♕f6+ ♖e7 15 ♕xf2 dxc4 16 ♘f3 ♘d7 17 ♔c2 ♔e8 18 ♕h4 f6 19 g5 f5 20 ♖d1 c3 21 g6 hxg6 22 ♕h8+ ♘f8 23 ♖d8+ 1-0 (L.Vicary-M.Horvat, correspondence 2000 demonstrate that Black's pieces aren't so hot when still at home.

6 ♗h4 ♗xc3+ 7 bxc3 e5

I am more used to seeing this and Black's next move played the other way round but, aside from the fact that White could now try 8 d6, probably it doesn't make much difference.

8 e3 d6 9 ♗d3

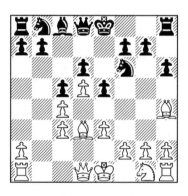

When I was a junior this was the position that I always associated with the Leningrad. This bishop move was played to facilitate ♘e2, and from there the knight may later find its way to g3 to hit e4 or to jump into f5. These days the concept of bringing the knight to d2 via f3 is more in vogue, and that plan will be discussed in Game 30.

9 f3 often transposes to the old main lines (i.e. the ones where ♗d3 and ♘e2 are still on the cards). However, some semi-independent possibilities include:

a) 9...g5 10 ♗g3 e4 (the almost ancient(!) 10...♕e7 11 ♗d3 ♘bd7 12 ♘e2 ♖g8 13 ♕c2 h5 14 h4 g4 15 ♖b1 ♔d8 16 a4 ♕c7 of J.Timman-L.Polugaevsky, Linares 1985 is more solid still and this type of position will be discussed in more detail throughout the chapter) 11 h4

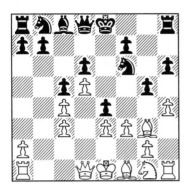

when Black can enter the complications of 11...g4 12 h5! or keep a little more dark-squared control via 11...♖g8!?.

b) 9...♕a5 10 ♕d2 ♘bd7 11 ♗d3 ♘b6 12 ♗xf6 gxf6 13 ♘e2 ♕a4 (a reason for the swing in popularity to the ♘f3-d2 manoeuvre was that on this square the knight covers e4; of course on d2 it also protects the c4-pawn, but in what follows White is evidently prepared to jettison that and more material in exchange for kingside action) 14 ♘g3 h5 15 0-0 h4 16 ♘e4 ♔e7 17 f4!? f5 18 fxe5! fxe4 19 ♕f2 f5 20 ♕f4 ♔d8 21 ♕g5+ ♔c7 22 ♕g7+ ♗d7 23 exd6+ ♔xd6 24 ♕f6+ ♔c7 25 ♕e5+ ♔d8 26 ♕xh8+ ♔c7 27 ♕e5+ ♔d8 28 d6 exd3 29 ♖xf5 ♗e6 30 ♕f6+ 1-0 T.Taylor-G.Hill, Los Angeles 2003.

c) 9...♘bd7 10 ♕c2 ♕e7 11 ♗d3 g5 12 ♗g3 b5 sees a crazy mix of many of this chapter's plans.

9...♕e7

As you will soon see, this move often features before ...e6-e5 when Black appears to be keeping his options open as to whether to keep the position blocked or not. One reason to place the queen here is to support the further advance of the e-pawn, although in fact even now 9...e4!? is a serious candidate. White can't take this pawn because of the unpinning ...g7-g5, while 10 ♗xf6? ♕xf6

leaves the black queen hitting c3. In fact the position after 10 ♗c2 ♘bd7 doesn't seem to have cropped up in tournament play for several years, with 11 f4 ♘b6! 12 ♗b3!? g5 13 ♗g3!? ♕e7 14 ♘e2 ♗g4 15 a4 0-0-0 16 h3 ♗h5 17 ♗h2 'unclear' being the assessment of Ivanchuk from a game that actually saw Black wind up with the slightly better position after 12 ♕e2 ♗g4 13 ♕f1 g5 14 fxg5? ♘h5! (V.Ivanchuk-V.Topalov, Wijk aan Zee 2001).

However, instead the simple 11 ♘e2 is likely to return us to the realms of our main game and possibly even a direct transposition.

10 ♘e2 ♘bd7

I would prefer 10...g5 here to avoid the option that White now doesn't take.

11 ♕b1

The next game investigates 11 f4!? which, in terms of specifics, I believe is a better move. However, that doesn't negate the validity of this game as Black could have played ...e5-e4 or ...g7-g5 earlier.

11...♔d8

This is the second main reason for the queen move. Rather than castling into a potential attack on the kingside, the black king travels to c7 where it also performs the useful function of guarding the b-pawn.

12 a4 a5

This looks like an ugly move to make but a white pawn on a5 would be very annoying. It would prohibit Black from ever going ...b7-b6 and the threat would always be there of a5-a6 to grasp the c6-square.

13 ♖a2 ♔c7 14 ♖b2 g5 15 ♗g3 e4

I am more used to Black's last two moves being inserted earlier, but the moves themselves come with pros and cons: ...g7-g5 escaped the pin but weakened the kingside and in particular conceded a big hole on f5; ...e5-e4 gained space and vacated the e5-square but the pawn is a target on e4 and White's dark-squared bishop has far more scope now.

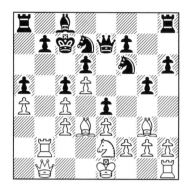

16 ♗c2 ♘e5 17 ♖b5!

Black can't now take the c4-pawn because of ♖xc5+. The d-pawn being pinned (with the knight absent from e5) plays a big part in what follows.

17...♘ed7?!

This is hardly progressive and 17...♖a7, intending to meet 18 ♗xe4?! with 18...♗d7, looks like a better way to go.

18 h4

Attacking on two fronts; this is the move Black must expect when ...g5 is employed. Nevertheless, quite a nice idea here is 18 h3!? with a plan of ♗h2, and ♘g3-f5.

18...♖g8 19 hxg5 hxg5 20 0-0

Rather audacious given the recent opening of the h-file, but White apparently wants his king's rook for active duty on the queenside.

20...b6

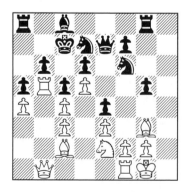

Now 21 ♗h2 ♖h8 22 ♘g3 doesn't work

because of 22...♕e5, and instead White really goes for it.

21 ♖xb6!!

The text is a stunning move although the theme isn't new. Coincidentally, it was seeing this same combination after having previously concluded that a breakthrough was practically impossible that persuaded me to take up the Leningrad again.

21...♘xb6 22 ♕b5

With a dual threat of ♕c6+ and ♕xc5+.

22...♘e8

22...♖a6! is probably the most challenging defence although 23 ♕xc5+ ♔d7 24 ♕b5+ ♔d8 25 ♘d4 looks worrying, and to show the strength of White's compensation, check out 25...♕d7 26 f3 ♕xb5 27 cxb5 ♖a8 28 fxe4 – the pawns are accruing!

23 ♕xc5+ ♔b7 24 ♕c6+ ♔a7 25 c5!

Time for the cavalry!

25...dxc5 26 ♖b1 ♖g6

After 26...♕b7 27 ♕xc5 Black has a rook for two pawns, but e4 is about to drop off and his poorly coordinated pieces must face the prospect of ♘d4.

27 d6!

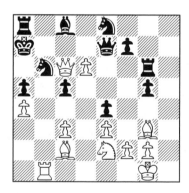

27...♖xd6

As 27...♕d8 28 ♕xc5 ♘xd6 29 ♕xa5+ ♗a6 30 ♘d4 looks pretty awesome, Black prefers to return material.

28 ♗xd6 ♕xd6 29 ♖xb6 ♕xc6 30 ♖xc6 ♗a6 31 ♘g3 ♖c8 32 ♖xc8 ♗xc8 33 ♘xe4 ♗f5

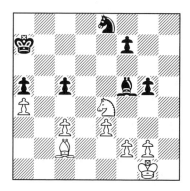

34 f3

It feels like a travesty of justice that Black escapes with a draw, but that might not have been the case in the event of 34 g4 ♗h7 35 ♗b1!.

34...♘d6 35 ♗d3 ♗xe4 36 ♗xe4 ♘xe4 37 fxe4 ♔b6 38 ♔f2 ♔c6 39 ♔f3 ♔d6 40 ♔g4 ♔e5 41 ♔xg5 c4! 42 g4 ♔xe4 43 ♔f6 ♔d3 44 ♔xf7 ♔xc3 45 g5 ♔b3 46 g6 c3 47 g7 c2 48 g8♕ c1♕ ½-½

Game 29
V.Misanovic-H.Hunt
Euro. Women's Team Ch., Batumi 1999

---

1 d4 ♘f6 2 c4 e6 3 ♘c3 ♗b4 4 ♗g5 c5 5 d5 h6 6 ♗h4 d6 7 e3 ♗xc3+ 8 bxc3 ♕e7 9 ♗d3 e5 10 ♘e2 ♘bd7 11 f4!?

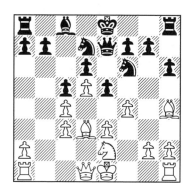

The first game in this chapter saw 11 ♕b1, whilst 11 ♘g3 ♘b6! isn't anything

special. On the other hand, the text gets straight to the point and sets about making Black regret not inserting ...g7-g5 earlier.

11...g5

The 11...exf4 12 exf4 g5 13 ♗f2 ♘g4 14 0-0 ♘xf2 15 ♖xf2 ♘f6 16 ♘g3 ♗g4 17 ♕e1 ♘h5 18 ♗f5 ♗xf5 19 ♖e2 1-0 of J.Parker-M.O'Cinneide, Dublin 1993 shows why it is detrimental to open the e-file, but I'm not enamoured by the text either. 11...g5 has been played on the vast majority of occasions but my preference is definitely for White.

12 fxg5 ♘g4

In light of how this game pans out, I'd have to say that 12...♘h5!? is a better practical try; rather than attacking the e3-pawn the knight stops its enemy number from getting too fruity. Now 13 ♘g3 (13 e4?! hxg5 14 ♗f2 ♘f4 was certainly okay for Black in L.Perdomo-E.Real de Azua, Buenos Aires 2001) 13...♘xg3 14 ♗xg3 hxg5 15 ♕c2 ♘f6 16 ♗f5 ♘h5 17 0-0 ♗xf5 18 ♖xf5 ♘g7 19 ♕a4+ ♔d8? 20 ♖f2 f5 21 ♖b1 f4?! 22 ♖fb2! was bad news for Black in Z.Basagic-R.Tischbierek, Ohrid 2001, but 19...♔f8 looks safer and earlier 18...♘xg3 can't be significantly worse.

13 ♘g3 ♘xe3 14 ♕f3 hxg5 15 ♕xe3 gxh4 16 ♘f5

White has sacrificed a pawn, but this is a wonderful square for the knight.

16...♕f6 17 0-0

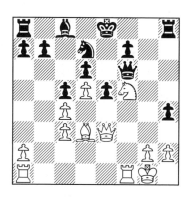

Already the reader should start to see the

---

attraction of 11 f4!?. Without too many pawns in the way, White's pieces flow.

17...♘f8 18 ♖ae1!

Most would probably have set about doubling rooks on the f-file, but whilst that plan has an obvious appeal to it, the text also sets Black a few problems.

18...♗xf5?

Few would blame the leading English lady player for wanting to remove this knight, but now Black seems to pretty much lose by force.

18...♘g6 19 ♖f2 ♔d8 on the face of it looks like a better practical try. However, as Black's pieces are poorly coordinated, White looks justified in trying 20 ♘xd6!? ♕xd6 21 ♗xg6 fxg6 22 ♕g5+: 22...♔c7? drops the queen to 23 ♖f6 and 22...♕e7 23 ♕xg6 leaves the black rooks relative bystanders, the bishop nowhere to go to and the king stuck in the middle.

19 ♖xf5 ♕e7

19...♕h6 walks into 20 ♖xe5+! dxe5 21 ♕xe5+.

20 ♖ef1

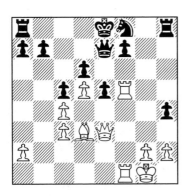

20...♖c8

20...♖h7 loses to 21 ♖5f3 ♖g7 22 ♕h6, and 20...♘g6 to 21 ♖xf7 ♕xf7 22 ♖xf7 ♔xf7 23 ♕h3. The text is no better though.

21 ♖xf7! ♕xf7 22 ♖xf7 ♔xf7

Black has two rooks for a queen but her remaining pieces lack cohesion.

23 ♕f3+ ♔e8

The fork on g4 prevents White from placing her king on the g-file.

24 ♕f6 ♖g8 25 ♗c2

A devastating check on a4 is threatened, leaving Black in a hopeless situation.

25...b5 26 cxb5 ♖g4 27 ♗f5 1-0

> *Game 30*
> # S.Mohandesi-E.Kengis
> Sautron 2003

1 d4 ♘f6 2 c4 e6 3 ♘c3 ♗b4 4 ♗g5 c5 5 d5 d6 6 e3 h6 7 ♗h4 ♗xc3+ 8 bxc3 ♕e7 9 ♘f3 e5

Again Black closes the centre. In the three games that follow this one, Black is not so eager to do this.

10 ♕c2

Obviously 10 ♗d3?? would run into a fork, and so the text is the best way to keep Black's bishop out of the immediate action. White has his knight's relocation in mind, but the immediate 10 ♘d2 can be punished by 10...g5 11 ♗g3 ♗f5!?.

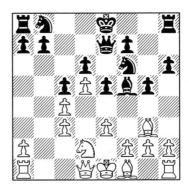

The black bishop operates well along the h7-b1 diagonal, and if White arranges e3-e4 then Black will be able to challenge with ...f7-f5. As it happens, that situation never came up in two of the many wins that Black has achieved from this position:

a) 12 f3 e4 13 h4 ♖g8 14 hxg5 hxg5 15 fxe4 ♗xe4 16 ♕a4+ ♘bd7 17 0-0-0 ♔f8 18 ♖e1 ♘e5 19 ♗e2 ♗xg2 20 ♖h2 ♗e4 21

♕d1 ♗g6 22 ♖f2 a6 23 ♖ef1 ♘fd7 24 ♔b2 b5 25 ♔a1 ♖h8 26 cxb5 axb5 27 ♗xb5 ♔g7 28 ♗xd7 ♘xd7 29 ♘c4 ♖a6 30 ♕g4 ♖ha8 31 ♗xd6 ♕f6!!

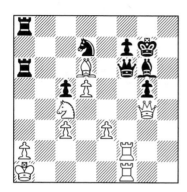

and White resigned in K.Sasikiran-R.Janssen, Calicut 1998.

b) 12 ♗e2 ♘bd7 13 h4 0-0-0 (of course this is also not possible with the bishop on c8) 14 ♕a4 ♔b8 15 ♕b5 a6 16 ♕b3 ♗a7 17 f3 e4 18 ♖b1 b6 19 f4 ♘g4 20 ♘f1 gxf4 21 ♗xf4 ♖hg8 22 g3 ♖b8 23 ♗xg4 ♗xg4 24 ♗xh6 ♘e5 25 ♗f4 ♘d3+ 26 ♔d2 b5 27 ♘h2 ♗d7 28 ♗g5 ♕e5 29 ♗f4 ♘xf4 30 gxf4 ♖g2+ 31 ♔c1 ♕h5 32 ♖b2 ♖xb2 33 ♕xb2 bxc4 34 ♕d2 ♕xh4 35 ♖g1 ♕d8 36 ♕c2 ♕a5 37 ♔d2 ♕a3 38 ♖b1 ♖g8 0-1 S.Ditiatev-S.Shipov, Cherepovets 1997.

I make no apologies for including all of the moves to these games because, from an entertainment point of view, I'm sure you'll agree that it was worth it!

10...♘bd7

It strikes me that some of Black's options are much of a muchness with a tendency to transpose down the line. Nevertheless, within some specific alternatives there are some different ideas:

a) 10...♔d8 11 ♘d2 ♔c7 12 ♗d3 g5 13 ♗g3 ♘h5 when each of 14 h3, 14 0-0 and 14 0-0-0 has previously been assessed by theory as 'slightly better for White'. Similar ideas feature in our main game.

b) 10...♗g4 11 ♘d2 g5 12 ♗g3 ♘bd7 13

♗d3 ♔f8 14 f3 ♗h5 15 ♖b1 b6 16 e4 with the better chances with White (he has a firm grip on f5) in I.Lempert-K.Lerner, St Petersburg 1993.

c) 10...g5 11 ♗g3 ♘h5 12 ♘d2 f5 is a little different, with 13 ♗e2 ♘g7 14 f4 0-0 15 ♔f2 h5 16 h4 gxf4 17 exf4 ♘d7 being fairly equally balanced in C.Gokhale-A.Zatonskih, Kapuskasing 2004.

11 ♘d2

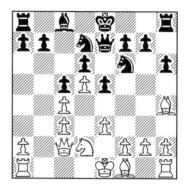

11...♔d8

So here we go again with the standard manoeuvre. Instead, upon 11...e4 12 ♗e2 Black can of course still go with 12...g5 13 ♗g3 ♔d8 when White would have to make that usual choice of castling (e.g. 14 0-0 ♔c7 15 f3 exf3 16 ♖xf3 ♘g4?! 17 ♘e4 ♘de5 18 ♗xe5 ♘xe5 19 ♖f6 ♖d8 20 ♖af1 a5 21 ♗h5 ♔b8 22 h3 ♘xc4 23 ♖xf7 ♕e5 24 ♕d3 ♘b6 25 c4 in which Black had got into a bit of a tangle in S.Matveeva-M.Maric, Belgrade 2000) or turning to usual 14 h4!?.

However, something less common is 12...0-0!? 13 0-0-0 ♖e8. This looks like a very sound way for Black to play and I especially like the 14 ♔b2 b5!? 15 cxb5 a6 16 a4 ♗b7 17 c4 axb5 18 axb5 ♕e5+ 19 ♕b3 ♘xd5! 20 ♗g3 ♕f6 21 ♕b2 ♘c3! of G.Gaertner-P.Wells, Oberwart 1995. To avoid the one way traffic of the game White might wheel out 14 g4!? instead.

After 11...g5 12 ♗g3 Black still has those ...♔d8 and ...e5-e4 moves, but 12...♘h5 13

♗d3 ♘df6 is a little different. As Black's 12th move obstructed the h-pawn, now 14 0-0 seems reasonable, but an interesting attempt at refutation was 14 h3!? intending ♗h2 and g2-g4. The other big idea is that after 14...♘xg3 (perhaps Black should avoid the opening of the f-file via 14...♖g8 with the intention of meeting 15 ♗h2 with the intercepting 15...g4) 15 fxg3 ♘h5 (15...g4 16 ♗f5 gxh3 17 gxh3 ♖g8 18 ♗xc8 ♖xc8 19 ♕f5 ♖c7 20 ♖f1 ♖g6 21 g4 ♕d7 22 ♔e2 ♕xf5 23 ♖xf5 ♔f8 24 ♖af1 ♔g7 25 ♔d3 was very passive for Black in E.Agrest-R.Akesson, Skara 2002) White can sacrifice the pawn via 16 0-0! ♘xg3 17 ♖f3. Should the knight retreat then ♗g6, ♖af1 and probably ♘e4 will feature anyway. However, 17...e4 18 ♘xe4 ♘xe4 19 ♗xe4 ♗d7? (19...g4 20 hxg4 ♗xg4 21 ♖f4 ♗h5 would be a slightly better defence, but the momentum is with White) 20 ♖af1 ♖f8 21 ♗g6! left White with a comfortable plus in A.Yusupov –R.Slobodjan, Nussloch 1996.

12 ♗d3 g5

A typical flow of play is something like 12...♖e8 13 f3 ♔c7 14 ♖b1 ♘b6 15 e4 g5 16 ♗f2 ♘h5 17 ♘f1 ♘f4 18 ♘e3. Black retains his good bishop and f4 is a nice square for a knight. However, it isn't an outpost as f5 is for White. Indeed, K.Sasikiran-M.Venkatesh, Mumbai 2003 slightly favoured White as he can play on either side of the board; one or even both of a2-a4 and h2-h4 could figure as White tries to make the most of the b- and h-files.

13 ♗g3 ♘h5 14 f3 ♘xg3

14...♘f4 15 ♗f1! doesn't get anywhere and it is wise to take this bishop before it runs away. Indeed, if ♗f2 is allowed then h2-h4 will appear later whilst the black knights will struggle to find good homes.

15 hxg3 ♔c7 16 g4

Of course the price of doubling White's g-pawns is the donation of a half-open h-file. The text appears to fix the target h6-pawn whilst securing the f5-square.

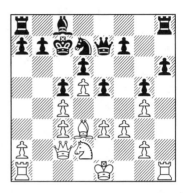

16...♘f6 17 0-0-0 ♗d7 18 ♘e4 ♘xe4 19 ♗xe4 ♕e8 20 ♖de1 a6

Correctly resisting the temptation of 20...b5?! 21 cxb5 ♗xb5 22 c4 ♗d7 23 ♔d2!? when it is Black's king rather than White's who may regret the opening of the b-file.

21 ♔d2 ♖b8 22 ♖b1 b6 23 ♗f5

23 ♖h5, intending to double on the h-file, looks like a sensible plan but ideally White would like at least four rooks. Indeed there could easily be repercussions of abandoning the b-file.

23...♗a4 24 ♕b2

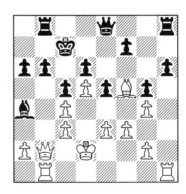

24...e4!?

Despite White's potential play on either the h-file or the b-file, because of the danger of a backlash I suspect that a draw is the most likely outcome if Black just sits (and plays ...h6-h5 should the white rook ever leave the h-file). The text sacrifice, however, highlights Black's own ambitions. He feels that it is worth donating a pawn in order generate play down the e-file and give his queen the e5-square.

25 ♗xe4 ♛e5

From here her majesty could invade further into g3 and the white monarch could get a little nervous. There shouldn't really be anything to panic about though.

26 ♔e2 ♗d7 27 ♗d3 h5

Throwing more temporary wood on the fire in the name of activity.

28 gxh5 f5 29 ♔f2 ♖h6 30 g3

This looks a little wet but there is no obvious way for White to make his material advantage count. The relative positioning of the queens summarise the extent of the compensation involved.

30...♛h8 31 ♔g2 ♖xh5 32 ♖xh5 ♛xh5 33 ♖h1 ♛f7 34 e4

This is White's extra pawn but as well as what follows, I would have thought that either of 34...g4 or 34...f4 is also adequate.

34...♖e8 35 ♖b1 ♖b8 36 exf5 ♗xf5 37 ♛e2 ♗d7 38 ♖h1 ♖f8 39 ♗e4 ♛f6 40 ♖h7 ♖f7 41 ♖xf7 ♛xf7 42 ♛d2 ♛g7

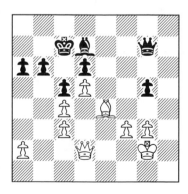

Some pieces have come off but the main thing is that the queens remain.

43 ♛d3 b5 44 cxb5 axb5 45 ♔f2 ♛h8 46 ♔g1 ♛e5 47 ♔g2 ♛h8

Yes, the strong Latvian grandmaster has correctly calculated that, with too many weaknesses elsewhere and with the black queen making a real nuisance of herself, White is not going to be able to make anything of that extra pawn. Instructive stuff!

48 ♔g1 ½-½

Game 31
C.Ward-J.Levitt
British Ch., Torquay 1998

---

1 d4 ♘f6 2 c4 e6 3 ♘c3 ♗b4 4 ♗g5 c5

Very hot off the press is the 4...h6 5 ♗h4 c5 6 d5 d6 7 e3 exd5 8 cxd5 0-0 9 ♗d3 ♛e7 10 ♘ge2 ♗g4 11 f3 ♗xc3+ 12 bxc3 ♗h5 13 e4 ♘bd7 14 0-0 of A.Ker-G.Thornton, Wanganui 2005. Incidentally, with his bishop pair and attractive centre, this is clearly better for White, but to be honest it is of very little theoretical interest.

In the system that Black employs in the main game you will see that the priority is ...♛a5 over ...0-0, and Jon also prefers to leave the white bishop on g5 for reasons that later become clear.

5 d5 d6 6 e3 exd5 7 cxd5 ♘bd7

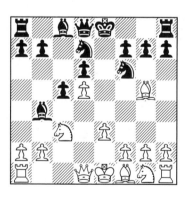

8 ♗d3

Theoretically, eliminating the possibility of ...♘e4 has always been deemed the most critical, although I need to mention others.

Firstly, after 8 ♗b5 Black can choose:

a) 8...0-0 9 ♘ge2 ♘e5 10 a3 ♗xc3+ 11 ♘xc3 ♘g6 12 ♛f3!? a6 13 ♗e2 (perhaps White should settle for 13 ♗xf6 ♛xf6 14 ♛xf6 gxf6 15 ♗d3 with a structural edge)

13...♞e5 14 ♛f4 ♛b6!? 15 ♗xf6 ♛xb2 16 0-0 ♛xc3 17 ♗e7 ♞g6 18 ♛xd6 ♜e8 19 ♗d8 ♗g4 20 ♗xg4 ♜axd8 21 ♛c7 ♛c4 22 ♗h5 ♛xd5 23 ♜ad1 ♛g5 24 ♗xg6 hxg6 25 ♛xb7 and an eventual draw in D.Glavas-D.Rajkovic, Bajmok 2001.

b) 8...h6!? 9 ♗h4 ♗xc3+ (9...0-0-0!? 10 ♞ge2 ♞e5 11 a3 ♗a5 12 0-0 ♞g6 13 ♗g3 ♞h5 14 ♜b1 a6 15 ♗d3 ♞xg3 16 hxg3 ♞e5 was also fine for Black in F.Vallejo Pons-J.Parker, Mondariz 2000) 10 bxc3 ♛a5 11 ♗xd7+ ♞xd7 12 ♞e2 ♞e5 13 0-0 ♗d7 14 a4 ♛a6 15 ♗g3 ♛c4 with an unbalanced position that Black actually went on to win in Y.Kruppa-M.Ivanov, St Petersburg 2002.

c) 8...♛a5 9 ♗xd7+ ♞xd7 10 ♞ge2 ♛c7 (10...♞e5 is the acceptable old move but the English GM's priority seemed to be making something of his queenside majority whilst facilitating a possible preservation of his dark-squared bishop) 11 0-0 a6 12 f4 (until of course White gives him something to think about!) 12...0-0 13 ♜f3 ♜e8 14 ♜g3 ♞f8 15 e4 ♚h8 16 f5. Certainly enterprising play by White, but with 16...f6 17 ♗h4 b5 18 ♜g4 g5 19 ♗f2 ♛f7 20 h4? ♗xc3 21 ♞xc3 b4 22 ♞e2 h5! 23 ♜g3 ♜xe4 he had overplayed his hand in P.Short-J.Levitt, Bunratty 2001.

Secondly, 8 ♞ge2 is solid and it's sad that the 8...0-0 (8...♞e5, with one idea being to exploit the d3-square, is possible, and 9 a3 c4!? certainly looks like fun) 9 a3 ♗a5 10 ♜b1 ♞e5 11 b4 ♗f5? was proven to be a bit too optimistic by 12 e4! cxb4 13 axb4 ♗b6 14 exf5 ♗xf2+ 15 ♚xf2 ♞fg4+ 16 ♚g1 ♛xg5 17 ♛c1 ♛xf5 18 ♛f4 ♛g6 19 ♞g3 f5 20 h3 ♞e3 21 ♗e2 ♜ac8 22 ♜b3 ♞c2 23 ♚h2. Very entertaining stuff, but Black had nevertheless seen his activity snuffed out in B.Korsus-B.Wittje, Germany 2003.

Finally, 8 ♞f3 h6 9 ♗h4 0-0 10 ♗d3 ♞b6 11 e4 ♜e8 12 0-0 g5 13 ♞xg5!? hxg5 14 ♗xg5 ♜e5 15 f4 ♜xg5 16 fxg5 ♞g4 was a fascinating experience in J.Richardson-S.MacDonald Ross, London 1995 but surely Black should employ 8...♛a5!?.

8...♛a5

After the less testing 8...♛e7 9 ♞ge2 h6 10 ♗h4 0-0 11 0-0 a6 12 ♞g3 ♞e5 13 ♞f5 ♗xf5 14 ♗xf5 White's bishop pair and extra central pawn left him on top in R.Hübner-J.Wintzer, Germany 2002.

9 ♞ge2

The advantage of 8 ♗d3 over 8 ♞f3 is that the bishop prevents a ...♞e4 incursion and the knight is left flexible with the option, as taken here, to slide to the supportive square e2. However, this whole set-up is essentially a gambit by White as his (in this instance, my!) d5-pawn is thrown to the wolves.

9...♞xd5

Declining the gambit via 9...♗xc3+ 10 bxc3 0-0 11 0-0 ♜e8 leaves White with a small but easy advantage whether he opts for the 12 a4 a6 13 ♗xf6 ♞xf6 14 c4 of W.Braun-A.Hellmayr, Vienna 1986 or plumps for 12 c4 immediately.

10 0-0

Offering a second pawn is the correct way to go.

10...♗xc3!?

Ironically my opponent offered a draw here and also later implied that I had perhaps played on a bit too long in a 'drawn' position; the point is that he could be right. There is an appeal to the compensation that White gets, but I have been unable to locate a significant improvement on the main game.

Instead 10...c4 11 ♗xc4 ♗xc3 (11...♘5b6 is no big deal here as White can avoid losing a piece by either of 12 ♗b5 or 12 ♗d5) 12 ♕xd5 ♕xd5 13 ♗xd5 ♗xb2 14 ♖ab1 ♘b6 gives White the choice of 15 ♗xf7+, 15 ♗xb7 and 15 ♖xb2 ♘xd5 16 ♖d1, all offering pleasant endgames.

Also 10...♘xc3 11 bxc3 is inaccurate as Black can't flick in ...c5-c4 as in the main game. Hence 11...♗xc3 12 ♘xc3 ♕xc3 when 13 ♗e2 0-0 14 ♕xd6 ♕e5 15 ♕xe5 ♘xe5 16 ♗e7 ♖e8 17 ♗xc5 is an endgame edge. The recent 13 ♗b5 f6 14 ♗f4 ♕a5 15 ♗xd7+ ♗xd7 16 ♗xd6 also looks interesting, although 16...♖c8 17 ♕d5 ♖c6?! 18 ♖fd1 ♕b6? 19 ♗xc5 ♕c7 20 ♗d6 ♖xd6 21 ♕xd6 ♕xd6 22 ♖xd6 wasn't the greatest ever defence in K.McPhillips-P.Makepeace, Millfield 2004.

11 bxc3

Not that it really crossed my mind, but 11 ♘xc3?? ♘xc3 12 bxc3 c4 is a bit of a disaster. White lost this way in M.Machius-D.Rajkovic, Baden 1987, and it is definitely a trick worth remembering.

11...c4!

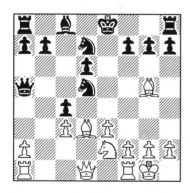

Instead 11...h6 12 ♗h4 ♘xc3 13 ♘xc3 ♕xc3 is just as my notes to 10...♘xc3 as the insertion of ...h7-h6 and ♗h4 doesn't change much. Now 14 ♗e2 0-0 15 ♕xd6 ♕e5 (15...♖e8 incurs more pressure after 16 ♖fd1 ♕e5 17 ♗b5) 16 ♕xe5 ♘xe5 17 ♗e7 ♖e8 18 ♗xc5 ♗g4 19 f3 ♗e6 20 ♖fc1 left

White's bishop pair giving him an endgame advantage in H.Eisterer-J.Rigo, Vienna 1986.

12 ♗c2

The c-pawn is out of bounds in view of 12 ♗xc4?? ♘5b6!, the double attack vindicating Black's decision to leave White's bishop on g5 by not inserting ...h7-h6 earlier.

Others have tried 12 ♗f5 but with no great success. Indeed 12...0-0 13 ♕d2 ♘xc3 14 ♘g3 ♘b6 15 ♗f6 ♗xf5 16 ♗xc3 ♕c5, as seen in A.Yuneev-R.Dautov, Russia 1989, looks rather speculative to me and certainly didn't get anywhere.

12...♘xc3

Previously much time had been spent analysing the complications of 12...0-0 13 ♘g3 (13 ♗h4 ♘xc3 14 ♗xh7+! ♔xh7 15 ♕c2+ ♔g8 16 ♘xc3 gave White reasonable play for the pawn in F.Gonzalez Velez-A.Ayas Fernandez, Barbera 1997, but Black could try 13...♘e5 instead) 13...h6 14 ♗xh6, but the text diminishes the importance of those results which, by the way, were fairly promising for White.

13 ♘xc3 ♕xc3

Definitely not 13...♕xg5? 14 ♘e4 as d6 drops with check.

14 ♕xd6

14 ♖c1 ♕a5 15 ♗f4 0-0 16 ♗xd6 does look playable but it's hardly stunning and Black could really test White's resolve through 15...d5 (although then 16 ♕g4! does look like 'game on'!).

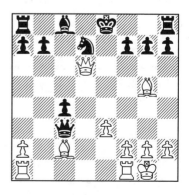

14...♕e5

14...f6 15 ♕e6+ ♔d8 16 ♖fd1 looks far too dangerous, and Black needs to stop the mate threat on e7.

15 ♗f4 ♕xd6 16 ♗xd6

Black is a pawn up, but his king is stuck in the middle and White retains those two bishops.

16...♘f6 17 e4 ♗d7 18 e5 ♘d5 19 ♗e4 ♗c6 20 ♖fc1 c3

20...b5? is far too loose, and indeed 21 a4! a6 22 ♖d1 ♘e7 23 ♗xc6+ ♘xc6 24 axb5 is virtually winning. Also, 20...♘b6 21 ♗xc6+ bxc6 22 a4 is definitely a niggling advantage for White and so instead my grandmaster opponent keeps things tight at the back and opts to defend the opposite-coloured bishops ending.

21 ♗xd5 ♗xd5 22 ♖xc3 ♗c6

I tried my best here, I really did, and perhaps there are different ways in which White can try to make Black suffer. However, the bottom line is that this endgame is probably just a draw.

23 f4 g6 24 ♔f2 ♖c8 25 ♖d1 a6 26 g3 h5 27 ♗b4 ♖d8 28 ♖cd3 ♖xd3 29 ♖xd3 ♗d7 30 ♖c3 ♗c6 31 a4 ♔d7 32 a5 ♖c8 33 ♔e3 ♗b5 34 ♗c5 ♔e6 35 ♔d4 f6 36 ♖e3 ♖d8+ 37 ♗d6 ♖c8 38 ♗c5 ♖d8+ 39 ♔c3 ♖d1 40 exf6+ ♔xf6 41 ♗e7+ ♔f7 42 ♗g5 ♖d7 43 ♔b4 ♖c7 44 ♖e4 ♗d3 45 ♖d4 ♗f5 46 ♖c4 ♖xc4+ 47 ♔xc4 ♔e6 48 ♔c5 ½-½

Game 32
J.Henriksson-Peng Zhaoqin
Rilton Cup, Stockholm 2004

---

1 d4 ♘f6 2 c4 e6 3 ♘c3 ♗b4 4 ♗g5 h6

Basically this game features the idea of Black placing his queen on e7 but then opting not to block things up with ...e6-e5. By leaving out ...h6 and thus ♗h4, Black retains the option of another trick but could also be tricked himself. To help me explain, firstly check out 4...c5 5 d5 ♗xc3+ 6 bxc3 d6 7 e3

♕e7 8 ♗d3 ♘bd7. Now 9 ♘e2 runs into 9...exd5 10 cxd5 ♕e5!.

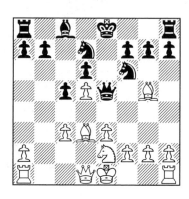

The key point is that Black is attacking the bishop on g5 as well as the d5-pawn, and he can therefore pretty much secure the bishop for the knight without compromising his pawn structure, for example:

a) I was watching 11 ♗f4 ♕xd5 12 ♗b5 ♕xd1+ 13 ♖xd1 a6 14 ♗xd7+ ♗xd7 15 ♖xd6 0-0-0 16 f3 ♗e6 when it was played in R.Sheldon-S.Prudnikova, Women's Olympiad, Yerevan 1996, and Black went on to win a superior ending.

b) 11 ♗xf6 ♘xf6 12 ♗b5+ ♔e7 13 c4 a6 14 ♗a4 b5 15 cxb5 ♗d7 16 ♖b1 axb5 17 ♗xb5 ♕xd5 18 ♕xd5 ♘xd5 19 ♗c4 ♘b4 with a much better ending for Black in O.Kirsanov-J.Emms, British League 2001.

However, regarding the alternative 5...d6, note that Black must be careful to flick in ...♗xc3+; if he doesn't know what he's doing, the delay could be fatal. For example, 6 e3 ♕e7 7 ♘ge2 exd5? (7...h6 is preferable, although it won't transpose to our main game as White should make the black queen move again; indeed 8 ♗xf6 ♕xf6 9 a3 ♗xc3+ 10 ♘xc3 is simply a little better for White because of his space advantage) 8 a3!.

This is very attractive pawn sacrifice, as demonstrated by 8...♗xc3+ (kind of forced as 8...♗a5 fails to 9 ♗xf6 ♕xf6 10 ♕a4+ ♗d7 – or 10...♘c6 11 cxd5 winning the knight – 11 ♕xa5 b6 12 ♘xd5 bxa5 13

♘xf6+ gxf6, leaving Black with an abysmal pawn structure) 9 ♘xc3 ♘bd7 (very strong players have fallen for this trick before, as the 9...dxc4 10 ♗xc4 ♗e6 11 ♘b5 ♗xc4 12 ♘xd6+ ♔f8 13 ♘xc4 ♘c6 14 0-0 of V.Hort-A.Miles, Porz 1982 proves) 10 ♘xd5 ♕d8 11 ♗e2 (Black's d-pawn is backward whilst White has an outpost on d5 and the bishop pair; one wouldn't expect the game to end quite as abruptly as it does but it is clear that, not even a pawn down, White already has quite a big advantage) 11...h6 12 ♗h4 g5 (escaping the pin but creating problems on a different diagonal) 13 ♗g3 ♘e4 14 ♕c2 ♘xg3 15 hxg3 ♘f6?? (losing, but arguably the best solution! Black's position is lousy) 16 ♕c3 1-0 J.Cooper-S.Giddins, British League 2000.

5 ♗h4 c5 6 d5 d6 7 e3 ♕e7

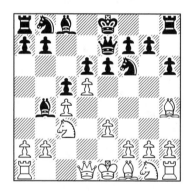

8 ♘ge2

8 ♘f3 and 8 ♗d3 are most likely to transpose either to the closed lines of Game 30 (i.e. in the event of a blocking ...e7-e5) or to the more open excitement of the encounter that follows this one. However, regarding the latter, note that there is no opportunity for Black to snatch the d5-pawn (8...♗xc3+ 9 bxc3 exd5?! 10 cxd5 g5 11 ♗g3 ♘xd5?? fails to 12 ♗b5+). Thus the only independent alternatives to the text are:

a) 8 ♕c2, e.g. 8...♘bd7 9 dxe6 ♕xe6 10 0-0-0 ♗xc3 11 ♕xc3 0-0 12 ♘e2 b5 13 ♘f4 ♕e8 14 ♗xf6 ♘xf6 15 cxb5 a6 16 b6 ♖b8

17 ♖g1 ♖xb6 18 g4 ♕e5 ½-½ J.Hjartarson-H.Stefansson, Reykjavik 1994. A surprisingly premature result given the exciting way both players handled the opening.

b) 8 ♖c1 ♘bd7 9 dxe6 ♕xe6 10 a3 ♗xc3+ 11 ♖xc3 ♘e4 12 ♖c2 g5 13 ♗g3 ♘b6 14 ♗d3 ♘xg3 15 hxg3 ♗d7 16 b3 0-0-0 17 ♔f1 d5 18 ♕e2 dxc4 19 bxc4 ♕f6 20 ♘f3 ♗e6 21 ♔g1 ♖d7 which, in view of his superior piece coordination and queenside pawn structure, was much better for Black in S.Vijayalakshmi-P.Motwani, British Championship, Edinburgh 2003.

8...exd5 9 cxd5 ♘bd7

9...0-0 10 a3 ♗a5 11 ♕a4 ♗d8 was very similar in the game F.Canabate Carmona-M.Suba, Villa de Albox 2001, when White decided to solve the problem of his awkwardly placed knight with the bizarre 12 ♘g1. However, after 12...a6 13 ♘f3 ♘bd7 14 ♕d1 b5 it feels like White had wasted too much time and 15 b4?! ♗b7 16 ♗e2 ♖c8 17 ♖c1 ♖e8 18 0-0 ♘b6 19 ♗xf6 ♕xf6 20 ♕b3 cxb4 21 axb4 ♘c4 22 ♖fd1 ♗b6 23 ♘d4? ♘xe3! 0-1 justifies that conclusion.

10 a3 ♗a5

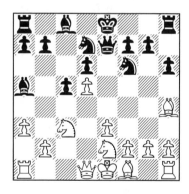

Basically this is the problem with 8 ♘ge2. White's intention was to use that knight to recapture on c3, but of course with ♕a4 not being check, Black is no longer compelled to make this concession.

11 ♕a4 ♗d8!

Black is still not obliged to play ball and

this bishop will find its way back into the game.

12 e4?!

I suspect that this (especially in conjunction with White's next move) is a little too ambitious, and instead White should focus on solving the problem of his 'in the way' knight.

12...0-0 13 f4 b5!?

13...♕e8, threatening ...♘xe4, and the slower 13...a6 also looked good but I like Black's style!

14 ♕xb5 g5!? 15 fxg5 ♘xe4 16 0-0-0 hxg5 17 ♗g3 ♖b8 18 ♕d3 ♘df6

Now Black's pieces start to surge forward.

19 h4 g4

Ensuring that there will be no play down the h-file and that the spotlight will be entirely on the white king.

20 ♖e1 ♗f5

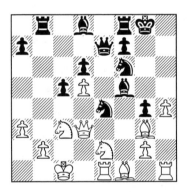

21 ♘d1?

This loses straight away, but White had an unenviable position.

21...♘xg3 22 ♕xg3 ♕e4!

And all of a sudden the white monarch appears to be getting mated.

23 ♔d2 ♕c2+ 24 ♔e3 ♖e8+ 0-1

Game 33
C.Ward-S.Gligoric
Malta 2000

---

1 d4 ♘f6 2 c4 e6 3 ♘c3 ♗b4 4 ♗g5 c5

---

5 d5 ♗xc3+ 6 bxc3 d6 7 e3 h6 8 ♗h4 ♕e7 9 ♗d3 ♘bd7 10 ♘f3

As Black hasn't castled there is some justification in trying to punish him via 10 dxe6. The point is that 10...fxe6 allows the check on g6, whilst 10...♕xe6 11 ♘e2 would see this knight aiming to occupy d5 via f4. That explains the 11...g5 12 ♗g3 ♘e5 13 0-0 ♗d7 of A.Yuneev-L.Yudasin, Leningrad 1989, which Black went on to win but not before both sides had their chances.

As usual White has to choose which track he wants his king's knight on, and although there is no longer a compatriot on c3 to support, 10 ♘e2 can't be too bad. However, the 10...0-0 (10...♘e5 11 h3 ♗d7 12 f4 ♘xd3+ 13 ♕xd3 exd5 14 ♗xf6 ♕xf6 15 cxd5 ♕h4+ 16 g3 ♕e7 17 e4 0-0 18 g4 ♖ae8 19 ♘g3 f5! saw White get punished for still having his king in the centre in J.Cantos Conejero-A.Delchev, Albacete 2001) 11 0-0 ♘e5 12 f4 ♘g6 13 ♗xg6 fxg6 14 ♕d3 exd5 15 cxd5 ♗f5 16 ♕d2 ♖ae8 of S.Boehm-K.Thiel, Leverkusen 1998 has previously been assessed as slightly better for Black, and I would go along with that.

10...♘b6

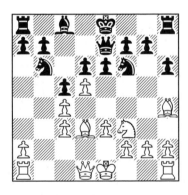

When you have finished playing over this game you will understand how pleased I was with it, although already at this point I was out of my theory. When this was played at the time I thought that it was extremely provocative and I simply couldn't resist sacrificing a pawn. Now I believe I understand the position more and consider 10...♘b6 to be quite reasonable.

Instead Black still has the option of returning to the realms of this chapter's early encounters via the closing 10...e5, and specifically to Game 30 following 11 ♘d2.

11 0-0

I make no apologies for including this game as it has some instructive points and I really enjoyed it! However, in light of the notes that follow, possibly 11 dxe6!? ♗xe6 12 0-0 could be employed instead. As far as I can see this sequence is yet to be tried out in tournament play but it looks like a sensible way of avoiding Black's 11th move improvement.

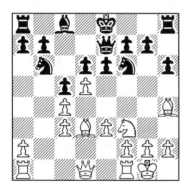

11...exd5?!

Grabbing the pawn is very risky, and 11...e5! is a much safer alternative. The black knight looks a little silly on b6 but the advantage of sealing off the centre now is that White has shown his cards by committing his king to the kingside. This feature is exploited in the variation 12 ♘d2 g5 13 ♗g3 h5 14 h4 ♘g4!, although with that in mind 14 f3! is more accurate. Now 14...h4 15 ♗f2 g4 16 ♕e1 ♘g8 17 fxg4 ♗xg4 18 h3 probably favoured White in S.Dolmatov-E.Geller, Moscow 1987 but I wonder whether Black gave much thought to 16...g3!? 17 hxg3 h3. It certainly looks very plausible.

12 cxd5 ♘bxd5 13 e4 ♘c7 14 e5

With the trusty bishop-pair advantage and a lead in development, I naturally wanted the position to be as open as possible.

14...dxe5 15 ♘xe5

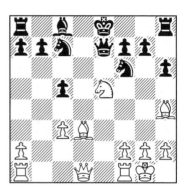

A nice square for the knight, which is effectively guarded by the ♖e1 pin.

15...♗e6?!

Presumably my famous opponent harboured some ideas of castling queenside. but this takes too much of a liberty. I was expecting 15...0-0 and, considering myself to have very reasonable compensation, was in the process of choosing between 16 ♖fe1 and 16 f4 (perhaps with ♕f3 and ♖ae1 to follow) when this move appeared on the board.

16 ♕a4+!

Throwing a spanner in the works. Now the black king is caught in a crossfire. I always teach juniors to look out for checks, and I'm glad that I was on the ball here!

16...♔f8

Ugly, but 16...♗d7 17 ♘xd7 ♕xd7 18 ♖fe1+ is no better.

17 ♖ae1!?

Here I had my longest think of the game and, as it transpires, the time spent was a worthwhile investment! I left a rook on f1 because I was anticipating that Black would have to turn to ...g7-g5 in order to try to solve his problems. In that instance (indeed the way the game panned out) I wanted utilise the f-file for some rook action.

17...g5 18 ♗g3 ♘fd5 19 f4!

I wasn't worried about my c-pawn, although it's true that I could also have considered 19 c4.

19...gxf4 20 ♗xf4 ♘xf4 21 ♕xf4

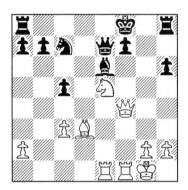

Now White's position is one of complete strength and, amongst other things, 22 ♘g6+ is threatened.

21...♔e8

Or 21...♔g7 22 ♘xf7 ♕xf7 23 ♕g3+.

22 ♘xf7

Ironically 22 ♕a4+ would again have been extremely strong, but I was never going to be able to resist the temptation of this visual continuation.

22...♔d7 23 ♘e5+ 1-0

White's position is crushing and a lot of fun to play. There was no way that I was going to be content with just 23 ♘xh8, as for starters I could win an exchange or more with ♘g6 next go anyway.

Game 34
V.Erdos-Z.Ilincic
Budapest 2004

---

1 d4 ♘f6 2 c4 e6 3 ♘c3 ♗b4 4 ♗g5 h6 5 ♗h4 c5 6 d5 0-0

This committal move is relatively rare in this position as Black usually holds back on deciding where to place his king. Though this hadn't been employed for a good three years, the fact that it is a strong grandmaster wheeling it out should make us sit up and take note.

As you'll see in this offbeat system, clearly 6...0-0 and 6...d6 are interchangeable. However, in a similar vein (i.e. black castling) but with a different configuration of white pieces is the continuation 7 e3 ♗xc3+ 8 bxc3 e5 9 ♕c2 ♘bd7 10 ♗d3 0-0 11 ♘e2

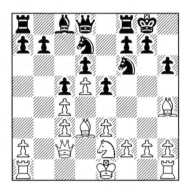

(White chooses the ♘e2 option rather than the main game's ♘f3-d2; I'm sure you've noted by now that these are the main two set-ups) 11...♖e8 12 f3. Now 12...g5 13 ♗g3 e4!? is a rarity. You won't find 14 ♗xe4 ♘xe4 15 fxe4 ♘f6 16 e5 dxe5 17 h4 ♘g4 18 ♔d2 b5! 19 e4 bxc4 20 ♕a4 ♗d7 21 ♕xc4 ♖b8 22 ♖ab1? ♖xb1 23 ♖xb1 gxh4 24 ♗e1 ♕g5+ 25 ♔d3 ♕e3+ 26 ♔c2 ♗a4+ 27 ♔b2 ♖b8+ 28 ♔a1 ♖xb1+ 29 ♔xb1 ♗d1 0-1 J.Richardson-C.Ward, Charlton 1995 on any other databases, and I was quite pleased by this original effort. Of course, on another day the black monarch might suffer because of those kingside pawn advances.

7 e3

In the few documented practical outings that have occurred White has tried 7 ♖c1 and 7 ♘f3, but presumably 7 f3 intending e2-e4 should be a consideration too.

7...d6 8 ♘f3

I don't want to give the impression that everything is new though, as the position after 8 ♗d3 brings us well back onto the transpositional map. Then Black has tried the standard 8...♗xc3+ 8 bxc3 e5, 8...♘bd7 and even 8...b5. However, presumably also critical is 8...exd5 9 cxd5 g5 (9...&bd7, just as we've seen before, is less greedy!) 10 &g3 &xd5 11 &ge2. The weak squares around Black's king form much of White's compensation, but I'm particularly interested by 11...Wf6 (rather than the 11...&g7?! 12 &c2 &e6 13 e4 &f4 14 &xf4 gxf4 15 &xf4 Wf6 16 Wf3 &c6 17 &xd6 that was just a pawn extra for White in H.Lehmann-H.Golombek, Zevenaar 1961) 12 0-0 &xc3 13 bxc3 &g4 14 Wd2 &xe2 15 &xe2 &xc3 16 &f3 which, despite Black's being two pawns ahead, Fritz seems to like for White even after 16...&c6 17 &fc1 &a4 18 &ab1 &e5 19 &xb7 &ab8 20 &xe5 Wxe5. Now White regains his second pawn via 21 Wa5 &b6 22 Wxa7 but after 22...&d5 23 Wa3 &b4 24 &f3 We6 25 &b2 g4 Black actually went on to win in the game D.Rogozenko-T,Tolnai, Debrecen 1992.

8...e5

After the alternative 8...exd5 9 cxd5 &bd7 10 &e2 White has managed harmonious kingside development compared to the same pawn structure of Game 32. His king's knight doesn't protect its partner but 10...Wa5 11 0-0 &xc3 12 bxc3 Wxc3 is asking for trouble, and 13 &d2 &b6 14 a4 We5 15 &f3 &d7 16 &g3 We7 17 e4 &fd8 18 &e1 &e8 19 Wb3 Wd7 20 a5 &c8 21 &c4 Wb5 22 Wc2 &h7 23 &g4 Wa6 24 &e2 b5 25 axb6 Wb7 26 &a5 Wxb6 27 &eb1 1-0 (J.Petkevich-S.Kislov Voronezh 1997) was certainly one way to get it!

9 &d2 g5!?

Definitely aggressive but also kind of inevitable as it is the only convenient way of escaping the pin. The obvious drawback of its employment here compared to the likes of Games 28 and 30 is that the black king is on g8 and thus advancing the kingside pawns could ultimately be punished.

Also of interest is the more restrained 9...&bd7 10 Wc2 Wa5 11 &d3 &xc3 12 bxc3 &e8 13 f3 a6 14 0-0 b5 15 &f5 &b8 16

a4 b4 17 &b3 Wc7 18 a5 bxc3 19 Wxc3 e4 20 f4 which Black actually went on to win in S.Khoroshev-A.Erikalov, Novosibirsk 2001. At this point, however, the advantage must be with White.

10 &g3

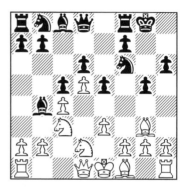

10...&xc3

Probably Black is wise to take this knight now whilst it still compromises the white pawn structure. Amazingly, as far as I can see this is the first time that this exact position has ever been reached.

11 bxc3 Wa5

And it's still unique here...

12 Wc2

And hence here too, which however is slightly surprising as the structure is very typical of the Leningrad. The key difference (and the main diverging characteristic of this game) is the unusual positioning of the black king. I never thought I'd ever hear myself saying that ...&d8-c7 is normal but in this opening it really is!

12...&bd7 13 &b1

In this particular position I think I prefer 13 &e2 with a likely follow-up plan of h2-h4. White should be eager to open the h-file and, with that in mind, I also see nothing especially wrong with the immediate 13 h4!? g4 14 h5 either. Black's pawn is a little stranded on g4 and the h4-square could prove very useful for White.

13...&h5!

Black takes his chance to play this while he can. White's last move was certainly not a bad one in principle, but perhaps it was lacking accuracy. Back to the topic of the black king, and if he hadn't already castled a typical plan would be the good old ...♔d8-c7 manoeuvre. As you should know by now, the king is usually safer on c7 than g8 and it also frequently provides the useful function of guarding the pawns on b7 and d6.

14 ♗d3 ♘df6 15 0-0 ♕d8 16 f3

Other ideas include 16 ♖be1, as part of a plan to arrange f2-f4, and 16 ♗f5, which is very possible here because after 16...♗xf5 17 ♕xf5 Black can not seek a trade of queens due to the hanging b7-pawn and/or the danger to d6 via ♘e4.

16...♘xg3 17 hxg3 ♔g7 18 ♔f2

Clearing the way for major piece play along the h-file.

18...♖h8 19 ♖h1 ♕a5

It's the to-ing and fro-ing of the black queen that leads one to the conclusion that it is White who is dictating the course of this game. Probably a fair assessment would be somewhere between equal and slightly better for White but the game continuation proves that he can easily go wrong.

20 g4 b6

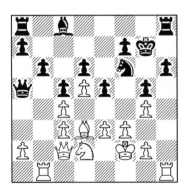

The black queen now looks committed to the queenside, but this was necessary to free the bishop from its defensive shackles.

21 ♖b2?!

This rook proves to be poorly placed on this square and I can only assume that it was played to avoid the variation 21 ♘f1 e4!? 22 ♗xe4 ♘xe4+. However, whilst 23 fxe4 ♗g4 24 ♘g3 ♖ae8 is far from clear, actually 23 ♕xe4!? ♕xa2+ 24 ♔g1 looks vaguely promising, e.g. 24...♗a6 25 ♘g3 when White is attacking with that deadly duo and the rook on h1 has a shout too. In the line 25...♖ae8 26 ♘f5+ ♔f8 27 ♕d3 ♗xc4 28 ♕d1 the knight is a real giant on f5.

21...♗d7 22 ♘f1 h5!

Eliminating an obvious weakness and reminding White that his rooks are no longer connected.

23 gxh5 ♖xh5 24 ♖xh5 ♘xh5 25 ♗f5

This is the square that White always looked most likely to invade on, but all is not that well at home for the first player.

25...♗a4 26 ♕d3 ♖h8 27 ♗g4 ♘f6 28 ♕f5 ♖h6!

Black is destined to lose his g-pawn but this rook now provides excellent cover. Meanwhile, back at the ranch White has some problems with his own queenside.

29 ♘g3 ♕xc3 30 ♖e2

After 30 ♕xg5+ ♖g6 31 ♘f5+ ♔f8 White would find himself with no checks and with his queen and rook both attacked.

30...♗d7! 31 ♖c2

After 31 ♕c2 ♕xc2 32 ♖xc2 ♗xg4 33 fxg4 the most accurate is 33...♔g6! – Black will enter an endgame at least one pawn up.

31...♕a3 32 ♕xg5+ ♖g6 33 ♘h5+ ♘xh5 34 ♕xh5 ♗xg4 35 fxg4 ♕d3!

Now White's position is all over the place. His queen is offside, his pawns are weak, his rook is attacked and his king is vulnerable. Taking everything into consideration, not great!

36 ♖e2 ♖f6+ 37 ♔e1 ♕c3+ 38 ♖d2 ♕c1+ 0-1

It's goodnight Charlie (mate comes via ...♕f1 or ...♕xe3 next turn)!

Game 35
C.Ward-T.Hinks-Edwards
British League 2000

---

1 d4 ♘f6 2 c4 e6 3 ♘c3 ♗b4 4 ♗g5 h6

It is less common to employ the gambit that follows without this insertion, but it is possible. The advantage is that a future ...♘e4 will hit the bishop and thus White may be inclined to volunteer ♗xf6, e.g. 4...c5 5 d5 b5 6 dxe6 fxe6 7 cxb5 0-0 8 e3 ♕a5 9 ♗xf6 ♖xf6 10 ♕c1 a6! 11 bxa6 ♘xa6 12 ♘f3 ♘c7 13 ♘d2 d5 with very reasonable play in P.Steneskog-P.Carlsson, Malmö 2004. The disadvantage though may be more relevant and is highlighted in the deviation 8 ♘f3 ♗b7 9 ♖c1 ♕b6 10 ♗d2!? ♗xc3 11 ♗xc3 ♕xb5 12 e3 which White went on to win in K.Sasikiran-R.Burnett, Hampstead 1998. I am talking about the option of the bishop retreat that White doesn't have when

it is on h4. It doesn't look that big a problem though and overall the '...h7-h6 or not?' debate is probably not that important.

5 ♗h4 c5 6 d5 b5!?

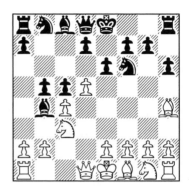

I have been known to play the Blumenfeld Counter Gambit (1 d4 ♘f6 2 c4 e6 3 ♘f3 c5 4 d5 b5) on the odd rare occasion and though with obvious similarities, this should be a better version. Black has the option to unpin with ...g7-g5, but his own pin on the white knight turns the heat up in the centre.

7 dxe6

This move accepts the pawn offering but is far from forced:

a) 7 e3 when:

a1) 7...0-0 8 ♕f3! ♗b7 9 ♗xf6 ♕xf6 10 ♕xf6 gxf6 11 0-0-0 was an endgame edge to White in Timman-Yusupov, Hilversum 1986; Black's b7-bishop is shut out of the game and his knight struggles too.

a2) 7...bxc4 8 ♗xc4 ♗b7 9 ♗xf6 (Black was threatening ...g5) 9...♕xf6 10 ♘ge2 ♕h4 11 ♕b3 a5 12 a3 a4 13 ♕a2 ♗xc3+ 14 ♘xc3 0-0 15 0-0 again with a niggling edge for White.

a3) 7...♗b7 8 dxe6 (8 ♕f3?! bxc4 9 ♗xf6 ♕xf6 10 ♕xf6 gxf6 looks good for Black) 8...fxe6 9 cxb5. Though this could transpose to our main game through 9...d5, now Black has other options, e.g. 9...0-0 10 ♘f3 (10 a3!? ♗a5 prevents the plan that follows, although the negative side is that this bishop can drop back to c7 later to help attack the white king)

10...♕a5 11 ♗xf6 ♖xf6. This position was reached in G.Campos-R.Markus, correspondence 1999. Black has pressure on both white knights and, even with ...d7-d5 available, the option to contemplate confirming the pawn as a sacrifice via ...a6.

b) 7 ♕c2 exd5 8 cxd5 d6 9 e4 a6 10 ♗e2 0-0 with a reasonable Benoni-style position in R.Gumerov-A.Shestoperov, Tula 2004. In fact, come to think of it, it's an ideal Snake Benoni for Black (1 d4 ♘f6 2 c4 c5 3 d5 e6 4 ♘c3 exd5 5 cxd5 ♗d6 intending ...♘c7-a5), although that's not saying that much!

c) 7 f3?! bxc4 8 e4 exd5 9 exd5 ♕e7+! 10 ♔f2 (or 10 ♗e2 ♕e5!) 10...♗xc3 11 bxc3 ♘e4+ when 12 fxe4 ♕xh4+ 13 ♔e3 ♕f6 14 ♕d2 0-0 15 ♗xc4 d6 16 ♗b5 a6 17 ♗a4 ♗d7 18 ♗c2?? ♕g5+ 0-1 V.Luciani-N.Aleksic, Pescara 2004 finished even earlier than it should have done.

d) 7 cxb5 g5 8 ♗g3 ♘xd5 (A.Kharitonov-T.Nyback, Chalkidiki 2003 continued 8...exd5 9 e3 ♗b7 10 ♘ge2 ♕e7 11 a3 ♗xc3+ 12 bxc3 ♘e4; it depends on whether Black feels that it is worth the tempi to keep his pawns undoubled) 9 ♖c1 when Black should have his fair of his play after 9...♗b7, although 9...♘f6, preparing to deploy the d-pawn, was tried in D.Rajkovic-A.Beliavsky, Yugoslavia 2000.

e) 7 e4

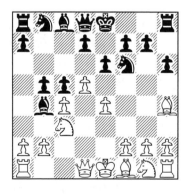

(declining Black's gambit in favour of offering one of his own!) 7...g5 8 ♗g3 ♘xe4 9

♕f3 f5 (the 9...exd5 10 0-0-0 ♗xc3 11 ♖xd5 ♕e7 12 bxc3 d6 of N.Murshed-S.Tiviakov, Calcutta 1993 has previously been assessed as 'unclear'; just what you wanted to hear!) 10 ♕h5+ ♔e7 11 d6+ ♘xd6 12 ♗xd6+ ♔xd6 13 0-0-0+ ♔e7 14 ♘xb5 ♘c6 15 h4 g4 16 ♘e2 ♕e8 17 ♕xe8+ ♖xe8 18 ♘c7 when all the fireworks frittered out into a dynamically equal endgame in D.Rogozenko-P.Charbonneau, Internet 2001.

To summarise then, aside from the 6 e4 counter gambit, there is a reasonable argument for White relinquishing his d-pawn to accept Black's offering on the grounds that it is difficult to keep his centre together anyway.

7...fxe6 8 cxb5 d5

8...0-0 9 e3 d5 would transpose, but 9...♕a5!? is definitely worth investigating. The point is that after 10 ♗xf6 ♖xf6 11 ♕c1 Black hasn't committed himself to either ...d7-d5 or ...♗b7. Though the former is likely eventually, in this position 11...a6 has scored quite well in practice. Instead 10 ♘ge2 was a more recent attempted improvement, when 10...♕xb5 11 ♕c2 d5 12 0-0-0 is a tough one to call: Black has the better centre but more pawn islands; he has a half-open b-file but a hole on g6. After 12...♕a5 13 a3, in S.Mohandesi-C.Mackenzie, Leuven 2003 Black mixed things up further with 13...♗d7. Although he went on to lose you'd have to say that, both with or without this move, his chances are not worse.

9 e3 0-0

9...d4?! 10 exd4 cxd4 11 a3 ♗a5 12 b4 dxc3 13 bxa5 ♕xa5 14 ♕c2 is clearly in White's favour.

10 ♗d3

Despite the 'knights before bishops' opening principle, this is more accurate than ♘f3 because it retains the option of ♘ge2.

10...♗b7

Although I certainly wouldn't blame Black's defeat on this move, at the very least here is a chance to ponder possible improvemenets:

a) 10...d4?! again looks premature in view of 11 exd4 cxd4 12 a3 ♗a5 13 b4.

b) 10...a6 11 ♘ge2! c4 12 ♗c2 axb5 13 0-0 ♘c6 14 ♘xb5 e5 15 b3 ♗g4 16 h3 ♗h5 17 ♗xf6 ♖xf6 18 bxc4 dxc4 19 ♕xd8+ ♘xd8 20 ♘ec3 ♖b6 21 a4 and White was essentially just a pawn up in N.Short-A.Aleksandrov, European Team Championship, Pula 1997. Black (who perhaps shouldn't let White have a second bite at the cherry and could instead employ 13...♕a5 or 13...♖a5!?) had his counterplay well nullified, although this encounter ended in disaster as, confused by the new style time control, Nigel later actually lost on time whilst putting the final touches on a won ending!

c) 10...♕a5 11 ♗xf6 ♖xf6 12 ♘ge2 a6 13 bxa6 ♗xa6 14 ♗xa6 ♕xa6 15 0-0 ♘c6 16 a3 ♗xc3 17 ♘xc3 ♖b8 18 b4 cxb4 19 axb4 ♕c4 20 b5! ♘b4 21 ♕d2 again just with an extra pawn for White, G.Gaertner-M.Grundherr, Austria 2000.

Overall then, nothing substantially better than what Black actually played.

11 ♘ge2 ♘bd7

This looks natural but two old references are:

a) 11...e5 12 a3 ♗a5 13 0-0 ♗b6 14 ♘a4 ♘bd7 15 ♘xb6 axb6 16 b4 ♕c7 17 f4 e4 18 ♗c2 ♖fd8 19 ♕d2 ♘f8 20 ♖fd1 ♖d7 21 ♗b3 ♔h8 22 a4 ♘g6 23 ♗xf6 gxf6 24 ♖ac1 ♕d6 25 a5 ♖ad8 26 ♕a2 ♘e7 27 bxc5 bxc5 28 ♕a3 when White inexplicably proposed an immediately accepted draw in T.Sorensen-L.Winants, Haderslev 1981.

b) 11...d4 12 exd4 g5 13 ♗g3 (although pieces are usually better than pawns in the opening/middlegame, I wouldn't say that this would be the case in the event of 13 dxc5 gxh4 14 c6 ♗c8 15 ♕b3!?) 13...♗xg2 14 ♖g1 ♗f3 15 a3 ♗xc3+ 16 bxc3 cxd4 17 cxd4 a6 18 h4 looked a bit ropy for Black in D.Rogozenko-R.Pogorelov, Odorheiu Secuiesc 1992.

12 0-0

12 a3 ♗a5 13 ♘f4 ♕b6 14 ♘g6 ♖fe8 15 0-0 e5 16 ♘a4 ♕e6 17 f4 exf4 18 exf4 ♘g4 19 f5 ♕e3+ all looks kind of plausible too, although not then the 20 ♗f2?? ♘xf2 21 ♖xf2 ♗e1! of P.Rietra-T.Dorland, Dieren 1981.

12...♕e8

Escaping the pin, this move is also designed to intercept the White's aforementioned ♘f4-g6 idea.

13 ♗g3 e5

Black's main compensation lies with his extra centre pawn and so advancing these pawns makes sense.

14 a3 ♗a5 15 ♕b1

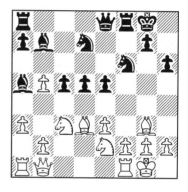

Eyeing the g6-square and preparing 16 b4. If Black's c-pawn is traded off then the power of his centre is significantly diminished as he can never really afford to concede the d4-square to a white knight.

15...♗b6

Although there will be some sceptics, I didn't actually select this game as the main example of the ...b7-b5 gambit because it was one of my wins! The truth (believe it or not) is that it does appear to be quite theoretically important. Black has had plenty of opportunities to deviate (as has White) although, apart from possibly 9...♕a5, there has been nothing that could be categorically classed as an improvement. If one believes that Black's big pawn centre is an adequate counterbalance for White's queenside pawn majority (and it's certainly not clear that this is the case) then we need to come up with a good move for him (sooner rather than later!).

Here Black retreated his bishop in anticipation of b2-b4 but perhaps this is the moment to reconsider. Certainly 15...♖ac8 and 15...♕e7 should come into Black's thoughts. However, 15...e4!? has a record in practical play of 100%: 16 ♗c2 ♗xc3 17 bxc3 ♘e5 18 a4 ♘h5 19 ♗xe5 ♕xe5 20 ♕d1 ♖ad8 21 ♕d2 ♘f6 22 ♘f4 ♘g4 23 h3 g5! 24 hxg4 gxf4 25 exf4 (25 f3!? appears to deal better with Black's pawn advances although would anyone then care to suggest 25...d4!?; crazy stuff, and to avoid all this perhaps White should have left his knight on e2 and gone with something like 22 a5 instead) 25...♖xf4 26 ♗d1 d4 27 cxd4 cxd4 28 ♖c1 ♖df8 29 ♗e2 ♔g7 30 ♕b2 ♖4f6 31 ♖c4 ♖d8 32 ♕d2 e3 33 fxe3 ♕g3 34 ♗d1 and when White resigned (arguably prematurely) in view of ...♖xf1+ and ...dxe3, G.Todorovic-P.Nikac, Kladovo 1992.

16 b4 c4 17 ♗g6

This tempo is required to prevent Black getting in ...d5-d4. White's next plan will be to further reduce Black's control over this key central area by pushing away the dark-squared bishop.

17...♕e7 18 ♖d1 ♖fd8 19 a4 ♘f8 20 a5 ♗c7 21 ♗f5 ♖ab8 22 ♕b2 ♘h5?

The first real mistake of the game. This is a reasonable idea but is played under the wrong circumstances. The game continuation suggests that Black can't really afford to remove a defender from d5, but problems only really mount there because of the lack of squares for the black rook. You'll have to play over the main game first to understand exactly what I'm talking about, but briefly I would say that Black would have better practical chances with 22...g6 instead, the point being that after 23 ♗c2, 23...♘h5 is okay. However, more testing is 23 ♗h3!? when the problem for Black is still this b5-b6 and a5-a6

danger. For example, although 23...♗c8 24 ♗xc8 ♖bxc8 gives Black more space in which to operate, in fact 25 b6! axb6 26 ♘b5 looks like a timely return of the pawn. One way to fend off (at least temporarily) White's plan is through 23...♖a8!?. Now if Black could get a knight to g5 then he would be doing well. However, I'm not sure he can with accurate white play, and indeed 24 ♖a4 ♘8h7 25 ♕c2 ♕f7 26 f4! is another variation that seems to suit White.

23 b6!

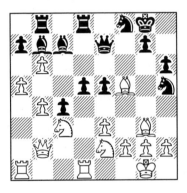

23...♘xg3 24 hxg3 axb6 25 a6 ♗a8

The bishop would obviously prefer to protect the d-pawn, and 25...♗c6 26 b5 is nothing but a delaying tactic.

26 a7

The key point that I alluded to earlier is that the c8-square isn't available to the black rook because of the placing of White's bishop.

26...♖b7 27 ♘xd5

So this pawn drops and with it goes Black's whole position.

27...♕f7 28 ♗e4 ♗d6 29 ♘dc3 b5 30 ♖a6 1-0

White is in no hurry to take the exchange just yet and I had sort of envisaged 30...♗e7 31 ♖xd8 ♗xd8 32 ♗d5 as being the end. Coincidentally, Black also obviously decided that there was no other way to grovel on and so threw in the towel here and now.

Summary

The Leningrad remains a dangerous weapon for the club player, but in recent times at the highest levels its popularity has dwindled. Whatever the rating of the competitors involved though, a Nimzo-Indian exponent should always be prepared to deal with 4 ♗g5. Arguably the most exciting lines for him are the ones involving a ...b7-b5 gambit, the likes of which Yusupov, Beliavsky, Tiviakov and Short have all been known to employ. Mind you, Nigel appeared happy with the white side of that line too (see the notes to Game 35), and whether or not Black gets enough for the pawn is still open to debate.

In contrast, playing à la Jon Levitt (Game 31) is not going to win over the audience but it's been tough for White to prove a significant advantage against the ...exd5 and ...♘bd7 lines. Indeed, in the modern Leningrad it seems that short castling for Black should certainly not be written off.

The main line, however, is probably still the closed positions that this chapter kicked off with. They tend to involve a ...♔d8-c7 manoeuvre; the king can be very usefully positioned here but both sides should pay heed to the sacrifice in Game 28 as clearly there is a possible way through for White on the queenside.

1 d4 ♘f6 2 c4 e6 3 ♘c3 ♗b4 4 ♗g5 c5 5 d5 h6
  5...d6 – *Game 31*
6 ♗h4 (D) ♗xc3+
  6...d6 – *Game 32*
  6...0-0 – *Game 34*
  6...b5 – *Game 35*
7 bxc3 d6 8 e3 e5
  8...♕e7 (D)
    9 ♘f3 – *Game 30*
    9 ♗d3 – *Game 33*
9 ♗d3 ♕e7 10 ♘e2 ♘bd7 (D) 11 ♕b1 – *Game 28*
  11 f4 – *Game 29*

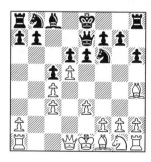

| *6 ♗h4* | *8...♕e7* | *10...♘bd7* |

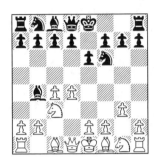

CHAPTER SIX

4 g3

1 d4 ♘f6 2 c4 e6 3 ♘c3 ♗b4 4 g3

Certainly in my time as a chess professional, 4 g3 is the continuation that I have employed most as White against the Nimzo-Indian. In this line pioneered by Romanishin, White fianchettoes his king's bishop in order to make Black's life a little difficult regarding developing his queenside. The bishop will sit pretty on g2, operating nicely on the long diagonal, which of course includes a nice view of the centre. The fact that White has no early obligation to advance his e-pawn means that the dark-squared partner on c1 will not be obscured, and in this line the advantage of the bishop pair often means quite a lot.

From the diagrammed position the majority of my opponents responded with 4...c5 which, after 5 ♘f3, transposes directly into the 'Kasparov Nimzo-Indian', and that itself is more commonly reached via the move order 4 ♘f3 c5 5 g3. While the variations that stem from that position are outside the scope of this book, I do want to concentrate on the other playable alternatives to 4...c5.

If a Nimzo player intends to meet 4 ♘f3 with 4...c5 then to avoid having to learn any more theory I guess treating 4 g3 in the same way makes perfect sense. However, in my opinion the plans discussed in this chapter with either ...d7-d6 or ...d7-d5 and a delay or

a complete omission of ...c7-c5 are perfectly playable and, to be perfectly frank, are the reason why I personally lost much of my enthusiasm for 4 g3. However, new plans crop up all the time and some fresh ideas have giving me some cause for a re-think!

Game 36
C.Ward-B.Gulko
Politiken Cup, Copenhagen 1996

---

1 d4 ♘f6 2 c4 e6 3 ♘c3 ♗b4 4 g3 0-0

Capturing on c3 first is fine. However, it is sensible to tuck the king away before advancing the d-pawn or at least ensuring that ♕a4+ won't be embarrassing!

5 ♗g2 ♗xc3+ 6 bxc3

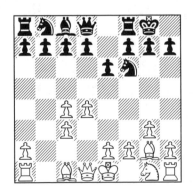

6...d6

Black must decide how he wants to develop his queenside and in particular his remaining bishop. The major alternative to...d7-d6 and ...e6-e5 is to try to get the bishop out to b7 or a6. The continuation 6...♘c6 7 ♘f3 ♖b8 (7...♘a5 looks premature in view of 8 ♕a4 b6 9 ♘d2 ♖b8 10 ♘b3) 8 ♕d3!? b6 9 ♗g5 brings back some very nice memories for me. After 9...h6 White has the attractive response 10 h4!?.

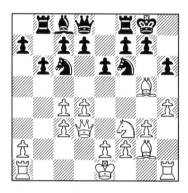

The basic idea is that if the piece sacrifice is accepted then Black will get into trouble down the h-file. However, White's h-pawn advance is more than just a cheapo as without a dark-squared bishop Black will find it tricky escaping the pin. 10...♖e8 11 ♘e5!? and now:

a) Upon 11...♘a5 both 12 ♗xf6!? ♕xf6 13 g4 and 12 g4 look encouraging; regarding the latter, now 12...d6 13 ♗xf6 gxf6 (observe 13...♕xf6 14 g5 hxg5 15 hxg5 ♕xg5 16 ♖h8+!) 14 ♘xf7 ♔xf7 15 ♕h7+ ♔f8 16 g5! ♕d7 17 ♕h8+ ♔f7 18 ♕h7+ ♔f8 19 ♕h8+ ♔f7 20 ♕xf6+ ♔g8 21 ♗c6!! (clearing the g-file) 21...♖f8 22 ♗xd7 ♖xf6 23 gxf6 ♗xd7 24 ♖g1+ ♔f8 25 ♖g7 was seen in the game S.Makarichev-A.Sokolov, Moscow 1982 – after all the fireworks White went on to convert the endgame.

b) One neat variation that I can recall memorising from the very old *New In Chess 1 d4 Keybook* is 11...♘xe5 12 dxe5 hxg5 13 hxg5

♘g4 14 f4 ♔f8 (or 14...g6 15 ♕f3 ♘xe5 16 fxe5 ♕xg5 17 ♕f6 ♕xf6 18 exf6 e5 19 ♗d5! c6 20 ♔d2 cxd5 21 ♖h6 ♖e6 22 ♖ah1 ♖xf6 23 ♖h8+ ♔g7 24 ♖1h7 mate!) 15 0-0-0 ♗a6 16 ♖h8+ ♔e7

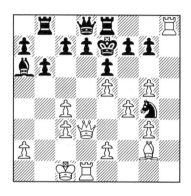

17 ♕d6+!! and a juicy checkmate.

A game that I won on route to my first GM norm continued instead with 10...♗a6 11 ♘e5 hxg5 12 ♘xc6 dxc6 13 hxg5 g6 14 gxf6 ♕xf6 15 ♗xc6, leaving White a pawn up. After 15...e5 16 ♗a4 c5 17 ♖h4 ♖fd8 18 ♖d1 cxd4 19 cxd4 exd4 20 ♖xd4 ♖xd4 21 ♕xd4 I eventually went on to convert the endgame in C.Ward-D.Leuba, Bern 1993.

7 ♘f3 ♘c6

7...♘bd7 is not a ridiculous move, but still Black has some problems activating his bishop. A recurrent theme running throughout this book is that just because Black has knights rather than bishops, he shouldn't always be happy to obtain a closed position. Indeed, the 8 0-0 ♖e8 9 ♘d2 ♖b8 10 e4 e5 11 f4! ♘f8 of C.Ward-H.Jensen, Copenhagen 1997 is not the sort of cramped scenario that Black should be aiming for. I played the obvious 12 f5 here, but I could equally have held back on that for a while.

Very provocative is the rather cheeky 7...b6 that English GM Jim Plaskett once played against me. That game continued 8 ♘d2 c6 9 0-0 e5 10 a4 a5 11 c5 bxc5 12 dxe5 dxe5 13 ♘c4 (C.Ward-J.Plaskett, Hastings 1998/99) when I felt that my two bishops offered me adequate compensation for 'half a pawn'. Looking back at it now though, certainly 11 f4!? is a candidate, while these days a less trusting Chris Ward may prefer 8 ♘e5!? as White may just be able to rescue the potentially cornered bishop following any exchange sacrifice.

8 ♕d3

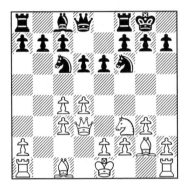

Although I was aware that 8 0-0 (see the next game) was the main line here, I always used to prefer this move. My logic was that although I fully intended to get in e2-e4 and hopefully f2-f4, I wanted my queen on d3 before employing a likely ♘d2. By delaying committing my king (or rather my king's rook!), those ♗g5, ...h6, h4!? ideas remained in the equation too. Above all, I don't think I liked the idea of my opponent parking a pawn on e4 himself, although we'll soon see why that may not be such a big problem anyhow.

I do feel though that the immediate 8 ♘d2?! is a little premature, and a rare outing of mine in which I was Black against my own pet variation continued 8...e5 9 d5 ♘a5 10 e4 b6 11 ♗a3 ♗a6 12 ♗f1 ♘d7 (G.Van Laatum-C.Ward Hastings 1996). White has handled this all wrong: he has conceded the c5-square cheaply and struggles to defend his c4-pawn.

8...e5

Personally I see no reason for Black to delay this although, as previously mentioned, 8...♖b8 9 0-0 b6 is the other main plan. As it happens, the actual final game that I needed

to win to secure my first GM norm (i.e. in that same Swiss tournament) reached this exact position. Play continued 10 ♘d2 ♘a5 11 ♘b3 ♗a6 12 ♘xa5 bxa5 13 ♗c6 ♘d7 14 ♗b5 ♗b7 15 c5 dxc5 16 ♗a3 f5 17 f3 ♖f7 18 dxc5 ♘e5 19 ♕d4 ♕f6 20 f4 ♘c6 21 ♕xf6 gxf6 22 ♗c4 ♖e8 23 ♖ab1 ♗a8 24 ♖fd1 ♔g7 25 ♔f2 ♖fe7 26 e3 ♔g6 27 ♖d2 ♔g7 28 h3 ♔g6 29 ♖bd1 ♔g7 30 ♗e2 ♔g6 31 ♗f3 ♖b8 32 ♗e2 ♖be8 33 ♖g1 h5 34 ♖dd1 e5 35 ♗d3 ♖d8 36 g4 e4 37 gxh5+ ♔xh5 38 ♗e2+ ♔h6 39 ♖xd8 ♘xd8 40 ♖d1 ♘c6 41 ♗b2 ♖e8 42 c4 ♘b4 43 ♗xf6 ♘d3+ 44 ♔g3 ♔g6 45 ♗d4 when, after plenty of cagey play, I had bagged an extra pawn which in a nervy ending eventually proved enough in C.Ward-J.Ambroz, Bern 1993. I do believe that White has an edge in such lines.

9 ♘d2

Part of White's plan, but in any case something was necessary to avoid the ...e5-e4 fork.

9...♘d7

The 9...♕e7 10 0-0 ♖e8 11 e4 b6 12 ♗a3 ♗a6 13 f4 ♕d7 14 fxe5 dxe5 15 d5 ♘a5 16 ♗b4 ♘b7 17 ♖xf6 gxf6 18 ♕f1 c5 19 ♗h3 ♕e7 20 ♗a3 ♘d6 of G.Van Laatum-V.Chuchelov, Belgian League 1997 is interesting, but White didn't get enough for the exchange. Instead of effectively wasting time with the bishop, 12 f4! would have been more to the point.

10 0-0 f5 11 c5

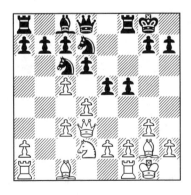

Adding extra tension to the centre and giving the white queen somewhere to flee to.

11...e4 12 ♕c4+ ♔h8 13 ♘b3 ♘f6 14 cxd6 cxd6 15 f3

White is naturally interested in opening up the position and, in particular, obtaining some air for his light-squared bishop.

15...♕e7 16 ♗g5

Placing further pressure on e4.

16...♗e6 17 ♕a4 ♖ae8 18 fxe4 fxe4 19 ♘a5

This game was played in my pre Grandmaster days and I was honoured to be playing such an illustrious opponent who was not only just a famous super-GM, but also a leading exponent of the 4 g3 Nimzo himself. I suspect that White should be a little better here, although perhaps the text is a little simplistic. Both 19 ♖ab1 and 19 ♕b5!? arguably keep Black under more pressure.

19...♘xa5 20 ♕xa5 ♗c4 21 ♖ae1 b6 22 ♕a4 d5

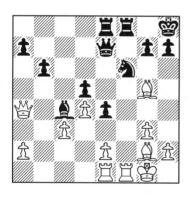

Black secures his bishop on c4, which attacks e2. However, whilst one of White's rooks is tied down to the defence of the e2-pawn, the other is experiencing some excitement along the f-file.

23 ♗h3 ♖f7 24 ♖f5 ♖ef8 25 ♖e5 ♕b7 26 ♕a3

Threatening ♗e6.

26...♕a6 27 ♕xa6 ♗xa6 28 ♗xf6 gxf6 29 ♖xd5 ½-½

Here I probably showed my opponent too

much respect. In view of 29...♗c4 30 ♖d7!, White should really play on.

Game 37
G.Fish-A.Lauber
Germany 2001

1 d4 ♘f6 2 c4 e6 3 ♘c3 ♗b4 4 g3 0-0 5 ♗g2 ♗xc3+ 6 bxc3 d6 7 ♘f3 ♘c6 8 0-0

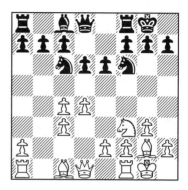

Taking stock of the diagrammed position, the white bishop can be very influential on g2 but the downside of the fianchetto is that the c4-pawn is more vulnerable. Black is about to put another pawn onto an opposite colour from his remaining bishop, but a blocked position could favour either side. The advantage of having a pawn on g3 is that the g-pawn supports an f2-f4 push. Remember, in the majority of occasions White will want to meet ...exf4 with gxf4 as this keeps control of the e5-square.

8...e5

The most obvious move, although others have also appeared in practice:

a) 8...♖e8 9 ♖b1 ♖b8 10 ♗g5 b6?! (White's interesting idea was to meet 10...h6 with 11 ♗xf6 ♕xf6 12 ♘d2 when after the knight-protecting 12...♗d7, White would have time to flick in 13 f4, inhibiting ...e5; nevertheless, the doubled f-pawns that Black soon gets are definitely undesirable) 11 ♘d2 ♘a5 12 ♘e4! ♗b7 13 ♘xf6+ gxf6 14 ♗h4 ♗xg2 15 ♔xg2 d5 16 e4 dxe4 17 ♕g4+ ♔h8

18 ♕f4 ♔g7 19 ♖b5! c5 20 dxc5 h5 21 cxb6 e5 22 ♕xe4 axb6 23 ♕f3 ♘xc4 24 ♖d5 ♕e7 25 ♕xh5 ♘e6 26 ♖fd1 ♖a8 27 ♗xf6+! ♕xf6 (or 27...♔xf6 28 ♕h6+ ♔e7 29 ♖d7+ ♕xd7 30 ♕h4+ ♔e6 31 ♕xc4+ ♔e7 32 ♕h4+ ♔e6 33 ♕g4+ f5 34 ♕g6+ ♔e7 35 ♕g7+) 28 ♕g4+ ♔f8 29 ♕xc4 ♖ac8 30 ♕b4+ ♔g7 31 ♖d6 ♕f5 32 ♖xb6 ♖h8 33 h4 e4 34 ♕d4+ ♔g8 35 ♖f6 ♕g4 36 ♖f4 1-0 A.Moiseenko-S.Halkias, Mureck 1998.

b) 8...♘a5 9 c5 d5 10 ♘d2 ♗d7 11 f3 ♗b5 12 ♖e1 b6 13 cxb6 axb6 14 e4 ♖e8 15 e5 ♘d7 16 f4, when Black had the better pawn structure but White had a kingside initiative in A.Bagonyai-R.Brajovic, Bucharest 1998. Approximately equal chances then, although White could probably improve with 10 ♘e5!?, and perhaps 9 ♕d3 is more accurate too.

c) 8...♕e7 9 c5 dxc5 10 ♗a3 ♘d7 11 ♘d2 ♖d8 12 ♘e4 ♘b6 13 ♗xc5 ♕e8 14 ♕c2 with a comfortable advantage for White, T.Reich-B.Stark, Augsburg 2001.

d) Finally, upon 8...♖b8 White should choose between 9 ♕c2, 9 ♕d3!? (for example, 9...b6 10 ♘d2 ♗b7 11 ♘b3 ♖e8 12 e4 e5 13 d5!? ♘e7 14 f4 ♘g6 15 f5 as seen in B.Gulko-A.Sokolov, USSR 1985) or 9 c5!?, which leaves White spatially well off in the case of both 9...d5 10 ♘e5!? ♘xe5 11 dxe5 ♘d7 12 ♕d4 and 9...dxc5 10 ♗a3 b6 11 dxc5 b5 12 ♘d4.

9 c5!?

Increasing the tension in the centre seems to me to be the most promising of White's options, but again it is useful to take a look other practical alternatives:

a) 9 ♖e1 ♖e8 10 e4 exd4 11 ♘xd4?! (the pawn sacrifice 11 cxd4!? ♘xe4 12 ♗b2 is more in the spirit of things and, looking back at this game, I'm sure White wishes he'd tried it!) 11...♘a5 (again Black is not interested in ironing out White's pawns and instead directs his attention towards the most advanced of the white c-file isolanis) 12 ♕a4 b6! (as well as protecting the knight, this puts paid to any

ideas White may have had of eliminating a weakness through c4-c5; Black now appears vulnerable along the g2-a8 diagonal but he has that situation well under control) 13 e5 ♗d7 14 ♕d1

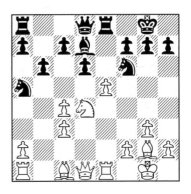

14...dxe5! (Black sacrifices the exchange with the expectation being that White will suffer on the light squares around his monarch in the absence of the fianchettoed bishop) 15 ♗xa8 ♕xa8 16 ♘c2 ♘xc4 17 ♗g5 ♘d5 18 ♘b4 ♗e6 19 ♕f3 h6 20 ♗c1 a5 21 ♘c2 f5 22 ♕d3 ♕c6 23 f4 e4 24 ♕d4 ♖d8 25 g4 ♖d6! 26 ♕f2 ♘xc3 27 ♗e3 ♕d7 28 ♗d4 ♘b5 29 ♗e5 ♘xe5 30 fxe5 ♖d2 31 ♖e2 ♖xe2 32 ♕xe2 ♘d4 33 ♕f2 ♘xc2 0-1 I.Sokolov-B.Kurajica, Sarajevo 1987.

b) 9 ♕c2 ♖e8 10 dxe5 (the 10 ♖d1?! e4 11 ♘g5 ♗f5 12 ♕a4 ♕c8 13 d5 ♘e5 14 c5 ♘ed7 15 c6 bxc6 16 dxc6 ♘b6 17 ♕b3 d5 18 a4 h6 19 a5 ♘c4 20 h4 ♖b8 21 ♕a2 ♖b5 22 ♖xd5 ♖xd5 0-1 of A.Botsari-P.Kiriakov, Halkida 1996 is exactly the sort of reason why as White I was always reluctant to allow a black pawn to e4) 10...dxe5 11 ♗g5 h6 12 ♖fd1 ♕e7 13 ♗xf6 ♕xf6 14 ♘d2 ♕e7?! (the queen was better off where it was on f6 supporting the steed on c6; I don't believe that Black should be worse after the simple 14...♗f5) 15 ♖ab1 f5?! (aggressive, but as Black's kingside attack plans never really bear fruit, this only serves to restrict the scope of Black's bishop) 16 ♗d5+ ♔h8 17 ♗xc6! bxc6 18 ♕a4 e4 19 ♘f1 ♕c5 20 ♖d5! cxd5

21 ♕xe8+ ♔h7 22 ♘e3 dxc4 23 ♖b5 ♕d6 24 ♖xf5 ♗xf5 25 ♕xa8 ♗g6 26 ♕d5. The greedy 26 ♕xa7 should also win but the main point has been made. The white knight was the boss and White went on to win in A.Moiseenko-T.Taenaev, Krynica 1997. This is an instructive game that demonstrates why White can certainly consider conceding his fianchettoed bishop.

c) 9 ♘e1 ♕e7 10 ♘c2 ♘a5 11 ♘e3 (a good square for the knight, although it has been time consuming to get it here and it is also somewhat in the way!) 11...c5 12 ♕a4 ♕c7 13 dxe5 dxe5 14 ♘d5 ♘xd5 15 cxd5 ♗d7 ½-½ I.Miladinovic-K.Sakaev, Tivat 1995 (although clearly there is play left in the position!).

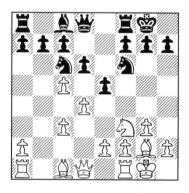

9...e4 10 ♘d2 ♖e8

10...d5 11 c4 ♖e8 (it's also not clear why Black can't just guzzle that d4-pawn now) 12 ♗b2 ♗e6 was a bit murky in L.Valdes-A.Rodriguez Cespedes, Cuban Championship 1995, although White should also consider 11 f3!? and 11 ♖b1!?. Nevertheless, our main game casts a cloud over 10...♖e8, and possibly 10...♗f5 is more accurate as well.

11 d5!

Ensuring that things get opened up.

11...♘xd5

The point was of course that 11...♘e5 allows the simple 12 ♘xe4 whilst 11...♘a5 leaves the knight offside after 12 ♕a4. Indeed 12...b6 13 ♘xe4 ♘xd5 leaves White

with some very attractive options, including 14 ♘xd6 and 14 ♗g5.

12 ♘xe4 dxc5

The only other way to solve the d-file problems was through the tricky 12...♗f5 13 ♕xd5 ♖e5. However, after 14 ♕b3 ♗xe4 15 ♗xe4 ♖xe4 16 ♕xb7 ♕e8 17 cxd6 cxd6 18 ♗e3 it's doubtful that Black has quite enough for the pawn.

13 ♗g5!

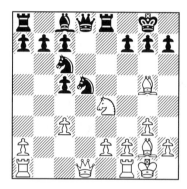

Really throwing the cat among the pigeons!

13...♘xc3

13...f6 would have walked into the standard tactic 14 ♕xd5+! ♕xd5 15 ♘xf6+.

14 ♕e1

This was always going to be hard to resist, although 14 ♗xd8 ♘xd1 15 ♗xc7 ♘b2 16 ♘xc5 ♖xe2 17 ♖fe1 should also leave White with a nice initiative. Note here the paralysing effect that White's light-squared bishop can have on Black's queenside.

14...f6 15 ♗xf6! gxf6 16 ♕xc3 ♘d4 17 ♕xc5 ♖e5

This appears to lose in a fairly straightforward manner, but nothing seems to be adequate. Upon 17...♘xe2+ 18 ♔h1 a big threat is ♕h5, hitting the black knight and threatening ♘xf6+. That aside, the steed could get trapped behind enemy lines, with 18...f5 19 ♖ad1 ♕e7 20 ♕xe7 ♖xe7 21 ♘f6+ ♔g7 22 ♘d5 ♖d7 23 ♖fe1 being one possible continuation.

18 ♘xf6+! ♕xf6 19 ♕xd4 ♗e6 20 f4
♖f5 21 ♕xf6 ♖xf6 22 ♗xb7

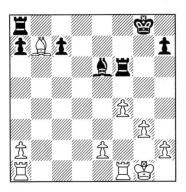

White is now two pawns up with an exceptionally attractive pawn majority on the kingside.

22...♖b8 23 ♖ab1 ♔g7 24 a3 ♗g4 25 ♖fc1 c6 26 ♗a6 1-0

Game 38
C.Ward-J.Timman
European Club Ch., Breda 1998

---

1 d4 ♘f6 2 c4 e6 3 ♘c3 ♗b4 4 g3 d5 5 ♗g2 0-0

And just as a final reminder, 5...dxc4?? is not too bright here in view of 6 ♕a4+!.

6 ♘f3

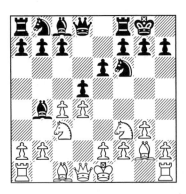

This game and the following one delve into the intricacies of this Catalan-style pawn sacrifice, whilst the final outing in this chapter studies the more cautious approach (specifically 6 cxd5 and 6 ♕b3).

6...dxc4

Overlapping with my book on the *Nimzo-Indian Kasparov Variation*, I have never been impressed with Black's position after 6...c5 (equally as often reached via 4 ♘f3 c5 5 g3 0-0 6 ♗g2 d5). I've just never found it very ambitious and my own results against it are excellent. For example, 7 cxd5 ♘xd5 8 ♗d2 ♘c6 (or 8...cxd4 9 ♘xd5 ♗xd2+ 10 ♕xd2 ♕xd5 11 ♕xd4 ♕a5+ 12 ♕d2 ♕b6 13 ♘e5 ♖d8 14 ♘c4 ♕c7 15 ♕a5 b6 16 ♕e5 ♕xc4 17 ♗xa8 ♗a6 18 ♗f3 ♘c6 19 ♗xc6 ♕xc6 20 0-0 f6 21 ♕e3 ♖d5 22 ♖fd1 with basically just an extra exchange for White, C.Ward-A.Salem, Lloyds Bank Masters, London 1993) 9 ♘xd5 ♕xd5 (or 9...♗xd2+ 10 ♘xd2 exd5 11 dxc5 ♖e8 12 0-0 ♕e7 where I suspect 13 e3 or 13 ♗xd5 may be the most precise but after 13 ♘b3 ♕xe2 14 ♕xe2 ♖xe2 15 ♖fe1 ♖xe1+ 16 ♖xe1 ♗e6 17 f4 g6 18 ♖d1 ♖d8 19 ♔f2 ♔g7 20 ♔e3 I went on to convert a comfortable ending in C.Ward-A.Lavie, Lloyds Bank Masters, London 1992) 10 ♗xb4 ♘xb4 11 0-0 ♖d8 (or 11...cxd4 12 ♘xd4 ♕d7 13 ♘b3 ♖b8 14 a3 ♘a6 15 ♘a5 ♕c7 16 b4 ♖d8 17 ♕b3 ♗d7 18 ♖ac1 ♕b6 19 ♖fd1 ♗b5 20 ♖xd8+ ♕xd8 21 ♗xb7 ♗xe2 22 ♕e3 ♗b5 23 ♗xa6 ♗xa6 24 ♘c6 1-0 C.Ward-P.Jaton, Mont St Michel 1994) 12 dxc5 ♗d7 13 a3 ♕xd1 14 ♖fxd1 ♘d5 15 ♘e5 ♗b5 16 ♗xd5 exd5 17 ♖d2 f6 18 ♘f3 a5 19 ♘d4 ♗d7 20 b3 g5 21 ♖c1 with the extra pawn eventually telling in C.Ward-P.Byway, British Championship, Swansea 1995.

You can see why I consider it a rather passive line for Black, and typical characteristics are the occasional black isolated d-pawn and nearly always the struggle to develop the queenside.

7 0-0

Taking the c-pawn on offer is a much more challenging route to take and, as stated previously, now the position resembles the

Catalan variation of the Queen's Gambit Declined but with key differences:

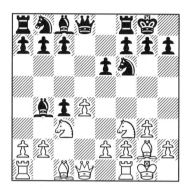

1) White's queen's knight has been committed to c3. This steed will not be able to regain the lost c-pawn and it also obstructs what is otherwise a typical ♕c2xc4 manoeuvre.

2) Black's bishop is on b4 rather than e7. It may have to retreat if it wants to be preserved or be used to escape any pin on the f6-knight. On the other hand, on b4 it does have an option to trade on c3 and it obstructs the ♕a4xc4 idea.

7...♘c6

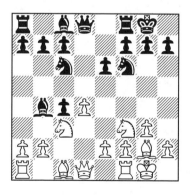

Just as with 6...c5, I'm also not a fan of 7...c5 as I believe that White can secure a comfortable middlegame or endgame advantage via 8 dxc5!; for example, 8...♕xd1 (or 8...♘c6 9 ♘d2 ♗xc5 10 ♘xc4 ♕e7 11 ♗g5 h6 12 ♗xf6 ♕xf6 13 ♘e4 ♕e7 14 ♘xc5

♕xc5 15 ♖c1, as in I.Miladinovic-R.Ferretti, Rome 2004) 9 ♖xd1 ♗xc5 10 ♘e5 ♘c6 11 ♘xc4 h6 12 ♗e3 ♗xe3 13 ♘xe3 e5 14 ♗xc6 bxc6 15 ♖d6 (C.Ward-T.Bjornsson, Reykjavik 1998). White's light-squared bishop always exerts that awkward pressure against Black's queenside and the option is often there for a bishop takes knight on c6 to split the black pawns.

A rare continuation, but incorporating a standard Catalan theme, is 7...♗d7 8 ♘e5 ♗c6. The position after 9 e4 ♗xc3 10 ♘xc6 ♘xc6 11 bxc3 is double-edged: White has the bishop pair but has yet to regain that pawn. Black should choose between 11...♖b8 to prepare ...b7-b5 and 11...e5 to challenge White's domination in the centre.

8 ♖e1

White's 8 ♖e1 clearly gets the e-pawn under starter's orders but it is often not clear whether White would rather have his rook on e1 or d1. Either way, vacating of the f1-square for the bishop is often a useful improvement to the white position.

8 e3 is a slower approach, after which 8...♘d5 9 ♕c2 ♗e7 10 ♖d1 can nevertheless reach some fairly unclear positions; for instance, 10...♘db4 (or 10...♖b8 11 e4 ♘cb4 12 ♕b1 ♘xc3 13 bxc3 ♘d3) 11 ♕e2 ♘d3 12 ♘d2 e5 13 ♘xc4 ♘xc1 14 ♖axc1 exd4 15 ♗xc6 bxc6 16 ♖xd4 ♕e8, P.Uhoda-A.Yusupov, Netherlands 1998. This certainly isn't forced though, and Black players may wish to study the 8...♖b8 9 ♕c2 b5 10 a4 a6 11 axb5 axb5 12 ♘g5 ♘e7 13 ♘ce4 ♘xe4 14 ♘xe4 ♗b7 15 b3 f5 16 bxc4 ♗xe4 17 ♗xe4 fxe4 18 c5 ♕d5 19 ♕b1 ♗c3 20 ♖a7 ♘c6 21 ♖xc7 ♗a5 0-1 of N.Gaprindashvili-J.Ehlvest, Tallinn 1998. Often Black has that choice of ...♖b8 or ...♘d5.

The other main move is 8 ♗g5 and that appears in the next game.

8...♘d5

Justifying my previous remark on the subject, here Black should make a decision over the text or 8...♖b8

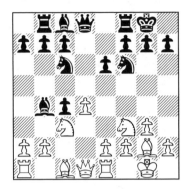

in which case it is White who has a choice:

a) 9 a3 when:

a1) 9...♗xc3 10 bxc3 ♘a5 11 ♖b1 b6 12 e4 does leave White with good compensation for the pawn as a black knight on b3 won't be a serious problem. Now 12...h6 13 ♘e5 ♗d7 14 g4!? ♗h7 15 h4 ♗e8 16 h5 b5 17 a4 ♘c6 18 ♗a3 b4 19 ♘xc6 ♗xc6 20 ♗xb4 could hardly have gone much better for in me in C.Ward-Erwando, Beijing 1993/94, whilst 12...♗b7 13 ♗g5 h6 14 ♗h4! ♕e8 (14...g5 15 ♘xg5! hxg5 16 ♗xg5 with e4-e5 up next is the big idea) 15 ♗xf6 gxf6 16 ♘d2 ♔h7 17 ♗f1 b5 18 ♕f3 f5 19 ♕f4 was definitely good value in O.Romanishin-V.Savon, Yerevan 1976.

a2) 9...♗d6 10 ♕a4 e5 11 d5 ♘d4 12 ♘xd4 exd4 13 ♕xa7 dxc3 14 ♕xb8 ♗e5 15 bxc3 ♗xc3 16 ♗f4 ♘xd5 17 ♖ad1 ♗xe1 18 ♗xd5 ♗e6 19 ♕xb7 ♗a5 20 ♕b5 with a clear advantage to White, S.Kindermann-M.Suba, Dortmund 1981 is a game I once had in my notes.

a3) 9...♗a5!? is rare but most definitely a candidate. Following 10 e4 h6 11 e5 ♘d5 12 ♗d2 ♘de7 13 ♘e4 ♗b6, up against a grandmaster opponent, a pupil of mine went for broke with 14 ♗xh6?! but alas 14...gxh6 15 ♘f6+ ♔g7 16 ♘h5+ ♔h8 17 ♕c1 ♘g8 18 ♖e4 ♘xd4 19 ♘xd4 f5 20 ♖h4 ♗xd4 21 ♘f6 ♖xf6 22 exf6 ♕xf6 saw his attack fizzle out in R.Cole-V.Kupreichik, Aarhus 1997. A calmer move than the bishop sacrifice would

obviously have been better. It's an imbalanced position and after the possible 13 ♕a4 ♗b6 14 ♖ad1 ♘a5 I'd have to say that the phrase 'dynamic equilibrium' springs to mind!;

a4) 9...♗e7 is sensible and not unlikely to transpose to the variation 'b3' below.

b) 9 e4

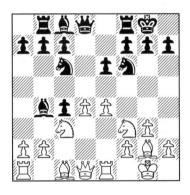

and now:

b1) 9...♖e8 10 ♗f4 ♘xd4!? 11 ♕xd4 ♕xd4 12 ♘xd4 e5 13 ♗e3 exd4 14 ♗xd4 c5 15 ♗e3 ♗e6 16 ♖ed1 ♗xc3 17 bxc3 b6 18 ♗f4 ♖bd8 19 ♗d6 ♗g4! saw Black ultimately go on to utilise her significant queenside majority in T.Vasilevich-C.Peptan, Istanbul 2003, but 10 e5!? must be more to the point.

b2) 9...b5!? 10 e5 (the 10 ♗f4 ♗b7 11 h3 ♘e7 12 ♘e5 ♘d7 13 g4 ♘xe5 14 dxe5 a6 15 ♗e3 ♘c6 16 f4 ♕e7 17 ♕e2 ♗c5 18 ♕f2 ♗xe3 19 ♕xe3 ♖fd8 20 ♖ad1 ♘b4 21 ♕e2 ♘d3 22 ♖f1 ♕b4 0-1 of G.Van Laatum-P.Kiriakov, Hastings 1998/99 never really saw White get going on the kingside) 10...♘d5 11 ♘g5 ♗e7 is the sort of position I always had my doubts about. White always has vague attacking chances but Black usually has that rock of a knight on d5 and menacing queenside pawns. I can recall feeling grateful that after 12 h4 ♘cb4 13 ♗e4 f5 14 exf6 my opponent accepted a draw in C.Ward-R.Fyllingen, Gausdal 1993, and this is the sort of variation that put me off 4 g3.

b3) 9...h6 10 a3 ♗e7 11 h3 ♘a5 12 ♗e3 ♘b3 13 ♖b1 c5?! (it's natural for Black to want to undouble the extra c-pawn, but this is a little premature) 14 dxc5 ♘xc5 15 ♘e5! ♗d7 16 ♘xc4 ♗c6 17 ♕c2 b5 18 ♖bd1 with a clear advantage to White in T.Vasilevich-A.Maric, Ulcinj 1997.

Backtracking a move, 8...♖e8 has apparently only ever been played once. Despite an eventual white win, 9 e4 e5 10 d5 ♘a5 11 ♕a4 ♗xc3 12 bxc3 b6 13 ♘d2 ♕d7 14 ♕c2 c6 15 ♗a3 ♗b7 looked more than fine for Black in C.Ward-J.Richardson, Isle of Man 1996. Looking at it now, perhaps White should switch plans back to 9 a3 or 9 ♗g5 instead, the question then being which of ♖e1 or ...♖e8 is more useful.

9 ♕c2 ♗e7

Black has no intention of playing ...♗xc3 now. Not only would that concede the valuable dark-squared bishop but it would donate to White control of the b4-square. In contrast, this retreat makes that square available to a black knight.

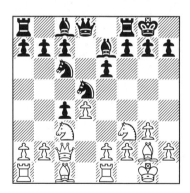

10 ♘e4

From White's point of view, the decision to play this type of position (i.e. a pawn for some play) is down to matter of taste. I just eventually decided that it wasn't very tasty! Actually, although I employed this move against three grandmaster opponents, perhaps it is not best. Let's take a look at some other tries:

a) 10 e3? ♘cb4! 11 ♕e2 ♘d3 12 ♖f1 c5 13 dxc5 ♘xc3 14 bxc3 ♕c7 15 ♘d2 ♕xc5 and there could be no disputing that Black was clearly better in N.Giffard-J.Speelman, Berlin 1980.

b) 10 a3 and now:

b1) 10...♘a5 11 e4 (11 ♗d2 ♘b3 12 ♖ad1 ♖b8 13 e4 ♘xd2 14 ♖xd2 ♘xc3 15 ♕xc3 b5 16 ♕e3 ♖b6 17 ♖c1 ♗b7 18 h4 ♖d6 19 ♖cd1 ♕a8 20 d5 exd5 21 exd5 ♖e8 22 ♘e5 ♗f6 23 f4 a6 was no better for White in the more recent encounter T.Vasilevich-H.Olsen, Copenhagen 2004; in my opinion Black is simply a pawn up!) 11...♘xc3 12 bxc3 ♘b3 13 ♖b1 b5 14 ♗f4 ♗b7 15 a4 a6 16 h4 h6 17 ♖bd1 ♗d6 18 ♘e5 ♕e7 19 ♕e2 ♔h7 20 ♕g4 ♖ad8 21 h5 ♔h8. Now Black is ready to play ...c7-c5, so White tried 22 ♘g6+ fxg6 23 e5 ♗xe5 24 ♖xe5 ♗g2 25 ♔xg2 g5 26 ♖xe6 ♕f7 27 ♗e3 ♘c5 28 dxc5 ♖xd1 29 ♕e4 ♕xh5 (0-1 J.Vilela-A.Yusupov, Cienfuegos 1979) and evidently it failed. I reiterate that this sort of thing is typical for this variation. Black will eventually realise his extra pawn and there often comes a point where White has to go for it!

b2) Similar, and also worth comparing with 'c', is the 10...♘b6 11 ♖d1 ♘a5 12 ♖b1 ♗d7 13 ♘e5 ♖e8 14 ♗e4 f5 15 ♗f3 ♕c8 16 e4 c5 17 ♗e3 cxd4 18 ♗xd4 ♗c5 19 exf5 ♗xd4 20 ♖xd4 ♗xf5 21 ♖e1 ♘c6 22 ♘xc6 ♗xc6 23 ♗g4 ♖f6 24 ♘e4 ♗xe4 25 ♕xe4 ♕c5 26 ♗xe6+ ♔h8 27 ♕e5 ♕c6 28 ♖f4 ♖xf4 29 ♕xf4 c3 30 bxc3 ½-½ of E.Van Beers-P.Wells, Antwerp 1997. With all things considered this was a fair result – White, who could also have considered 14 d5!?, gets some play for the pawn.

c) 10 h4 h6 11 a3 (this is of course similar to 10 a3) 11...♘b6 12 ♗e3 ♗d7 13 ♖ad1 ♗e8 14 d5! exd5 15 ♗xb6 axb6 16 ♘xd5 ♗d7 17 ♕xc4 ♖e8 18 ♕c3 and White definitely obtained a reasonable advantage in R.Vera-A.Franco Alonso, Linares 2002. Perhaps there is something to be said for this controlled approach, although Black's play looks a little passive and one would have thought that a ...♘a5-b3 manoeuvre should feature somewhere.

10...♘db4 11 ♕c3

The problem with 11 ♕xc4?! now is 11...♕d5! because after 12 ♕xd5 exd5 13 ♘c3 Black has 13...♘c2.

11...b5 12 a3 ♘d5 13 ♕c2

All this to-ing and fro-ing by White was designed to sidestep ...♘xc3. Not that I think it was worth it!

13...♗d7

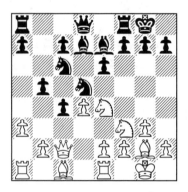

Sooner or later Black needs to make a decision on this bishop and this looks just as good as 13...♗b7. Amazingly, two of the fives times that the position after 13 ♕c2 has ever been reached occurred within two days! The other was with 13...♗b7 and continued 14 ♗d2 ♖b8 15 ♖ad1 h6 16 ♗c1 ♘a5 17 ♘e5 ♕e8 18 ♘c5 ♗xc5 19 dxc5 ♘c6 20 ♘xc6 ♕xc6 21 e4 ♘f6 22 ♗e3 ♘g4 23 ♗d4 e5 24 ♗c3 ♖fc8? 25 ♖d5 ♕g6 26 ♖d2 ♗c6 27 f3 ♘f6 28 ♗h3 ♕h5 29 ♔g2 ♖d8 30 ♖ed1 ♖xd2+ 31 ♖xd2 ♕g5 32 ♕d1 ♘h5 33 ♔f2 ♕e7 34 ♗b4 ♘f6 35 ♔e2 ♖a8 36 ♕g1 a5 37 ♗c3 ♗d7 38 ♗xd7 ♘xd7 39 ♖d5 f6 40 c6 ♘b8 41 ♖xb5 ♘xc6 42 ♕c5 ♕e6 43 ♕d5 ♘d4+ 44 ♔e3 ♕xd5 45 ♖xd5 ♘b3 46 f4 exf4+ 47 gxf4 ♖e8 48 e5 fxe5 49 fxe5 ♔f7 50 ♖d7+ ♖e7 51 e6+ ♔xe6 52 ♖xe7+ ♔xe7 53 ♗xg7. To be brutally honest, I think that C.Ward-V.Bogdanovski, European Club Championship, Breda 1998 was a pretty poor

game. I actually went on to win this endgame but my general feeling is that, although I was better at some stage of the middlegame, probably Black's position was superior for the majority of the early part. Basically, it's just a mess; if I'd had more than an evening's preparation then I most certainly wouldn't have repeated this variation as I do in the main game.

Incidentally, previously the 13...h6 14 ♗d2 ♗d7 15 ♖ad1 ♖b8 16 ♗c1 b4 17 ♘c5 ♘xd4 18 ♘xd4 ♗xc5 19 ♕xc4 ♕e7 20 ♗xd5 exd5 21 ♕xd5 ♖fd8 22 ♕c4 ♗xd4 23 ♖xd4 ♗e6 ½-½ of C.Ward-A.Yusupov, European Club Championship, Eupen 1994 hadn't seen me prove an edge for White either, although my illustrious opponent was never going to be a pushover!

14 ♘eg5 ♘f6 15 h4

And so here we go with more speculative kingside play. To me it always seemed to be the same story!

15...h6 16 ♘h3 ♗d6 17 ♗f4 ♘d5

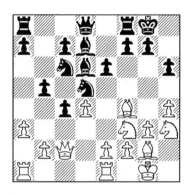

More sensible play. Fair swaps are just going to promote the importance of Black's extra pawn, and rather than retreat I engaged in some dubious tactics!

18 ♗xh6?! gxh6 19 e4 e5

Not surprisingly Fritz isn't impressed by my sacrifice and would quite happily enter 19...♘b6 20 e5. My opponent prefers the more human neutralising response.

20 dxe5 ♘xe5 21 ♘xe5 ♗xe5 22 exd5

♕f6

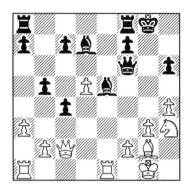

Black has the bishop pair and White has a ridiculously placed knight! Rather than grimly defend b2, I again opted to concede material.

23 ♖xe5 ♕xe5 24 ♘f4 ♖fe8 25 ♕d2 ♖ab8 26 ♗f3 ♖b6!

Unfortunately Black finds a good way of making his exchange count.

27 ♖c1 ♖f6 28 ♔g2 ♖xf4

Yes, giving it back, this time wrecking my pawn structure.

29 ♕xf4 ♕xf4 30 gxf4 ♗f5

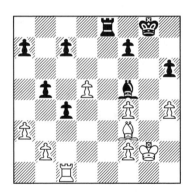

Black dominates the open e-file and it's only a matter of time before that queenside majority will have a big impact.

31 a4 a6 32 axb5 axb5 33 ♖a1

Could anyone blame me for wanting some activity?

33...b4 34 ♖a7 c3 35 bxc3 bxc3 36 ♖xc7 c2

Alas, ...♖c8 is next and my final attempt is a feeble one!

37 ♗g4 ♗xg4 0-1

Game 39
J.Gonzalez Garcia-S.Tiviakov
Mallorca Olympiad 2004

1 d4 ♘f6 2 c4 e6 3 ♘c3 ♗b4 4 g3 0-0 5 ♗g2 d5 6 ♘f3 dxc4 7 0-0 ♘c6 8 ♗g5

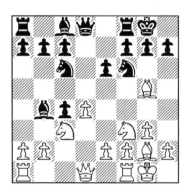

8...h6

This is the most solid response but, going on the accuracy of this game, Black should probably opt for something else if he is eager to win. One alternative is to ignore this pin and continue with 8...♖b8, preparing ...b7-b5. In that instance White has some interesting possibilities:

a) 9 ♖c1 b5 10 b3!? h6 (upon 10...cxb3 both 11 ♕xb3 and 11 ♘e4 leave Black, and particularly his knights, under pressure) 11 ♗xf6 ♕xf6 12 bxc4 bxc4 13 ♘e4 ♕e7 14 ♖xc4 ♘a5 15 ♖c1 ♖d8 16 ♕c2 ♗b7 17 e3 ♗a3 18 ♖b1 ♗d5 19 ♘e5 ♗d6 20 ♕c3 ♗xe5 21 ♕xa5 and White's structural superiority slightly outweighed Black's bishop pair advantage in A.Moiseenko-L.Christiansen, Internet 2004.

b) 9 e3 b5 10 ♘d2 ♗d7 11 ♘ce4 ♗e7 12 ♘xf6+ ♗xf6 13 ♗xf6 ♕xf6 14 b3 e5 15 bxc4 exd4 16 cxb5 ♖xb5 17 ♘b3 ♖b4 18 ♖c1 ♖d8 19 ♕c2 ♖b6 ½-½ F.Levin-M.Wahls, Bundesliga; White's active play never looked like amounting to more than a draw.

c) 9 a3 ♗xc3 (9...♗e7!? makes a lot of sense now too that White has weakened the b3-square) 10 bxc3 h6 11 ♗xf6 ♕xf6 12 ♘d2 e5 13 e3 exd4 14 exd4 b5 15 ♘e4 ♕g6 16 ♘c5 ♘d8 17 ♖e1 ♘e6 18 ♖e5 ♖b6 19 ♘xe6 ♗xe6 20 ♖c5 when White should have just about enough compensation for a draw but actually went on to win in J.Nilssen-D.Palo, Koge 2004.

Another lesser-seen move is 8...♗e7. This unpins the knight and thus avoids White's ♘e4 ideas. Now 9 e3 (the usual purpose of this move is to vacate the e2-square for the queen and to protect the d-pawn to enable the f3-knight to go walkabout) 9...♘d5 10 ♗xe7 ♕xe7 11 ♘d2 ♘b6 12 ♕e2 ♘a5 13 b3 cxb3 14 axb3 ♘c6 15 ♗xc6 bxc6 16 ♖a5 ♕b4 17 ♖c5 e5! was if anything very slightly better for Black in A.Moiseenko-O.Budnikov, Kharkov 1999. Instead 13 ♕h5 f5 is a tough one to call; White has some reasonable pieces and squares but Black continues to hang onto that extra pawn.

9 ♗xf6 ♕xf6 10 ♖c1

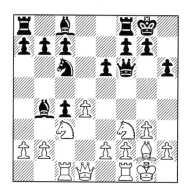

Looking to ultimately regain the c-pawn with the rook.

10...♖d8 11 e3 e5

Black now enters a pretty forcing variation, but I don't believe that 11...♕e7 12 ♕e2 ♘a5 13 ♘e5 ♗d7 constitutes an improvement. White can win back the c4-pawn, al-

though as there doesn't appear to be any need to hurry, 14 ♖fd1 is sensible.

12 ♘xe5 ♘xe5 13 dxe5 ♕e7

13...♖xd1?! 14 exf6 ♖xc1 15 ♖xc1 would leave White with a superior endgame as Black still has difficulty developing his queenside.

14 ♕h5

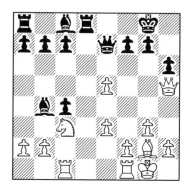

White opts to hang on to his e5-pawn as the alternative 14 ♕e2 ♕xe5 15 ♕xc4 ♗d6 would see Black escaping with two bishops.

14...♗xc3

Now though this bishop had nowhere to run, whilst the white knight threatened to hop into d5.

15 ♖xc3 ♖d2

15...♗e6 16 f4 (I think I prefer the white pawns in the major piece ending arriving from 16 ♗xb7 ♖ab8 17 ♗a6 ♖xb2 18 ♗xc4 ♗xc4 19 ♖xc4 ♖xa2 20 ♖fc1, but it's probably a draw) 16...♖d2 17 ♗e4 (presumably White didn't fancy 17 f5 ♖xg2+!? 18 ♔xg2 ♗d5+ 19 ♔g1 ♕xe5) 17...♖ad8 18 f5 was a riskier road for Black to take in K.Oreopoulos-S.Zagrebelny, Thessaloniki 2004, but that game ended in a draw anyway!

16 ♖b1 ♕b4 17 a3 ♕b5 18 ♖d1 ♕xb2

Or 18...♕xe5 19 ♕f3. Black doesn't want a white queen or rook on his back rank but his bishop is tied to the defence of his b7-pawn.

19 ♖xc4 ♕xe5 20 ♕f3

Of course not 20 ♕xe5?? ♖xd1+ 21 ♗f1

&h3. Both sides have had their little tactical episodes, but a neutraliser has always been on hand.

20...&e6 21 &xd2 &xc4 22 &f1! &xf1 ½-½

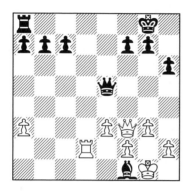

Black offered a draw knowing full well that the 23 ♕xb7 intermezzo would come before the bishop is recaptured.

Game 40
J.Nilssen-N.De Firmian
Politiken Cup, Copenhagen 2003

---

1 d4 ♞f6 2 c4 e6 3 ♞c3 &b4 4 g3 0-0 5 &g2 d5 6 cxd5

This is certainly one way to make sure that Black doesn't snatch the c-pawn (as in our previous two games), and 6 ♕b3 is another. Regarding the early queen sortie though, her majesty does have a tendency to get into hot water. Black has two ways to try to exploit this, with the second obtaining particularly good results:

a) 6...♞c6 7 ♞f3 ♞e4 8 ♕c2 ♞d6 9 cxd5 exd5 10 0-0 &f5 11 ♕b3 &xc3 12 ♕xc3 ♖e8 13 ♖e1 &e4 14 ♖d1 f6 15 &f4 ♞f5 16 ♖ac1 g5 17 &d2 ♞d6 18 &e1 ♕d7 19 &f1 &f5 20 ♕b3 ♞e7 21 &b4 c6 22 ♞e1 a5 23 &c5 b6 24 &a3 ♖ab8 25 ♞g2 &h3 26 ♕f3 ♞e4 27 ♞e3 &e6 28 &g2 ♔g7 29 &xe7 ♖xe7 (O.Romanishin-V.Ivanchuk, Yerevan 1989) was I would say approximately equal throughout, but I guess the feature of

White's superior pawn structure eventually told in an emphatic collapse: 30 ♖c2 h6 31 ♖dc1 ♖c8 32 g4 ♞d6 33 ♕g3 ♔g8 34 h4 &f7 35 ♖c3 ♞e4 36 &xe4 ♖xe4 37 f3 ♖e6 38 ♞f5 ♖xe2 39 ♞xh6+ ♔g7 40 ♞f5+ ♔g6? 41 hxg5 &e6 42 ♖xc6!! 1-0.

b) 6...c5!?

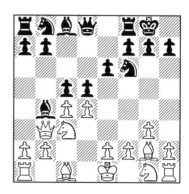

and now:

b1) 7 a3 &a5! 8 ♞f3? cxd4 9 ♞xd4 e5! 10 ♞c2 d4 and yes, that was a free piece in G.Fish-A.Morozevich, Alushta 1993. It's amazing that such an early natural move (8 ♞f3?) can be such a mistake, but that's just the way it is! With the white queen out on b3, d4 is simply too vulnerable.

b2) 7 dxc5 ♞c6 8 &g5 h6 9 cxd5 exd5 10 &xf6 ♕xf6 11 &xd5 ♞d4 12 ♕d1 when 12...♖d8!? looks attractive but 12...♞b5 13 ♖c1 &xc3+ 14 bxc3 ♞xc3 15 ♕d2 ♞xd5 16 ♕xd5 ♖d8 left Black with excellent compensation for a measly pawn in J.Pisulinski-K.Panczyk, Bydgoszcz 1990.

6...exd5

6...♞xd5 7 &d2 ♞c6 8 ♞xd5 &xd2+ 9 ♕xd2 exd5 has also been seen before, but I prefer the text.

7 ♞f3 c6

This bolstering move is probably inevitable, and certainly 7...&g4 (aggressive but leaving the b7-pawn unprotected) 8 0-0 ♞bd7 9 ♕b3! saw Black suffer without it as he was forced to concede his dark-squared bishop in I.Miladinovic-S.Hondrogiannis,

Thessaloniki 1999.

The pawn on c6 obviously supports d5, but it also covers the b5-square and offers the black queen some options. However, it could be held back for a move or so, with 7...♖e8 certainly not ridiculous either.

8 0-0

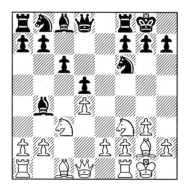

As White against the Queen's Gambit Declined I have always been fond of the 'Exchange variation' (1 d4 d5 2 c4 e6 3 ♘c3 ♘f6 4 cxd5 exd5 5 ♗g5). There is obviously a similarity in the structure here but there also some key differences:

1) Black's dark-squared bishop is on b4 rather than e7. It would probably rather not give itself up for a knight, and thus time is eventually going to have to be expended on a retreat.

2) The usual pin ♗g5 doesn't fit in well with a kingside fianchetto as after ...h7-h6 the bishop only gets trapped if it retreats to h4.

3) White's light-squared bishop has essentially been fianchettoed against a wall of black pawns. On d3 this bishop may restrict the activity of its opposite number, but as it stands here the early cxd5, ...exd5 has merely provided Black's light-squared bishop with some options.

4) Whilst a 'minority attack' is not out of the question for White, the location of his light-squared bishop means that the c4-square is potentially much weaker.

8...♘bd7

The text prevents 9 ♘e5 but nevertheless 8...♖e8 must also be sensible. Play could easily turn out as in our main game, whereas the 8...♗d6 9 ♘e1 ♖e8 10 f3 ♘bd7 11 ♘d3 ♗c7 12 ♖b1 a6 13 b4 ♘f8 14 ♘f2 h5 15 ♖b2 h4 of R.Albrecht-V.Eingorn, Bad Wiessee 2003 was certainly something a little different. Lunging with the h-pawn is certainly an idea worthy of Black's consideration, whilst in general White should strive to get in b2-b4-b5 or e2-e4.

9 ♘e1

As Black's previous move took away an attractive post for this knight, White dabbles in a spot of repositioning. Instead 9 a3 ♗d6 10 b4 a6 11 ♕b3 ♕e7 12 ♖e1 ♘e4 13 ♘xe4 ♕xe4 14 ♗b2 ♕g4 15 e4 dxe4 16 ♘e5 ♘xe5 17 dxe5 ♗e7 18 ♗xe4 ♗e6 19 ♕c2 ♕h5 20 ♗d4 ♖fd8 21 ♗b6 ♖d7 22 ♖ad1 ♖xd1 23 ♕xd1 ♕xd1 24 ♖xd1 g6 25 f4 f6 26 exf6 ♗xf6 27 ♖d2 ♖e8 ended drawn in J.Agirretxe San Sebastian-J.Gomez Esteban, Portugalete 2004.

9...♖e8 10 ♘d3

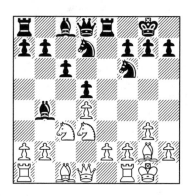

10...♗d6

After 10...♗xc3 11 bxc3 ♘e4 12 ♕c2 ♘b6 13 f3 ♘d6 14 ♘f2 ♗f5 15 e4 ♗g6 16 ♗f4 Black's position was solid in I.Miladinovic-A.Kanengoni, Elista 1998. However, those white bishops always have potential and inroads have already been made in the centre. I think it makes more sense to preserve the bishop and 10...♗f8 would be a another typical grandmasterly retreat.

11 ♕c2 ♘f8

The usual stop off point for the knight in the QGD Exchange variation. From here the knight may emerge on g6 or could have other options from e6. On its new location though, it no longer obstructs the bishop.

12 ♗f4 ♗f5 13 ♗xd6

White gets to trade off his 'bad' bishop, but Black isn't losing any sleep over the fact that he is left with his light-squared bishop here as at the very least it can give itself up for a knight.

13...♕xd6 14 a3 ♘e6 15 e3 ♘g5

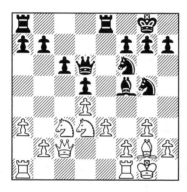

Black has excellent control over the e4-square, and there are some holes in White's kingside that he can try to probe too.

16 ♖ae1 ♗h3 17 f3 ♗xg2 18 ♔xg2 ♘e6

White would dearly love to get in e3-e4 but, as his d-pawn is always likely to hang, that probably won't happen.

19 ♘a4 ♘d7 20 ♖c1 ♖e7 21 ♕b3 ♕c7 22 ♘b4 ♕d6 23 ♘d3 ♕c7 24 ♘b4 ♘b6

Good lad! Black spurns a repetition of moves to go for a win. Unfortunately though, if that is going to happen he really needs to play on the kingside and he seems to have become sidetracked.

25 ♘xb6 ♕xb6

Structurally 25...axb6?? would be better but, in view of 26 ♘xd5!, tactically it's not!

26 ♖c3 ♘c7

If allowed this knight would head for c4 or f5 via b5 and d6.

27 a4 ♖ae8 28 ♘c2 ♘a8 29 ♕xb6 ♘xb6 30 b3 ♘c8 31 ♔f2 ♘d6 32 h4 f6 33 ♘a3 ♔f7 34 b4 a6 35 ♖b1

If White could swap the knights off and get in b4-b5 then he could make something of his structural advantage. However, there are a few technical problems involved in obtaining a successful minority attack.

35...♘f5 36 ♘c2

One being that he needs to defend his e-pawn.

36...♘d6 37 ♘a3 b5!?

Again refusing the repetition.

38 ♘c2

38 ♖xc6 ♖xe3 39 ♖xd6 ♖xa3 would encourage a double rook invasion of the seventh rank, but I'm not that keen on allowing a black knight to set up camp on c4 either.

38...♘c4 39 a5

I think it's fair to say that White's intentions were pretty clear throughout this game. Unfortunately, Black is running out of ways to make progress.

39...h5 40 ♖e1 ♔e6 41 ♘a1 f5 42 ♘b3 ♔f7 43 ♘c5 ♖a8

Now Black has to go on the defensive and so the die is cast.

44 ♘d3 ♔f6 ½-½

Summary

I'm not too impressed with this last game as a winning attempt for White but Games 38-39 certainly question whether or not he gets enough compensation if he leaves his c-pawn to be taken. The only real question is whether Black can hack playing these Queen's Gambit Declined style positions. Indeed, if White plays the Catalan against the QGD (1 d4 d5 2 c4 e6 3 ♘f3 ♘f6 4 g3) then he may have more experience in this type of position. On the other hand, perhaps the Semi-Slav variation 1 d4 d5 2 c4 e6 3 ♘c3 c6 4 ♘f3 dxc4 5 g3 bears just as many similarities as it is definitely a gambit.

What is clear is that against 4 g3, Nimzo-Indian players shouldn't automatically transpose to the Kasparov stuff via 4...c5 5 ♘f3 as he could well do better. The lines without ...c7-c5 and ...d7-d5 seen in Games 36-37 also come with a solid reputation, although my personal opinion is that White holds the initiative there.

1 d4 ♘f6 2 c4 e6 3 ♘c3 ♗b4 4 g3 0-0 5 ♗g2 (D) d5

      5...♗xc3+ 6 bxc3 d6 7 ♘f3 ♘c6 (D)

            8 0-0 – *Game 37*

            8 ♕d3 – *Game 36*

6 ♘f3

      6 cxd5 – *Game 40*

6...dxc4 7 0-0 ♘c6 (D) 8 ♗g5 – *Game 39*

      8 ♖e1 – *Game 38*

      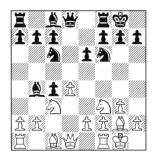

    5 ♗g2   *7...♘c6*   *7...♘c6*

CHAPTER SEVEN

4 ♕b3

1 d4 ♘f6 2 c4 e6 3 ♘c3 ♗b4 4 ♕b3

The truth about this move is that it is the poor relation to the Classical variation, with the one advantage that it does have over 4 ♕c2 being that Black's bishop is under immediate attack. Indeed, should Black respond with 4...♗xc3+?, then after 5 ♕xc3, having saved on a2-a3, White could view the opening as a categorical success. Of course Black shouldn't be so obliging, and the 4...c5 of this chapter's first three games is the most principled response. The reason for this is that White is now weak on d4 and his queen can prove to be vulnerably placed too. Unfortunately, most of this chapter is probably best used to aid sleep, and arguably the most interesting move, 4...a5 (Game 44), is probably just inferior.

Game 41
J.Fries Nielsen-C.Ward
Politiken Cup, Copenhagen 1994

---

1 d4 ♘f6 2 c4 e6 3 ♘c3 ♗b4 4 ♕b3 c5

One drawback of the early white queen move is that the d4-square is weakened. Also, on b3 rather than c2 her majesty gets in the way of a b-pawn advance and is vulnerable to attack from a ...♘a5 thrust as well as a ...♘d4.

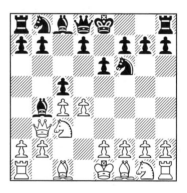

5 dxc5

Relinquishing a centre pawn but creating a half-open d-file.

The advance 5 d5 is asking a bit much as White is in danger of overextending. Whilst Black could consider the immediate 5...b5!?, very convincing was the 5...0-0 6 f3 b5!? 7 cxb5 exd5 8 ♗d2 d4 of S.Bergsson-H.Olafsson, Reykjavik 2000.

5...♘c6

Game 43 looks at the alternatives to this natural move. Note for now though that Black can regain the c5-pawn at any time.

6 ♘f3

Preventing a possible ...♘d4; 6 ♗g5 is covered in the next game.

6...♘e4!?

6...♕a5 7 ♗d2 ♕xc5 8 e3 0-0 9 a3 ♗xc3 10 ♗xc3 ♘e4 is an alternative solid approach, but arguably 11 ♗d3 ♘xc3 12 ♕xc3 b6 13 0-0 ♗b7 14 ♖fd1 ♖ac8 15 ♖ac1 ♖fd8 16 b4 ♕f8 left White with a slight nibble in J.Piket-L.Ljubojevic, Monte Carlo 1994.

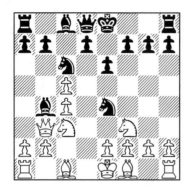

7 ♗d2

Preventing the queenside pawns from being splattered.

7...♘xd2

Instead 7...♘xc5 8 ♕c2 0-0 9 a3 ♗xc3 10 ♗xc3 a5 11 b3 f5 12 e3 b6 13 ♗e2 ♗b7 14 0-0 left White with the two bishops in D.Garcia Roman-A.Ayas Fernandez, Mislata 2003; I definitely prefer my move!

8 ♘xd2 f5

Slightly different was the 8...0-0 9 e3 ♗xc5 10 ♗e2 b6 11 ♖d1 f5 12 ♘f3 ♕f6 13 0-0 g5 of L.Christiansen-J.Speelman, Munich 1992. Clearly Black can play to win here, although he certainly has some weak points in his camp. The d7-pawn is a target whilst White should try to park a knight on d6. Indeed it was my eagerness to keep a white knight out of e4, thus avoiding the likes of 9 ♘de4 f5 10 a3 ♕a5 11 ♖d1 fxe4 12 axb4 ♘xb4 13 e3 ♕xc5 14 ♘xe4 ♕a5 15 ♘c3, that lead me to 8...f5.

Incidentally 8...♗xc5 9 e3 b6 10 ♘de4 0-0 11 ♗e2 ♗e7 12 ♖d1 a6 13 0-0 ♕c7 14 ♖d2 f5 also worked out okay for Black in J.Piket-Ki.Georgiev, Corfu 1991.

9 e3 ♗xc5 10 ♗e2 b6 11 0-0 ♗b7 12

♘a4

I was naturally very happy with the ultimate outcome of this game. I have sympathy for my opponent's decision to seek out my bishop but, as you'll soon see, exchanges seem to help my structure. Black's way of tackling 4 ♕b3 here clearly offers some winning chances but, objectively speaking, if White just did something sensible now like parking a rook on d1 then he shouldn't be worse.

12...♖b8 13 ♘xc5 bxc5 14 ♕c3 ♕f6 15 ♕xf6

15 ♗h5+ is possible but the black king won't be unhappy in the centre.

15...gxf6

Now Black has three pawn islands compared to White's two, but I was pleasantly surprised as to just how useful the half-opened knight's files became.

16 f4 ♖g8

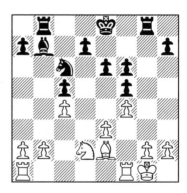

17 g3

This pawn was a target on g2, but now it is in the way of the 'rook swinger' ♖f3-h3 that would have been perfect for hitting my isolated h-pawn.

17...♗a8 18 b3

And now the same thing has happened on the queenside. For the foreseeable future at least, my isolanis look safe from the attentions of the enemy rooks.

18...♔e7 19 ♔f2 a5

What's more, now my 'weakness' is being used as a weapon!

20 a4?!

Conceding b4 was hardly desirable but if ...a5-a4 had appeared, White's b-pawn would have been a target. Of course it is now anyway, but at least White can dream of parking a knight on b5 and one day attacking Black's a-pawn. Unfortunately, we don't deal in dreams and this is reality!

20...♘b4 21 ♗f3 ♖b6!

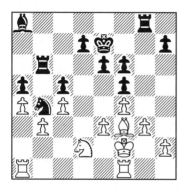

This rook prepares to infiltrate White's position.

22 ♗xa8 ♖xa8 23 ♔e2 ♖d6

Yes, adding insult to injury, it is Black who has achieved the 'rook swinger'!

24 ♖fc1 ♖d3 25 ♖ab1 ♖b8 26 ♘f3 ♖d6

That was fun but now it's time for plan B!

27 ♖c3 ♖db6 28 ♖b2 ♘a6

The start of a long but rewarding journey.

29 ♘d2 ♘c7 30 ♖b1 ♘e8 31 ♔f3 ♘d6 32 g4

This looks like desperation but White's pieces are extremely passive and, in conjunction with a possible ...♖b4xa4 plan, Black intends plonking his knight on e4.

32...fxg4+ 33 ♔xg4 ♖g8+ 34 ♔f3 ♘f5

Sadly for White it is Black who gets to use the g-file first.

35 ♔f2 ♘h4

A black rook is destined to infiltrate down either of the g- or the d-files.

36 ♖g1 ♖xg1 37 ♔xg1 ♖d6

Black is coming at White from all angles.

38 ♘f1 ♖d1 39 ♔f2 ♘f5 40 ♔e2 ♖b1 41

♖d3 ♘d6

Now the knight is heading for the e4-square; this would completely paralyse White.

42 ♘d2

Hence White opts to concede a pawn and effectively the game.

42...♖h1 43 e4 ♖xh2+ 44 ♔d1 ♖h4 45 ♖f3 f5 46 e5 ♘e4 47 ♘xe4 fxe4 48 ♖f1 ♔f7 49 ♔e2 ♔g6 50 ♖d1 ♔f5 51 ♖xd7 ♔xf4 52 ♖c7 ♖h2+ 53 ♔d1 ♔e3 0-1

Game 42
V.Kosyrev-A.Mastrovasilis
Aeroflot Open, Moscow 2004

---

1 d4 ♘f6 2 c4 e6 3 ♘c3 ♗b4 4 ♕b3 c5 5 dxc5 ♘c6 6 ♗g5

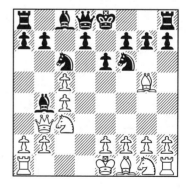

Preventing Black's king's knight from having the same involvement that it did in the previous game. Note that because White has no d-pawn, now the unpin/pin 6...♕a5 is well met by 7 ♗xf6.

6...h6

This is the simplest route to clear equality, with 6...♗xc5 7 ♘f3 b6 8 e4 (White could also settle for 8 e3, but not for the first nor the last time the white queen is not best placed on b3) 8...♗e7 9 ♗e2 ♗b7 10 e5 ♘g4 11 ♗f4! the more lively option seen in V.Akopian-A.Shneider, USSR Championship, Moscow 1991.

Incidentally 6...♘d4 7 ♕a4 ♗xc3+ 8 bxc3 ♘c6 is not that clever as White's trebled isolated pawns control many useful squares and are not easy to remove.

7 ♗xf6

Black gets too much action after 7 ♗h4?! g5! 8 ♗g3 ♘e4.

7...♕xf6 8 ♖c1

The structurally preferable move. Upon 8 ♘f3 ♗xc3+!, whichever way White recaptures, when the trebled pawns appear Black can always make the pawn deficit permanent with ...b7-b6!?. Such a continuation (similar to a theme we encountered in Chapter 1) guarantees adequate play on the queenside.

8...♗xc5 9 e3 b6 10 ♘f3 ♕g6

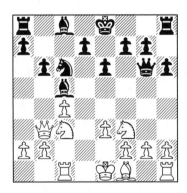

Attacking the g2-pawn and thus making life difficult for White's remaining bishop.

11 ♕c2

White's solution is to propose a queen trade. A swap here and now doesn't look much for White, but there is that d-file to be

working with.

11...f5 12 g3 ♗b7 13 ♗g2 0-0 14 0-0 ♕g4 15 b3 ♖ad8 16 ♖cd1 ♗a8

The last few moves have been fairly natural and this retreat is to place the bishop on a protected square so as to avoid ♘e5.

17 ♕e2 ♗b4 18 ♘b5 a6 19 ♘bd4 ♘xd4 20 ♖xd4 ♕h5

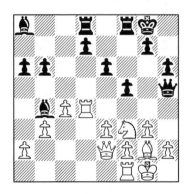

21 ♕d1

Or 21 ♖fd1 ♗c6, when White can't do much as his own queen is unprotected.

21...♗c5 22 ♘e5 ♕xd1 23 ♖dxd1 d6 24 ♘d3 ½-½

Game 43
V.Epishin-P.Nielsen
Hastings 2003/04

---

1 d4 ♘f6 2 c4 e6 3 ♘c3 ♗b4 4 ♕b3 c5 5 dxc5 ♘a6

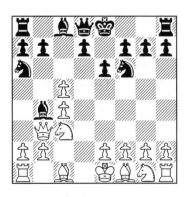

Aside from the text and the 5...♘c6 of the two previous games, the other move played in this position is the simple recapture 5...♗xc5. As developing the queen's knight protects the bishop anyhow, it seems a shame to move the bishop again so soon, but there is certainly an argument for it. Compared to the similar line in the Classical variation (4 ♕c2 c5 5 dxc5 ♗xc5), White queen is detrimentally placed in that it obstructs the b-pawn. Also, if Black wants to get in ...b7-b6 and ...♗b7 before committing the b8-knight then obviously this makes sense too. After 6 ♘f3 typically there is a branch in proceedings (although not surprisingly transpositions are common):

a) 6...b6 7 ♗g5 ♗b7 and now:

a1) 8 e3 ♗e7 9 ♗e2 ♘a6 10 0-0 ♘c5 11 ♕c2 ♘ce4 12 ♘xe4 ♘xe4 13 ♗xe7 ♕xe7 14 ♖fd1 0-0 15 ♘d2 ♘xd2 16 ♖xd2 ♖fc8 17 ♕d1 ♖c7 18 ♗f3 ♖b8 19 ♗xb7 ♖bxb7 20 ♕a4 ♕c5 21 ♖ad1 g6 22 g3 b5 23 cxb5 d5 ½-½ J.Galianina Ryjanova-K.Arkell, Cappelle la Grande 2002 was a not very thrilling but also not an uncommon scenario for this system; if White lacks ambition then with sensible play Black can easily equalise.

a2) J.Piket-A.Karpov, Roquebrune (rapid) 1992 followed along similar lines, but after 8 ♖d1 0-0 9 e3 ♗e7 10 ♗e2 ♘a6 11 0-0 ♘c5 12 ♕c2 ♘ce4

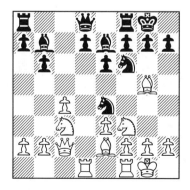

the Dutch GM made the surprising decision to concede the bishop pair with 13 ♗xf6 13...♘xf6 and then to put his pawns

on light squares. After 14 e4 d6 15 ♖d2 ♕c7 16 ♖fd1 a6 17 ♘d4 ♖fd8 18 ♕d3 ♗f8 19 ♕h3 e5 20 ♘f5 ♘xe4 21 ♘xe4 ♗xe4 22 ♘e3 b5 White had to work hard just to draw. Upon 13 ♘xe4, a recapture with the knight should transpose to the Keith Arkell game above, whilst 13...♗xe4 should also be fairly equal.

b) 6...0-0 7 ♗g5 ♗e7 (7...♘c6 8 e3 b6 9 ♖d1 ♗e7 10 ♗d3 ♗b7 11 0-0 h6 12 ♗h4 ♘a5 13 ♕c2 ♖c8 14 ♕e2 ♗xf3 15 gxf3 d5 16 cxd5 ♘xd5 17 ♗xe7 ♘xc3 18 ♗xd8 ♘xe2+ 19 ♗xe2 ♖fxd8 was also rock-solid in the drawn game J.Piket-B.Gelfand, Monte Carlo [blindfold] 2001) 8 e4!? (easily the most aggressive approach) 8...d6 (the provocative 8...h6 9 ♗xf6!? ♗xf6 10 e5 ♗e7 11 ♗d3 ♘c6 12 0-0 b6 13 ♖ad1 a6 14 ♗b1 ♕c7 15 ♕c2 ultimately saw White capitalise on his space advantage in J.Piket-L.Zsinka, Corfu 1991) 9 ♗e2 ♘bd7 10 0-0 b6 11 ♖fe1 a6 12 ♗f1 ♕c7 13 ♕c2 ♗b7, reaching the formidable 'hedgehog' structure in A.Lein-V.Epishin, Philadelphia 1998.

6 ♗d2

6 a3 ♗xc3+ 7 ♕xc3 ♘xc5 transposes to a main line of the Classical where perhaps Black may have been railroaded into his wrong variation (i.e. 4 ♕c2 c5 rather than the 4...0-0 or the 4...d5 that he may prefer). If that is the case then he should opt for 6...♗xc5 instead, when 7 ♘f3 is comparable to the lines I have just discussed under 5...♗xc5 only with White having expended time on a2-a3. Repeating a familiar theme, very reasonable is the 7...b6 8 ♗g5 ♗b7 9 e3 ♗e7 10 ♗e2 0-0 11 0-0 ♘c5 12 ♕c2 ♘ce4 of M.Hochstrasser-F.Jenni, Silvaplana 2003. Note that 7...0-0 8 ♗g5 ♗e7 allows White to get in 9 e4, with 9...h6 10 ♗h4 d6 11 ♗e2 ♘c5 12 ♕c2 a5 being played in the game V.Kosyrev-A.Aleksandrov, Internet 2004. Ironically, perhaps Black should not attempt to dissuade White's e-pawn from moving two squares if he wants the game to have more of an unbalanced feel!

6...0-0

Though some of the moves are the same you will notice that, compared to our main game, 6...♕e7 7 a3 ♗xc3 8 ♕xc3 ♘xc5 9 f3 a5 10 e4 d6 11 ♘e2 0-0 12 ♘g3 h6 13 ♗e2 ♗d7 14 0-0 a4 wastes a bit too much time. Although it does seem attractive to fix White's queenside pawn structure in this manner, in fact the knight isn't guaranteed a permanent home on c5 as there are things going on elsewhere. Indeed 15 e5! dxe5 16 ♕xe5 leaves White with two excellent bishops (particularly the dark-squared one). One big threat is ♘f5, and now 16...♘a6 17 ♗e3 ♘e8 18 ♖ad1 f6 19 ♕d4 ♗c6 20 ♗d3 ♘ec7 21 ♗c2 ♖ad8 22 ♕g4 f5 23 ♕f4 ♖xd1 24 ♖xd1 ♖d8 25 ♖xd8+ ♕xd8 26 ♕e5 saw White turn his domination into points (well, one!) in V.Epishin-R.Pogorelov, Catalan Bay 2004.

7 ♖d1 ♕e7

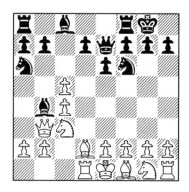

A useful move that includes a sneaky idea. Black is now threatening to take on c5 with the knight as the bishop wouldn't really be en prise on b4 because of the knight check on d3. I still feel that it is my duty to talk about the likes of 7...♗xc5 8 ♘f3 b6 9 ♗g5 ♗b7 10 e3 ♗e7 11 ♗e2 h6 12 ♗h4 ♘c5 13 ♕c2 ♘fe4 14 ♗xe7 ♕xe7 15 0-0 again. It is really difficult to believe that White has much of an advantage (if indeed any) in this type of position but there is clearly one super-GM who perseveres with this variation. Check out

15...f5 16 ♘b5 a6 17 ♘bd4 a5 18 ♘e5 ♕f6 19 ♘df3 ♖ad8 20 ♘d3 ♗c6 21 ♘d4 ♗a8 22 f3 ♘xd3 23 ♕xd3 ♘c5 24 ♕c3 f4 25 exf4 ♕xf4 26 ♘b3 ♘a4 27 ♕d2 ♗c6 28 ♘d4 ♗b7?? 29 b3 (overlooking 29 ♕xf4! ♖xf4 30 ♘xe6; we shouldn't read too much into this blitz game but I'm still going to leave you with the rest of it as the general flow is a good indication of how Black can be ground down) 29...♘c5 30 ♕xf4 ♖xf4 31 g3 ♖ff8 32 f4 ♔f7 33 ♗f3 ♗xf3 34 ♘xf3 d6 35 ♖fe1 ♖fe8 36 h4 ♖d7 37 ♔g2 ♖ed8 38 h5 ♔e7 39 f5 e5 40 g4 ♔f6 41 ♔g3 ♖b8 42 ♖d5 ♖c8 43 ♘d2 ♖c6 44 a3 ♔e7 45 ♖e3 ♔d8 46 b4 axb4 47 axb4 ♘b7 48 g5 hxg5 49 ♔g4 ♔e7 50 ♔xg5 ♘d8 51 ♔g6 ♔e8 52 b5 ♖cc7 53 ♘e4 ♘f7 54 f6 gxf6 55 ♘xf6+ ♔e7 56 ♘xd7 ♖xd7 57 ♖f3 ♔f8 58 h6 ♔e8 59 h7 ♘h8+ 60 ♔h6 ♔e7 61 ♖d1 ♔e6 62 ♖g1 e4 63 ♖f8 1-0 V.Epishin-V.Bologan, playchess.com 2004.

Recently I must confess to being a bit dismayed when preparing for a tournament and observing so many Internet blitz games on the likes of Mega Database 2005. However, in all fairness I believe that weaker players can find a lot of instruction in encounters of such a type between two strong players as the positional play (rather than all the tactics) is often of a good quality. The instinctive judgement calls of the top players are certainly something to learn from.

8 a3

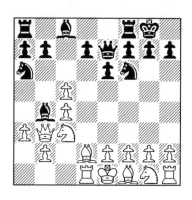

8...♗xc3

Of course 8...♘xc5?? 9 ♕xb4 ♘d3+ doesn't work now as the queen is protected.

9 ♕xc3 ♘xc5 10 f3 d6 11 ♗g5

11 b4 is possible, but with White's kingside development being so poor such an expansion could easily backfire.

11...♗d7

Compared to the line I just gave in the note to 6...♕e7, here Black has forgone pawn moves in favour of swift piece development. Things could easily go horribly wrong for White, and I'm sure this concept was very much taken into consideration in the route this game takes.

12 e4

The Spielmann variation expert decides against the greedy 12 ♕d4 ♗a4 13 ♕xd6 ♕xd6 14 ♖xd6 ♖fd8 and who could blame him? With more than half of White's army still at home, such pawn grabbing is asking for trouble.

12...♗a4 13 ♖d2

13 ♗xf6 gxf6 may double a set of black kingside pawns, but that bishop is one of the few pieces in play!

13...♘b3 14 ♖d1 ♘c5 15 ♖d2 ♘b3 16 ♖d1 ♖fc8

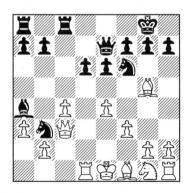

Suddenly fancying his chances, Black eschews the draw by repetition here as he appears to go for the win.

17 ♘e2 ♘c5 18 ♖d2 ♘b3 19 ♖d1 ♘c5

In truth, not for very long though! Black could have tried the aggressive 19...b5 or

perhaps 19...e5 to seek a possible knight outpost on d4. Things would be fairly unclear though and so instead Black errs on the side of caution!

20 ♖d2 ♘b3 ½-½

Game 44
N.Pedersen-S.Kristjansson
Budapest 2002

1 d4 e6 2 c4 ♘f6 3 ♘c3 ♗b4 4 ♕b3 a5

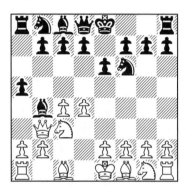

Guarding the bishop and certainly putting the clamp on any of White's queenside expansion plans for the foreseeable future. Aside from this and 4...c5, a couple of other ideas have appeared in practical play:

a) 4...♘c6 5 ♘f3 (not falling for 5 a3? ♘xd4! 6 ♕xb4? ♘c2+) 5...d6 6 a3 ♗xc3+ 7 ♕xc3. We have now reached a position that could have come from a Classical Nimzo (4 ♕c2), a Kasparov Nimzo (4 ♘f3) or even a 'Two Knights' Tango' (1 d4 ♘f6 2 c4 ♘c6). Planning for ...e6-e5, Black's structure is very solid but theoretically speaking White has a very slight edge because of his bishop pair advantage.

Although 4...c5 is probably the 'best' way to deal with 4 ♕b3, there is also an element of taste present in Black's decision making. In the previous variation, for example, 5...d5 is possible if Black is happy with that whole QGD scene. After 6 ♗g5 dxc4 7 ♕xc4 ♕d5 8 ♕xd5 ♘xd5 9 ♖c1 ♗d7 10 e4 ♘xc3 11 bxc3 ♗a5 12 ♗d3 f6 13 ♗e3 e5 14 ♘d2 ♗b6 15 ♘b3 0-0-0 16 ♔e2 Black actually went on to win in L.Van Wely-V.Bologan, playchess.com 2004, although that wasn't really down to the opening.

b) 4...♕e7 5 ♗g5 b6 is slightly reminiscent of a Bogo-Indian, only after 6 a3 ♗xc3+ 7 ♕xc3 ♗b7 White has no need to commit his knight to f3. Indeed 8 f3 d6 9 ♘h3 h6 10 ♗h4 ♘bd7 11 e3 c5 12 dxc5 bxc5 13 ♗e2 d5 14 ♗f2 0-0 15 0-0 again left White with a minute plus in L.Christiansen-A.Karpov, Wijk aan Zee 1993. Now the position has Classical traits and once more it's the bishops that have the potential.

5 a3

White could of course consider 5 ♗g5 and 5 ♘f3 but this gets straight to the point.

5...♗xc3+

Black was a strong player, but I don't buy the 5...♗e7 6 e4 d6 7 ♘f3 e5 8 ♕c2 ♘bd7 9 b3 0-0 10 ♗e2 ♖e8 11 0-0 of V.Malaniuk-A.Onischuk, Hamburg 1993. Black may just as well have played the Old Indian (1 d4 ♘f6 2 c4 d6 3 ♘c3 ♘bd7 4 e4 e5) from the off!

I must confess that what first attracted me to 4...a5 was the possibility of 5...a4?! 6 ♕xb4 ♘c6 7 ♕c5 (definitely best!) 7...♖a5 8 ♘b5 ♘e4 9 ♕h5 ♘xd4 10 ♖b1 ♘c2+ 11 ♔d1 ♘xf2+. I remember analysing these sort of crazy lines with John Emms before we were both Grandmasters, and I have to say that I'm disappointed that it seems nobody has ever played this. I don't blame them though, as despite being a bit of fun it is probably complete rubbish for Black, who looks set to get a knight or two trapped in a corner!

6 ♕xc3 h6

Regarding that previous fantasy variation, my idea had been to get in ...a5-a4 for free. Of course 6...a4 is possible now but, although the existence of the en passant rule means that White's queenside pawns are fixed, this seems a bit time consuming. To go with his bishop pair White has a free hand in the centre. Specifically, as a reply White could

employ 7 g3, 7 ♗g5 or even the move that is utilised in the main game.

Maybe Black should settle for 6...d6, but I don't like the 7 ♘f3 b6 8 b3 ♗b7 9 ♗b2 ♘bd7 10 e3 ♖a7 11 ♘d2 c5 12 ♗e2 ♕a8 13 f3 ♕b8 14 0-0 of N.Pedersen-I.Csom, Budapest 2002 as Black's queenside looks awkward.

7 ♕g3!?

Black's previous move was obviously designed to prevent the ♗g5 pin, but now the h-pawn becomes a target itself. The immediate threat though is to the g7-pawn.

7...g5

Unattractive, but nevertheless somewhat better than 7...0-0? 8 ♗xh6.

8 h4!

Correctly exploiting Black's pawn weaknesses and his lack of a dark-squared bishop. **8...g4 9 e4!?**

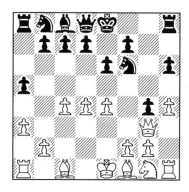

I can't vouch for the quality of my books, but even the harshest of critics would have to acknowledge that I do pick some entertaining games!

9...♘xe4 10 ♕xg4 ♘f6 11 ♕g7 ♔e7 12 ♕g3

Twelve moves into the game and White's main army languishes at home. Black's situation is no better though, with just a knight and a king to show in terms of development.

12...d6 13 ♗d3 ♘bd7 14 ♕f3

I think I might have preferred a knight move here but there is a definite appeal to the way that White has handled this opening, and I think that we should just let him get on with it!

14...♕g8 15 ♖h3!

Consistent!

15...♖b8 16 ♖g3 ♕f8 17 ♗d2 b6 18 ♗c3 ♗a6

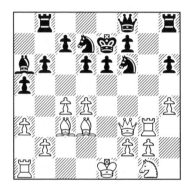

19 b4

I'm not so sure about White's next few moves, and the more mundane 19 d5!? makes more sense to me.

19...axb4 20 axb4 ♗b7 21 ♕e2 ♖a8 22 0-0-0?!

Unbelievable stuff!

22...♔d8

With or without the ridiculous placing of both kings, 22...b5! battling for the d5-square would be a good positional move here.

23 ♘h3 ♖g8 24 ♖xg8 ♕xg8 25 ♘f4 b5!

He's found it now though, and here the situation is rather unclear.

26 c5 ♘d5 27 ♘xd5 ♗xd5 28 g4 ♖a3 29 ♗b2 ♖xd3?

Although Black's bishop is dominant now, I really don't think that this was necessary. The simple 29...♗b3 was fine.

30 ♖xd3!

I suspect that Black had expected 30 ♕xd3 ♕xg4 when there is a pawn plus plenty of compensation for the exchange.

30...♗c4 31 ♖a3

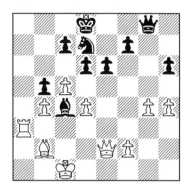

This and the similar idea 31 ♕f3 were probably what Black had overlooked.

31...♗xe2 32 ♖a8+ ♔e7 33 ♖xg8 ♘f6 34 ♖h8 ♘xg4 35 ♔d2

In this endgame, one pawn is not going to be enough compensation.

35...♗f3 36 ♔e1 h5 37 ♗c1 dxc5 38 bxc5 c6 39 ♗g5+ f6 40 ♖h7+ ♔f8 41 ♗f4 e5 42 dxe5 fxe5 43 ♗g3 ♘f6 44 ♖a7 ♘g4 45 ♖a3 ♗d5 46 ♖a7 ♔e8 47 ♖h7 ♘f6 48 ♖h8+ ♔f7 49 ♗xe5 ♘e4 50 ♗d4 ♔g6 51 ♖f8 ♗f7 52 ♖d8 ♗d5 53 f3 ♘g3 54 ♖d6+ ♔h7 55 ♖f6 ♗c4 56 ♔f2 ♘e2 57 ♗b2 b4 58 ♖xc6 ♘c3 59 ♗xc3 1-0

Summary

In my opinion 4 ♕b3 isn't a serious try to get an advantage from the opening. However, given that 4...c5 is probably the best response, if White is in a solid mood, it could be extremely difficult to defeat. Having said all that, Epishin is just one strong grandmaster who seems to be persevering with it, and Black often needs to be comfortable with a hedgehog formation to put up a good defence.

Rarely a variation for excitement lovers!

1 d4 ♘f6 2 c4 e6 3 ♘c3 ♗b4 4 ♕b3 (D) c5

　　　4...a5 – *Game 44*

5 dxc5 (D) ♘c6

　　　5...♘a6 – *Game 43*

6 ♘f3 (D) – *Game 41*

　　　6 ♗g5 – *Game 42*

4 ♕b3　　　　　*5 dxc5*　　　　　*6 ♘f3*

CHAPTER EIGHT

Very Rare Fourth Moves for White

1 d4 ♘f6 2 c4 e6 3 ♘c3 ♗b4

Here I want to tie up all the loose ends starting with the amazingly cheeky 4 e4?. If you are a Nimzo-Indian player then you could easily go through your whole life without encountering any of the lines that follow, and I strongly urge White players to stay well away from this chapter's contents!

Game 45
V.Chemin-J.Sunye Neto
Brazilian Ch., Sao Luis 1981

---

1 d4 ♘f6 2 c4 e6 3 ♘c3 ♗b4 4 e4?

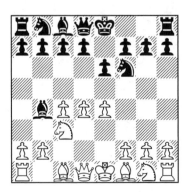

This is a pretty old game to be using considering I promised to base most of my lines on modern ideas. However, if this move worked then this book and indeed every book ever written on the Nimzo-Indian would be made redundant. It doesn't!

In light of trendy lines such as the Semi-Slav's 1 d4 d5 2 c4 c6 3 ♘f3 ♘f6 4 e3 e6 5 ♘c3 ♘bd7 6 ♕c2 ♗d6 7 g4!?, I thought it might only be a matter of time before 4 g4?!

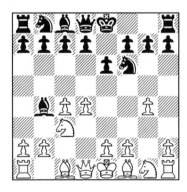

(see diagram) was wheeled out against the Nimzo. Surprisingly there seemed to be no trace of it until I located 4...♘xg4 5 e4 f5 6 ♘h3 0-0 7 f3?! ♕h4+ 8 ♔e2 in the game J.Hvenekilde-E.Bang, Copenhagen 1973. The less said about that the better, except that the enigmatic pipe-smoking Mr Hvenekilde was clearly a man ahead of his time!

4...♘xe4

To consider anything else would be pure

lunacy, and indeed 4...d6?? 5 ♕a4+ ♘c6 6 d5 got all it deserved in R.Schoengart-A.Cotaru, Hamburg 1997.

5 ♕g4

The only justification for White's apparent contempt of the Nimzo. However, compared to the next game's notes to 4 ♗d2 b6 5 e4!? ♗xc3 6 ♗xc3 ♘xe4 7 ♕g4, White isn't going to get a chance to take on g7 because of the problems on c3.

5...♘xc3

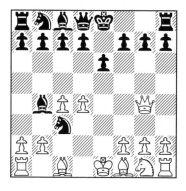

6 a3

6 ♗d2 0-0 7 bxc3 ♗e7 8 ♗h6 ♗f6 9 ♘h3 e5! 10 ♗e3 exd4 11 ♗xd4 ♗xd4 12 cxd4 d5 13 ♕f3 dxc4 14 ♗xc4 ♕xd4 was no improvement in C.Risueno-G.Jimenez, Albacete 1991, and of course 6 ♕xg7?? is rubbish in view of 6...♘e4+ 7 ♔e2 ♕f6.

6...♗e7 7 bxc3

Or 7 ♕xg7? ♗f6.

7...♗f6

7...0-0 8 ♗d3 f5 9 ♕e2 ♗f6 was equally adequate in M.Roeder-G.Volpert, Unterfranken 1987 – White is simply a pawn down.

8 ♗d3 b6 9 ♘e2 c5 10 ♕e4

This would be an excellent move were the black king on h7. Unfortunately, it's not!

10...♘c6 11 d5 ♘e5 12 dxe6

I could criticise this move but I would just be splitting hairs. 4 e4? is a complete failure!

12...♘xd3+ 13 ♔f1

13 ♕xd3 dxe6 leaves White a pawn down,

with the worse structure and up against the two bishops on a reasonably open board.

13...d5! 14 exf7+ ♔xf7 15 ♕xd3 ♗a6

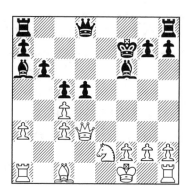

Black's point: a6-f1 is a tasty diagonal!

16 ♕xd5+ ♕xd5 17 cxd5 ♖ad8 18 ♗e3 ♖xd5 0-1

White's cause is a hopeless one.

Game 46
F.Vanlerburgh-C.Ward
Ghent 2004

---

1 d4 ♘f6 2 c4 e6 3 ♘c3 ♗b4 4 ♘f3

Although 4 ♘f3 is the specific move here (destined to transpose next turn), I just want to stop for a moment to talk about 4 ♗d2.

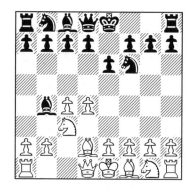

I had this move played against me many times when I was a young junior and I'm sure that other relative beginners can relate similar Nimzo-Indian experiences. Indeed, if a novice playing White has no real theoretical knowledge of 3...♗b4 then this is going to be a popular response. The logic of course is that the text unpins the knight and prevents the doubling of the c-pawns. It's a bit harsh to call it a bad move but the reason why it is virtually never seen at high levels is because it seriously lacks ambition. Although it purports to win a bishop for a knight without compromising the pawn structure, that is not actually the reality; after a ...♗xc3, ♗xc3 trade Black will have available ...♞e4 to, if desired, redress the minor piece balance. As it is generally the case that White has a space advantage in this 1 d4 opening, it is not in his interest to encourage fair swaps and, besides, Black may well prefer his knight on e4 to White's dark-squared bishop.

Although 4...d5 would not be ridiculous here and 4...c5 has also been seen, I'd prefer to focus on two more Nimzo-style plans:

a) 4...b6

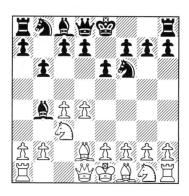

and now

a1) 5 ♘f3 would transpose to our main game.

a2) 5 e4!? ♗xc3 6 ♗xc3 ♞xe4 7 ♕g4 is the same theme seen in the first game of this chapter, but under better circumstances; That's not saying an awful lot but at least here White hasn't got real problems on c3. Instead of this, bizarre and not to be recommended is the 7 ♕f3?! ♗b7 8 0-0-0 ♕g5+ 9 ♔c2 ♞c5 10 d5 0-0 11 h4 ♕g6+ 12 ♗d3

♞xd3 13 ♖xd3 exd5 14 cxd5 ♗a6 of W.Zichler-D.Paashaus, Bad Zwesten 1998.

Back to 7 ♕g4, we have 7...♞xc3 (7...f5 8 ♕xg7 ♕f6 9 ♕xf6 ♞xf6 10 f3 is objectively a bit better for White) 8 ♕xg7 ♗e7 9 bxc3 ♕g8 10 ♕h6 ♗b7 11 f3 ♕g6 12 ♕e3 with equal chances in O.Jakobsen-Cu.Hansen, Vejle 1982.

a2) 5 f3 ♗xc3 (not forced, but the immediate 5...d5?? is of course not possible because of 6 ♕a4+) 6 ♗xc3 d5 7 e3 ♗a6 8 ♕a4+ ♕d7 9 ♕xd7+ ♞bxd7 10 cxd5 ♗xf1 11 ♔xf1 and whichever way Black recaptures (the knight in the case of Z.Nikolic-I.Csom, Nis 1981) it's no great shakes for White.

b) 4...0-0 5 a3 ♗xc3 (gaining control of the e4-square is the most obvious but 5...♗e7 6 e4 d5 7 e5 ♞e4 8 ♞xe4 dxe4 9 ♗c3 f6 ½-½ N.Ostojic-S.Martinovic, Belgrade SCG 2004 is food for thought) 6 ♗xc3 ♞e4 7 ♕c2 (or 7 ♖c1 d6, for example 8 ♞f3 ♕e7 9 g3 ♞xc3 10 ♖xc3 e5 and Black had easily equalised in A.Ascic-E.Dizdarevic, Porec 1998 and actually went on to win) 7...f5

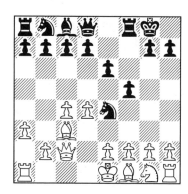

when Black has no worries in any of the three different white approaches:

b1) 8 ♞f3 d6 9 g3 b6 (9...♞c6 and the plan of playing for ...e6-e5 is also reasonable) 10 ♗g2 ♞xc3 11 ♕xc3 ♗b7 12 c5 ♗d5 13 0-0 ♕f6 14 cxd6 cxd6 15 ♞h4 ♗xg2 ½-½ H.Schaufelberger-O.Cvitan, Switzerland 2004.

b2) 8 g3 d6 9 ♗g2 ♘xc3 10 ♕xc3 ♘d7 11 ♘f3 ♕e7 12 ♖c1 e5 again with equality, and the 13 0-0 e4 14 ♘d2 ♘f6 15 e3 c6 16 f3 ½-½ of H.Schaufelberger-P.Hardicsay, Balatonlelle 2004 suggested that both players concurred!

b3) 8 e3 b6 9 ♘e2 ♗b7 10 f3 ♕h4+! 11 g3 ♕h5 12 ♗g2 ♘xc3 13 ♕xc3 ♗xf3 14 ♘f4 ♕g4 with very minimal play for the pawn, D.Cavero Cavero-Z.Franco Ocampos, Javea 1992.

4...b6 5 ♗d2?!

Although 4 ♘f3 shouldn't strictly speaking belong in this book, in my recent *Nimzo-Indian Kasparov Variation* I really only focussed on 5 ♗g5 here (with 5 g3 getting a small mention). Therefore this game gives me an excellent opportunity for completion in that department whilst also being able to cover 4 ♗d2. Regarding this move now, perhaps the symbol '?!' is a little unfair but, as I have already implied, my own experiences of such a move for White in the Nimzo is that it rarely causes Black any problems.

5...♗b7

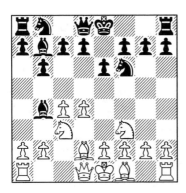

Okay, a confession here: the real move order to this game was 1 c4 b6 2 ♘c3 ♗b7 3 d4 e6 4 ♘f3 ♗b4 5 ♗d2 ♘f6. Had the game really come via the text moves, I may have selected 5...0-0 over 5...♗b7 on the grounds that it is more flexible. Of course it would be very harsh to criticise the also very obvious 5...♗b7.

6 a3 ♗xc3 7 ♗xc3 ♘e4 8 ♕c2 0-0

Unless the e1-square is vacated to facilitate a retreat, Black can always redress the bishop-for-knight balance with ...♘xd2. However, I was in no hurry to take White's bishop; the knight is an excellent piece on e4 and White has his work cut out trying to budge it.

9 e3 d6 10 ♖d1 ♘d7

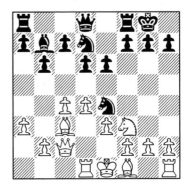

I certainly toyed with the idea of 10...♘xc3 11 ♕xc3 ♗xf3 12 gxf3 ♘d7 with the intention of bringing the queen out to h4 or f6. Yes, I was happy with the concept of mixing things up but I was also attracted to the road I took.

11 d5

Things work out quite nicely for Black despite this being the thematic approach. White wants to open up the c3-g7 diagonal and shut out my bishop on b7.

11...♘xc3 12 ♕xc3 ♘f6!

With my f-pawn at home rather than on f5 (where it had previously seemed destined to end up) I am not remotely weak on e6. Hence the decision to test White's mettle.

13 ♕b3

Hardly desirable, but after the alternative 13 dxe6 fxe6 Black would have reopened the diagonal for his bishop as well as having an f-file to play with.

13...a5! 14 a4

This is an incredibly ugly move but, as well as helping to secure the c5-square, the threat that Black's last move carried is evident in the following variation: 14 ♗e2 a4 15 ♕a2 exd5 16 cxd5 ♖a5! 17 ♗c4 ♕a8 when the d5-pawn will drop.

14...♘e4 15 ♕c2 ♘c5 16 ♗e2 e5

Black's bishop is currently locked out on b7 but it has an obvious way back into the game.

17 h4?!

One can understand why White played this move but it is wildly optimistic. Probably he should just sit back and take his medicine.

17...♗c8

This and ...f7-f5 were on my mind in any case and White's previous move wasn't going to put me off.

18 ♘g5 f5 19 f4

It's very logical for White to want to fix some pawns on dark squares, but now White will experience difficulties on the e-file.

19...exf4 20 exf4 ♕e8!

Looking to invade down the e-file but also eying up the a4-pawn.

21 b3 ♕e3!

Suddenly White's position collapses: he can't guard both his b-pawn and his f-pawn.

22 ♖f1

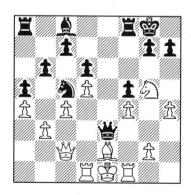

22...♕xb3

I was also attracted by the idea of 22...♕g3+ 23 ♖f2 h6 but decided it was simpler to net pawns rather than the exchange.

23 ♕xb3 ♘xb3 24 ♖d3 ♘c5 25 ♖a3 h6 26 ♘f3 ♗d7 27 ♗d1 ♖ae8+ 0-1

This rook is heading for e4. Black has by far the better pieces and will soon be plenty of pawns up too.

Game 47
D.Kudischewitsch-I.Manor
Israel Team Ch., Ramat Aviv 2000

---

1 d4 ♘f6 2 c4 e6 3 ♘c3 ♗b4 4 ♕d3

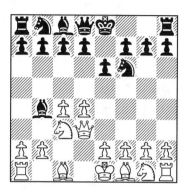

I'm going to finish off this book with another odd move. Its offbeat nature justifies its inclusion and at least it is a game between two strong players and in the same millennium!

Before I go into detail about the text though, for completion let me eliminate all the other dregs!:

a) 4 ♕a4?!

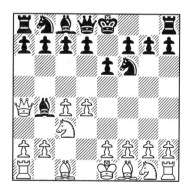

Given that I was never likely to cover 4 ♕d2?, this is the only remaining queen move!

Unlike 4 ♕b3, it doesn't get in the way of the b-pawn. However, whilst it does attack the black bishop, it doesn't support the knight. Thus it is never likely to compare with the Classical (4 ♕c2) as a2-a3 isn't a threat. Now 4...c5 5 ♘f3 ♘c6 6 e3 0-0 7 ♗d2 b6 8 ♗d3 ♗b7 9 0-0 d5 10 cxd5 exd5 11 ♗b5 ♕c7 12 ♗xc6 ♗xc6 13 ♕b3 a5 14 a3 c4 15 ♕c2 ♗d6 had highlighted the poor positioning of her majesty in G.Sull-Z.Hajnal, Hungary 1999 and I suspect that Black could do even better.

b) 4 ♗f4

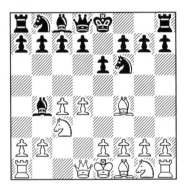

As this is neither pinning nor unpinning, it is difficult to justify it right now (if ever). This move is not to be confused with 1 d4 ♘f6 2 c4 e6 3 ♘f3 b6 4 ♗f4, which was a favourite variation of the English GM Tony Miles.

After 4 ♗f4 Black has several very satis-factory plans but one very entertaining game (particularly from Black's point of view!) was 4...0-0 5 e3 d6 6 ♗d3 ♗xc3+ 7 bxc3 ♕e8 8 ♘e2 ♘bd7 9 h3 e5 10 ♗h2 b6 11 g4 ♗b7 12 ♖g1 ♘e4 13 g5 f6 14 gxf6 ♖xf6 15 ♕c2 exd4 16 cxd4 ♘xf2 17 ♗xh7+ ♔h8 18 ♗f5 ♘e4 19 ♘g3 ♘g5 20 0-0-0 ♕xe3+ 21 ♔b1 ♘f3 22 ♖d3 ♕e7 23 ♕g2 ♘xg1 24 ♕xb7 ♕e1+ 25 ♔c2 ♖xf5 26 ♘xf5 ♕f2+ 27 ♔b3 ♖b8 28 ♕e4 ♘c5+!! 29 dxc5 bxc5+ 30 ♔c3 ♕b2 mate!, J.Jansson-J.Tisdall, Asker 1988.

4 ♕d3 has a little more sense. We have seen in the kingside fianchetto variations

how the queen often comes here and White's light-squared bishop could still come out to d3 if the queen recaptures on c4 in the near future.

4...d5

Switching to a QGD set-up makes sense, although 4...c5!? also looks like a good way of exposing the white queen. Now:

a) 5 d5 0-0 6 ♗d2 exd5 7 cxd5 d6 8 g3 b6 9 ♗g2 ♗a6 10 ♕c2 ♘bd7 11 ♘h3 ♖e8 12 ♘f4 ♗xc3 13 bxc3 g5 14 ♘d3 ♖xe2+ 15 ♔xe2 ♘e5 16 ♔d1 ♗xd3 17 ♕a4 b5 18 ♕a6 ♕d7 19 ♔c1 b4 20 ♕a5 a6 0-1 was pretty impressive in V.Mikenas-P.Keres, Moscow 1949

b) 5 dxc5 ♘a6!? 6 a3 ♘xc5 7 ♕c2 ♗xc3+ 8 ♕xc3 0-0 leaves Black a tempo up on the equivalent Classical line because the white queen has triangulated!

On top of this, a transposition back into the Classical could easily occur, say, after 4...0-0 5 a3 ♗xc3+ 6 ♕xc3 but the feeling is that Black should be striving for more.

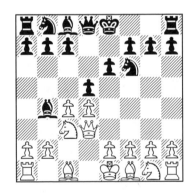

5 cxd5

5 ♗g5 shouldn't be worse for White al-though 5...c6 (certainly not forced) 6 ♘f3 ♘bd7 7 e3 ♕a5 was a Cambridge Springs but with the white queen on d3 rather than c2. Now the 8 ♗xf6 ♘xf6 9 ♘d2 0-0 10 ♗e2 ♖e8 11 0-0 e5 12 ♘b3 e4 of G.Grassmehl-M.Usachyi, Bad Liebenzell 1996 proved that to be an inferior square.

Upon 5 a3, 5...♗xc3+ 6 ♕xc3 ♘e4 would

transpose to a main line of the Classical, but instead a retreat along the diagonal seeks to punish White more.

5...exd5 6 ♕b5+

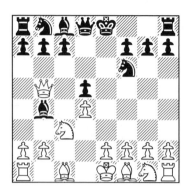

I would have said 'A kingside fianchetto would ultimately see the light-squared bishop biting on granite so instead White vacates the d3-square for it.' However, read on!

6...♘c6

Black gets to develop another piece, although in truth he would rather not obstruct his c-pawn. In queen's pawn openings, c-pawns (be they white or black) are used to attack or to support the centre.

7 ♗g5 h6 8 ♗xf6 ♕xf6 9 e3

9 ♕xd5? ♗e6 10 ♕e4 ♕xd4 clearly favours Black who would have the bishop pair and a big lead in development.

9...♕d6 10 ♘ge2 a6 11 ♕d3 ♘e7 12 a3 ♗a5

The other bishop makes it to f5 soon anyway. Regarding this one, there is no point in trading on c3 because the other knight is waiting to replace its compatriot.

13 b4 ♗b6 14 g3 a5

I think I prefer 14...c6!? as it offers other possibilities to this otherwise 'out of it' bishop. Black is probably slightly better here.

15 b5 h5

With White still to sort out his kingside

this was always going to be tempting. It's too late for the ...c7-c6 idea now as effectively White will have executed a successful minority attack.

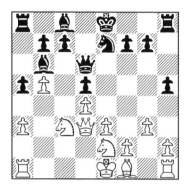

16 h4 ♗f5 17 ♕d2 0-0-0 18 ♗g2 ♔b8 19 ♘f4 ♗e6

Required to protect the d-pawn.

20 ♘a4 f6 21 ♘xb6 cxb6 22 ♘xe6 ♕xe6 23 ♕d3 g5

Structurally White stands better. However, his problem is what to do with his king.

24 ♗h3 ♕d6 25 ♔e2 ♖dg8 26 ♖ac1 ♖d8 27 ♖c3 g4 28 ♗g2 ½-½

In my opinion White should play on, although he has a hard graft ahead of him and whether he would actually win is a different matter.

Summary

What can I say? In one way 4 e4(?) is critical, but basically it's rubbish. Discounting 4 ♘f3, of all White's fourth move alternatives covered here, I would have to say that 4 ♕d3 is the 'least bad'! Black doesn't have the advantage after that (well, not yet anyway!) but has several reasonable responses available. Essentially then, a warning to White players: Keep clear!

1 d4 ♘f6 2 c4 e6 3 ♘c3 ♗b4 4 ♕d3 (D) – *Game 47*

    4 e4 (D) – *Game 45*
    4 ♘f3 – *Game 46*
    4 ♗d2 (D) – *Game 46* (notes)

    4 ♕d3   *4 e4*   *4 ♗d2*

INDEX OF COMPLETE GAMES

Beliavsky.A-De Firmian.N, Sigeman & Co, Malmö 2004............................*34*

Beliavsky.A-Kunte.A, Pune 2004...*37*

Berkes.F-Cao Sang, Hungarian Ch., Budapest 2004....................................*64*

Chemin.V-Sunye Neto.J, Brazilian Ch., Sao Luis 1981..............................*135*

Danilov.V-Hernandez.H, Pedrido 2004..*85*

Epishin.V-Nielsen.P, Hastings 2003/04...*128*

Erdos.V-Ilincic.Z, Budapest 2004..*100*

Fish.G-Lauber.A, Germany 2001..*111*

Fries Nielsen.J-Ward.C, Politiken Cup, Copenhagen 1994........................*125*

Gonzalez Garcia.J-Tiviakov.S, Mallorca Olympiad 2004..........................*119*

Henriksson.J-Peng Zhaoqin, Rilton Cup, Stockholm 2004........................*96*

Hillarp Persson.T-Lehikoinen.P, Reykjavik 2004.......................................*28*

Hofstra.H-Ikonnikov.V, Vlissingen 2000..*77*

House.G-Ward.C, Jersey 2002..*72*

Ivanchuk.V-Csom.I, Yerevan 1989...*61*

Kosyrev.V-Mastrovasilis.A, Aeroflot Open, Moscow 2004........................*127*

Kudischewitsch.D-Manor.I, Israel Team Ch., Ramat Aviv 2000.................*139*

Lalic.B-Jovanic.O, Zadar 2004..*23*

Martic.Z-Jankovic.A, Zadar 2004...*69*

Milov.V-Polgar.J, FIDE World Ch., Moscow 2001......................................*80*

Misanovic.V-Hunt.H, Euro. Women's Team Ch., Batumi 1999...................*89*

Mohandesi.S-Kengis.E, Sautron 2003...*90*

Moskalenko.V-Gonzalez Rodriguez.J, Barcelona 2003..............................*40*

Moskalenko.V-Lopez Martinez.J, Paretana 1999.......................................*75*

Nguyen Chi Minh-Van den Doel.E, French League 2003............................*20*

Nilssen.J-De Firmian.N, Politiken Cup, Copenhagen 2003........................*121*

Norberg.M-Sasata.R, Correspondence 1999..*45*

Pedersen.N-Kristjansson.S, Budapest 2002..*131*

Sagalchik.G-Akopian.V, New York 1998..*9*

Saric.I-Nikolac.J, Pula 2001..*79*

Shirov.A-'Canchess', Internet (Simultaneous Display) 2000..........................*26*

Summerscale.A-Yudasin.L, World Open, Philadelphia 2002.....................*47*

Tipu.V-Henry.L, Canadian Ch., Toronto 2004...*16*

Van Buskirk.C-Del Pilar.R, Agoura Hills 2004...*50*

Vanlerburgh.F-Ward.C, Ghent 2004..*136*

Volkov.S-Bartel.M, playchess.com (blitz) 2004 ....*54*

Volkov.S-Ionov.S, Russian Ch., St Petersburg 2004.....................................*57*

Volkov.S-Istratescu.A, Korinthos 2002..*13*

Volkov.S-Jeremic.V, Korinthos 2004...*31*

Volkov.S-Vekshenkov.N, Russian Team Ch., Togliatti 2003 ....*58*

Ward.C-Gligoric.S, Malta 2000...*98*

Ward.C-Gulko.B, Politiken Cup, Copenhagen 1996.....................................*108*

Ward.C-Hinks-Edwards.T, British League 2000 ....*103*

Ward.C-Levitt.J, British Ch., Torquay 1998 ....*93*

Ward.C-Timman.J, European Club Ch., Breda 1998.....................................*114*

Yakovich.Y-Campora.D, Santo Antonio 2001..*18*

Yakovich.Y-Tunik.G, Russian Ch., Krasnodar 2002.....................................*43*